The Fieldston Guide to American History for Cynical Beginners

Other books by Jim Cullen

The Civil War in Popular Culture: A Reusable Past (1995)

The Art of Democracy:
A Concise History of Popular Culture in the United States (1996, 2002)

Born in the U.S.A.: Bruce Springsteen and the American Tradition (1997, 2005)

Editor, *Popular Culture in American History* (2001)

Restless in the Promised Land: Catholics and the American Dream (2001)

The American Dream: A Short History of an Idea that Shaped a Nation (2003)

Editor (with Lyde Cullen Sizer), *The Civil War Era:*
An Anthology of Sources (2005)

The Fieldston Guide to American History for Cynical Beginners

✦

Impractical Lessons for Everyday Life

Jim Cullen

The Ethical Culture Fieldston School

For the Zambellis,
Nettner cynical
na beginners.

—Jim Cull
2005

iUniverse, Inc.
New York Lincoln Shanghai

The Fieldston Guide to American History for Cynical Beginners
Impractical Lessons for Everyday Life

iUniverse books may be ordered through booksellers or by contacting:

iUniverse
2021 Pine Lake Road, Suite 100
Lincoln, NE 68512
www.iuniverse.com
1-800-Authors (1-800-288-4677)

Chapter Six was originally published as "Fools Paradise: Frank Sinatra and the American Dream," in *Popular Culture in American History*, edited by Jim Cullen (Oxford: Blackwell Publishers, 2001).

ISBN: 0-595-34342-2

Printed in the United States of America

For Theodore Ryland Sizer and Nancy Faust Sizer,

teachers

Hope is the thing with feathers
That perches in the soul
And sings the tune without the words
And never stops at all

—Emily Dickinson

Contents

Acknowledgments

It's a little ironic that you're reading this book, because while a book is what I originally imagined this would be, that's not how it initially ended up. A few chapters had been drafted by January 2004, when I attended the New York State Association of Independent School (NYSAIS) Experienced Teacher's Institute in Rensselaerville. It was at the conference that I described my idea during one of the sessions, and the conference organizer, Ann Mellow of St. Luke's School in Manhattan, said, "This would make a great Web site." Upon reflection, I decided she was right, and approached Mary McFerran, who was at the time the Director of Educational Technology at the Ethical Culture Fieldston School (ECFS), where I teach. She agreed it was a good idea. So did the Venture Grant Committee at ECFS, which gave us the funding to launch it, which we did in the summer of 2004. You can have a look for yourself:

www.ecfs.org/projects/jcullen

I never quite let go of the idea of making a book out of the project, though. This was partly pragmatic. The Web site works well for browsing small pieces, but downloading and printing more than a chapter or two can be tedious and not especially user-friendly. Books, by contrast, are still a very good format for extended reading, and the medium closest to my heart. I'm grateful once again to the Venture Grant Board—Beryl Dorsett, Nina Freedman, Geoffrey Gund, Donald Sussman, and Linda Viertel—for their support. Rita McRedmond administered the grant. Former principal Rachel Stettler and History Department Chair Andy Meyers provided welcome and necessary support, as has the current principal of Fieldston, John Love. Thanks also to some of the colleagues who offered positive feedback, among them David Swartwout and Bob Montera in the History Department, Kate Fox Reynolds and Dotty Hanson in the English Department, and Robert Schaecher, Debbie McFall, and Mara Gross in the Ethics Department. ECFS head Joe Healey has been a stalwart supporter of my work and a valued colleague, as has Beth Beckmann, the associate head of the school. Joel Levin and Vasil Bury provided valuable technical support for the site and the book. Kristin Oomen and the staff at iUniverse worked with notable professionalism and dispatch in moving it through the (print) publishing process.

My four children—Jay, Grayson, Ryland, and Nancy—remain the largest undertaking I have ever embarked on and an endless source of lessons, some of them humbling. But they are a gift, one conferred on me by my wife Lyde, who has given me so many of the things that have made my life worthwhile. God bless you all.

Jim Cullen
February 2005

Introduction:
The End of American History

OF ALL THE THINGS you could be doing right now, here you are, reading a history book.

And why is that? Most likely, it's because a teacher has asked—told—you to, and you need to at least partially heed that teacher's instructions to get a decent grade, finish the semester, graduate, and get on to a future that's as likely to be as hazy as it is hopeful. Maybe you bought this book; maybe somebody else, like your parents, paid for it; maybe you borrowed a copy from a library or a friend. But while you may not have spent money on it, you certainly are spending time on it. There are other things you could be doing right now (sleep may seem like a particularly attractive alternative). In any event, it's virtually certain that at some point amid these sentences, your attention will be broken by any number of welcome or unwelcome distractions: a noise down the hall; a phone ringing; the appearance of a friend at the door. Real life—often ordinary yet vivid and insistent—must take precedence over freeze-dried thought. So you'll put this aside. Maybe you'll pick it up again later.

If and when you do, I'll need to be clear and compelling if anything I say will last longer than, say, next weekend. And just what is my point? This: the idea that history, American history in particular, is worth your time—so much so that you'll not only study it for credit, or even for pleasure, but that it will seep into your consciousness, even become a way of life.

Now I realize that amid the finite space we all have in our lives for work, family, and other obligations, there are any number of things that may compete for your interest, things as exhaustingly variegated as life itself: gardening, babysitting, cooking, sex, poker, yoga, an argument with your mother that you're conducting in your head. Even if one limits the domain to the life of the mind—those of us who have ended up as teachers have perhaps a charming belief that books and ideas are intrinsically superior to other pursuits—the choices range from astronomy to zoology. Far be it for me to suggest that any of these subjects is less worthy of a lifetime's pursuit; variety is the spice of life, and there's something usefully humbling about knowing that there are people out there who

1

have mastered topics you haven't even begun to understand. But at the very least, history is certainly one of those topics, and one that can inform and animate many of the others. It may even help you do some good in the world (something that's always an option).

Still, you may be asking yourself: What's so great about history? "History is bunk," Henry Ford once reputedly said. Actually, what he really seems to have said, in a 1916 interview with the *Chicago Tribune,* is that "History is more or less bunk. We don't want tradition. We want to live in the present, and the only history that's worth a tinker's damn is the history we make today." (Ford's attitude lives on in contemporary lingo, where the phrase "that's history" is meant to connote the irrelevance of the topic in question, like a relationship you consider convenient to forget.) Yet the man whose cars and the assembly line he perfected symbolized modernity a century ago was obsessed by the past. In the 1920s, he built an entire town, Greenfield Village, as a museum of American life as he remembered it from his childhood. It was a pretty good re-creation, and remains a model for living history museums. Nevertheless, Ford's memory was somewhat selective: It had no bank, no lawyer's offices, and no bars. Facts, it's clear, don't always get in the way of history.

When history isn't irrelevant, it can be a crushing burden. "History is a nightmare from which I'm trying to awake," thinks the main character in James Joyce's 1922 novel *Ulysses.* In the classic socialist anthem "The Internationale," tradition is a chain that the workers of the world must shatter to usher in a better world. Maybe Henry Ford was right: Some things—most things?—are better off forgotten.

Indeed, you really do have to wonder whether learning about the past can make all that much of a positive difference in a person's life. I mean, sure, it might be useful to be aware, for example, that you have a family history of alcoholism. But you don't need a three-credit class for that. Really: Is learning *anything* about, say, the Ming Dynasty going to make a difference? For a while, I would open my U.S. history courses by asking my students about why, other than some tedious distribution requirements, anyone should bother. Invariably, I heard variations on George Santayana's famous dictum, echoing Euripides and Thucydides, that "those who cannot remember the past are condemned to repeat it." All right, then, I would tell the students wryly, you'll know better than to start a land war in Asia. But of course, virtually nobody is ever in position to start a land war in Asia. Nor, for that matter, is virtually anybody in a position to stop one once one starts.

I should add that large numbers of people may collectively stop a war they find problematic or wrong, and that a sense of history can shape the perceptions that make opposition possible. But the "lessons" of the past are nothing if not slippery. The classic example is the so-called Munich analogy, wherein American policymakers wished to avoid the mistakes of European leaders in appeasing Hitler, as British Prime Minister Neville Chamberlain did at a 1938 meeting, only to have their determination to stand fast against Communist aggression lead to a quagmire in Vietnam in the 1960s. Hence an affirmation of the truism that one should never to start a land war in Asia, which U.S. policymakers nevertheless ignored by going to war with Iraq in 1991 and again in 2003 (with very different results). Go figure.

So: History is irrelevant, history is depressing, history is maddeningly ambiguous. But what may be worst of all is that history is boring. Or, more accurately, History—the professional kind, with teachers and classrooms and assigned reading, which we'll designate with a capital "H"—is, shall we say, less than incredibly exciting. Movies like *Gladiator* and *Saving Private Ryan* are okay, but History books are often deadly. Actually, reading *itself* is often deadly. Well, maybe that's an exaggeration. (I myself think of reading the way I think of exercise: Once you get in shape, it's something that's good for you that you actually enjoy, even crave.) Still, so much of what you're asked to read doesn't seem to be addressed to you in an especially compelling way. So what's the point? *Why* is history worth your time? Why *should* it seep into your consciousness?

The answer is hope. Good history gives you hope.

This may strike you as a thin, vague, even foolish, assertion. One reason why I say so is that I myself am only a recent—and, truth be told, intermittent—convert to hope. I don't know about you, but for most of my life, I've looked upon hope with suspicion. Hope means potential disappointment. It means failure that's all the more acute when there's a belief that things could have been otherwise. Hope is risky, It may lead you to commit to things that could hurt you—and it's painful even before the outcome whatever it is you're hopeful about, because it often leads to stress and anxious uncertainty. In many respects, life would be easier without hope.

As a practical matter, however, life without hope is impossible. You need at least some, whether it's faith there will be food in the cafeteria when you get there at lunchtime, or an assumption you'll live long enough to actually use that education you're acquiring amid a lot of exertion and boredom. Even suicide attempts involve the hope they'll actually work. So hope is inescapable. But that's my point, you see: Hope is a trap. It's a problem that has to be dealt with, for better or worse.

But even if we grant the desirability and utility of hope, you still have to wonder if *history* is really the best source of it. Remember that James Joyce line: "History is a nightmare from which I'm trying to awake." Of course, if you're an Irishman in the early twentieth century, history, particularly that of Ireland in the preceding 350 years or so before Joyce wrote, may be a particularly dreadful nightmare. American history isn't so bad—unless, perhaps, you're an African American born before, say, 1950, or a Chinese immigrant born, say, after 1850, or someone with a family history of alcoholism. And yet there have been lots of people and movements in American history, from the Puritan migration of the early seventeenth century to the Civil Rights Movement of the mid-twentieth, that have not only made life better for people of the time, but have also given justified hope to succeeding generations that they too can wage and win comparable struggles. Even Ireland is now a sunnier place for many of its people than it has been for centuries. Then again, intolerance, poverty, and racism have not exactly disappeared, either. It sort of depends on how you look at it.

To put it another way, I'm suggesting that you might do well to have faith in history, and more generally, to have hope in hope. In this sense, I'm asking you to view history as something closer to a religion than a science, even if it borrows the means, and maybe even some of the ends, of science. By asking you to have faith, I don't mean for this to be considered a mindless confidence that things will turn out for the best. More often than not, they won't. In his 1991 book *The True and Only Heaven*, the late historian Christopher Lasch makes as an arresting distinction between optimism and hope. Optimism, Lasch says, is a fatuous belief in Progress, a misguided confidence in human knowledge, power, and goodness—all of which are real, but limited. Hope, by contrast, "implies a deep-seated trust in life that appears absurd to those who lack it." That trust, Lasch explains, comes from early memories—not necessarily accurate memories, but nevertheless happy ones, moments that lodge in our consciousness and remain there as touchstones. Such experiences, Lasch says, leave as its residue "the unshakable conviction, not that the past was better than the present, but that trust is never completely displaced, even though it is never completely justified either and therefore destined inevitably to disappointments."

So hope is a different thing than optimism. But optimism isn't the opposite of hope, only a simple-minded version of it. Nor is worry, the fear that the future may not turn out the way one wants. Worry can be painful and even paralyzing, but it has the potential to motivate people to do constructive things that may allay fears or even avert a negative outcome. Nostalgia, a belief that the past will always be better than the future, isn't quite the opposite of hope either, because the nostalgist will settle for a facsimile of past, and grant the existence of good outcomes, even if they've already happened. Nor is despair, which is grief about an outcome and an inability to believe that future good outcomes are possible. None of these are especially happy or productive states, as you may know first-hand. But they are not implacable enemies of hope. Someone in despair, for example, *wants* to hope but simply cannot.

The real opponent of hope is cynicism: a *refusal* to believe. The cynic does not simply assert things will not turn out for the best, but that they *can't*. Insofar as history matters, it's as a track record of failure, and attempts to say otherwise are simply rationalizations by people unable to face reality, whatever the textbooks might say. The cynic, for instance, notes the South won the Civil War. Sure, Lee surrendered to Grant on April 9, 1865. And yes, slavery was abolished as a result of the Thirteenth Amendment to the Constitution, also ratified in 1865. But the tenant farming system that replaced slavery was simply peonage by a different name. A hundred years later, the Civil War was fought all over again, led by people like Martin Luther King Jr. and his army of nonviolent protesters. He lost, too. (Like Lee, he had decent tactics, but insufficient numbers.) Sure, African-Americans don't have separate water fountains, Michael Jordan is a multimillion-aire, and President Bush gets some of his best advice from a black woman named Condoleezza Rice. But are schools or neighborhoods any less segregated? And what flag is it that flies over the South Carolina statehouse a century-and-a-half after the state seceded? "What's new?" an old joke among African Americans asks. Nothing much, is the answer: "White folks still on top." It's not so much the version of the story that matters here; even the optimist may accept its outlines. It's more the tone, a complacent confidence that true wisdom lies in detached amusement. True love does not conquer all, and you can't fight City Hall. Do you really need to be told?

I don't want to be cynical about cynicism: It's an understandable, even attractive option. Nor is it necessarily the domain of the old and jaded: You might say the smartest cynic is a young one, because she's figured things out so quickly. But every cynic arrives at such a destination from experience: from actually listening to (if not actually following) parental advice; from watching what teachers do (as opposed to what they say); from seeing peers who jumped to conclusions (and landed on their asses). Cynicism is best treated sympathetically, and seriously.

By some lights, this is also an especially good time to be a cynic—or to become one. You have come of age in an era of presidents who evade personal responsibility by asking what the meaning of "is" is, and who proclaim their intent to "leave no child behind" when that's precisely what has happened on their watch. You live in a time when *what* people say—or, more precisely, *how* they say what they say—seems to be of paramount importance, from corporate pronouncements about "service" that are really about profit to ideologues who more anxious to get people to resign for saying tasteless things than for actually doing hateful things. My best guess is that this era will later be viewed as an Age of Debt, a time when even affluent individuals, families, and governments lived beyond their means and denied the deprivations of others even as they lightened their own burdens. Speculation, not production, has been the order of the day.

A good cynic would point out that such remarks could be made about many times and places, and would be correct. But I write out of a sense of worry, a long-standing but intensifying concern that our national self-indulgence is on the cusp of catching up with us, and that there will be consequences for this that you'll experience in your lifetime. Am I wrong? Quite possibly, though it will be a while before we know. And if I'm right, it may not matter, because there may be nothing you can do.

Then again, there might. And this is where I try to convert my worry into something better: This book is an act of hope. It takes the form of history, more specifically a series of snapshot accounts of how other people have dealt with difficult, even hopeless, situations. Like other historians, I make arguments, chiefly in the form of saying that what these people did—or what these people did *not* do—is worth keeping in mind as you live your life and exercise your judgment about others (such as those who represent you). It's possible you'll find directly applicable lessons here about what do to if you find yourself fighting a land war in Asia. But I doubt it. If anything, the lessons here may seem almost perversely impractical. That's a big part of their appeal.

I believe the habit of absorbing such stories will engender a sympathetic imagination. Over time and with practice, you'll develop your ability to relate to other people, past and present. (Perhaps you'll find that you don't really *need* to defeat, or even argue with, your mother anymore.) You'll see that you're not alone, that you've never been alone. And this will engender confidence with which to face an uncertain future, to believe that conditions will change for the better, and that what once seemed impractical once may be possible, even necessary. Indeed, to my way of thinking, history is nothing more than the story of how common sense changes.

The following biographical sketches explore a series of questions. How does one keep true to one's vision in the face of social pressure? What strategies will work in persuading reluctant people to do the right thing? Can public acts successfully atone for private flaws? The following chapters attempt to provide answers such questions—not definitive answers, but real ones. You can weigh them, accept them, reject them, and maybe even apply them. Is history the only way to answer such questions? Certainly not. Is it the best way? Perhaps not. But it's certainly one way, a way that can inform and leaven others. Poker, gardening, and history make for a nice mix.

So what do you say? Shall we move forward by going back?

1

General Washington Says No

A fragile country wracked by war and dissent. A ragged army restless with neglect. Angry creditors demanding payment. And in the capital, government officials plotting intrigue. The looming question: What will army officers—particularly in the man in charge—do when they're invited to march in and take over?

The scenario described here has come to pass any number of times in any number of places over the last few hundred years. One of those places was the United States, specifically the town of Newburgh, New York. It was there, in the winter of 1783, that General George Washington became aware of a conspiracy, one which he was being urged to join by one of his closest aides. What did he do? The answer may prove surprising to the cynical beginner.

CHAPTER 1:
GENERAL WASHINGTON SAYS NO

in which we see the limits of power
—and the power of limits

IT IS EARLY MARCH, 1783. Almost eight years earlier, in April 1775, the American Revolution began with pitched battles in the Massachusetts towns of Lexington and Concord. The following days, weeks, and months have mostly been times of defeat and deprivation for the rebel cause. The armed forces of Great Britain—the greatest in the world—have imposed their will by occupying, or threatening to occupy, vast stretches of the thirteen colonies, only some of whose residents are in active revolt.

Now, after almost a decade of active fighting and another one of seemingly endless riots, boycotts, and other forms of agitation, it's precisely Britain's will that has become the defining issue. One rare but decisive defeat, at Saratoga, New York, in 1777, led to the capture of an entire British army and brought the Empire's longtime adversary, France, into the war. French aid proved decisive in another such defeat at Yorktown, Virginia, in October 1781, resulting in the capture of a second British army. The government of His Majesty George III has reluctantly concluded the war is simply not worth the mounting aggravation of time, money, and imperial jockeying with France (and its ally, Spain—both of whom are more daunting adversaries than those pesky rebels, particularly in the Caribbean, whose vulnerable sugar plantations might well be worth more than anything on the mainland anyway). And so it is that after months of delays and haggling, his negotiators are in Paris, haggling over a peace treaty that would grant the Americans their independence. Though the deal isn't official, and the war could resume after almost eighteen months of relative quiet, it really does look like the end is near.

All of this is exciting, amazing, even surreal. (The surrendering British army band at Yorktown had played a tune called "The World Turned Upside Down.") And yet, you, a junior officer in the American Continental Army, the army that has made this astounding turn of events possible, are absolutely furious—and so is everyone else around you. Despite the fact that victory is at hand, you're actually *afraid* of peace, because you fear it means you're going to get shafted—again. Ever since you joined the army, the divided and feckless politicians of the Continental Congress have provided you with nothing but misery: poor or insufficient supplies, little or no pay, and a string of broken promises. If the war actually does end now, then Congress will have no incentive to address these issues. It will simply send you all home, impoverished, to face families that have themselves endured years of hardship. This, apparently, is what "freedom" is going to mean.

And so you're asking yourself: When Congress does disband the army, are you just going to stand there and take it? Should you even *wait* to give them the chance to abuse you any more? What kind of man would do that?

You've heard that some members of the Continental Congress are themselves disgusted with the government, though for reasons that have little to do with the army. (Apparently, some rich people are mad they haven't been paid what they're owed either.) Rumor has it that congressional leaders have been talking with a small group of officers, and that they're planning to take matters into their own hands. They will *make* the government do the right thing—whatever it takes. The whispering around army headquarters in Newburgh, New York, about seventy miles up the Hudson River from British-occupied Manhattan, suggests the call to action will come any day now.

How do you feel about these plans? Do they make you nervous, relieved, depressed, giddy? Maybe it doesn't matter. Maybe the only real question is whether anyone is going to try to stop this secret plan once it's in motion. Then you'll decide what to do—and whom to follow.

Oh, God, why did you ever join this army in the first place?

◆   ◆   ◆

"These are times that try men's souls," Thomas Paine had written in December 1776. Paine, whose wildly popular pamphlet *Common Sense* has spurred the colonials to revolt back in January, penned these words while traveling with the infant Continental Army, seeing firsthand that the Americans were proving exasperatingly independent-minded about their pursuing their independence. Paine's new pamphlet was titled *American Crisis*, which is what he saw when he looked at the situation of that army. The opening battles of the Revolution, Lexington and Concord, had been fought by local militias, the legendary "Minutemen," so named because they were ready to fight at a moment's notice. Such organizations could be effective in localized combat precisely because their members were volunteers who were fighting for their homes. Yet for this very reason, they were reluctant to travel very far—and, especially, to submit to control by outsiders. (This was the source of much British exasperation and disdain toward them when used in colonial wars against the French and Indians.) The colonists had long been notable for their deep aversion to professional soldiers; indeed, one of the

major factors in the coming of the Revolution involved the presence, and require-
ment to support, a standing British army in North America. Many were afraid
that any such army, even one they raised themselves, was capable of all kinds of
mischief—or worse.

As a practical and even symbolic matter, however, Americans of the thirteen
colonies were going to need a standing professional army if they were going to
win their independence as a group. As Paine observed, "the summer soldier and
sunshine patriot" would likely wilt in the face of adversity or a long struggle, and
only an organization of paid soldiers contractually committed for the long haul
(such as a three-year enlistment) was likely to stand up to the British in a sustained way. And so it was that Congress borrowed money and issued currency to
recruit, pay, and outfit the Continental Army in 1775. While local militias continued to play a major role throughout the Revolution, especially in the South,
the existence—and survival—of the army was the key to the outcome of the
struggle. The British would control the seas and take cities from New York to
Charleston, but as long as there was an army to fight them, the Revolution could
go on.

The problem was that the colonies were often ambivalent about giving the
army the resources necessary to even wage, never mind win, the war. Jealous of
their own authority, they had difficulty coordinating even the most ardently
shared objectives, and were notoriously bad about sustaining the national government financially: that meant taxes, and nobody likes being taxed. The result was
vividly on display in the winter of 1777–1778, when the Continental Army win-
tered at Valley Forge, Pennsylvania. A sick, hungry, cold, and half-naked collection of men tottered on the edge of destruction.

You might well ask yourself: Why was there an army at all under such circumstances? Why didn't the men simply say "the hell with this!" and go home? Many
did, of course. As to why more didn't, well, this is something of a mystery in the
American Revolution, as it is in many wars. In part, the men fought in this one
because they believed in the cause, which, whether framed in terms of the gran-
diloquent phrases of the Declaration of Independence or the hardheaded defense
of one's home from invaders, was usually more compelling than that of their
opponents, many of whom were mercenaries strictly in it for the money. And
American soldiers, like virtually all soldiers throughout history, fought for each
other, bound by ties that transcended (and, at times, even defied) civilian standards and values. But financial incentives were by no means absent. A typical
member of the Continental Army received a $10 bonus upon enlistment (a salary
that varied depending on rank) and a promise of 100 acres of land upon the com-

pletion of his service. In 1780, Congress sweetened the offer for officers by promising them they would receive pensions at half-salary in recognition of their service.[1]

By the end of 1782 though, promises weren't good enough. Unpaid for months, there was widespread doubt among soldiers they would ever see their pensions, and they began setting their sights on getting a lump-sum payment now rather than hoping for more later. In December of that year, a group of officers at the army's headquarters in Newburgh, New York, sent a delegation led by Major General Alexander McDougall to the national capital at Philadelphia to make such a deal. "We have borne all that men can bear—our property is expended—our private resources are at an end, and our friends are wearied out and disgusted with our incessant applications," their petition read. These men were willing to negotiate for less than they had been promised, but something had to be done—*now*. If not, "Any further experiments on their patience may have fatal effects." This was a vague but unmistakable threat that the army might have to take matters into its own hands.

There were men in Congress who were sympathetic to this delegation and willing to act on its behalf. These people, who were dismayed by the lack of a strong central authority in a government where unanimous consent among the colonies was required to get anything of consequence done, were known as Nationalists. Among the Nationalists were figures that would later rise to fame in working with (and sometimes against) each other: Alexander Hamilton of New York, James Wilson of Pennsylvania, and James Madison of Virginia. For some of these men, however, among them Hamilton, Congressional Treasurer Robert Morris, and his assistant, Gouverneur Morris (no relation), concerns for the army and administrative efficiency were only part of the problem: They were worried that speculators, domestic and foreign, who had loaned the United States money, would not see a return on their investments and thus be unwilling to finance the government any further. Under the leadership of all these men, a proposal was made in January 1783 whereby the colonies would agree to tax imports in order to pay the army as well as government creditors. To support it, the Newburgh delegation testified that Congress could expect "at least mutiny" if the army wasn't satisfied, and Robert Morris abruptly resigned as finance minister to impress upon wavering congressmen just how serious the state of the nation's finances were.

Despite the high-pressure tactics, the proposal failed. In the course of debate, it became clear that Congress was willing to raise the money for overdue bills and salaries, but New Englanders in particular were unwilling to commit to any deal on pensions. The backdrop for the argument was the prospect of peace with England. Many members of Congress were reluctant to make major financial commitments that perhaps they would not have to, while the Newburgh delegation and Hamilton in particular grew increasingly anxious that peace would make it hard, if not impossible, to convince Congress to act. When a second vote failed, they concluded more radical measures were necessary.

What kind of radical measures? From this point, the story begins to get murky. A series of letters went out from Philadelphia to General Henry Knox, a senior officer and activist for the soldiers. One told him the pension proposal had failed. Another suggested the army might have to get tough if it wanted to see results. A third, written by McDougall under a pseudonym, was more explicit: The army just might have to mutiny, or, in the event of peace, refuse to disband until it was satisfied. Knox was to wait for instructions and "not to lose a moment in preparing for events."[2]

But would Knox actually go along with something like this? Even those who wanted him to must have known that this was very unlikely. A dedicated patriot who had distinguished himself as an artillerist, he was an avowed champion of the disgruntled officers. He was willing to push hard on their behalf—but not *that* hard. After a silence of about two weeks, Knox replied. "I consider the reputation of the American Army as one of the most immaculate things on earth," he wrote to the head of the Newburgh delegation. "We should even suffer wrongs and injuries to the utmost verge of toleration rather than sully it in the least degree." To Gouverneur Morris, Knox said the army would make no coercive moves unless directed by "proper authority."[3]

Well, no coercive moves made under *his* direction, anyway. On February 13, 1783, while Knox was mulling over the situation, news arrived in Philadelphia that King George III had told his Parliament that preliminary articles of peace had been signed the previous month accepting the independence of the United States. (The often-glacial pace of events in the eighteenth century, in which news took weeks to travel over oceans and wars were suspended for months because of the weather, represents perhaps the greatest barrier between that time and ours.) Those who wanted Congress to address the army/creditor problem concluded it was now or never. From Philadelphia, McDougall wrote Knox in late February that there was no hope their pay claims would be resolved and that Congress might split the army into detachments to prevent insurrection. More importantly—and this is where the story gets really murky—an emissary, Colonel Walter Stewart, sent instructions to a secret group of conspirators who were aides of, but not necessarily working with, Major General Horatio Gates, an ambitious man with a mottled reputation and a well-known frustration with his status.

On Monday, March 10, amid rumors the army would join with public creditors to move on Philadelphia, where even many members of Congress would welcome an army takeover, an unsigned manifesto began circulating at army headquarters. This first "Newburgh Address," as it has come to be known, exhorted officers to reject "the meek language of entreating memorials" and "change the milk-and-water style" of their correspondence with Congress. "If the present moment be lost," the document read, "every future effort is in vain; and your threats then, will be as empty as your entreaties now." If the war was indeed over, then no one should surrender his arms until his grievances had been met. And if the war wasn't over…well…they should "retire to some unsettled country, smile in your turn, and 'mock when their fear cometh on.'" If the politicians and civilians weren't willing to support the army, then let *them* fight the war. Regarding patience as a form of cowardice, the First Newburgh Address exhorted the officers to "suspect the man who would advise to more moderation and longer forbearance."[4]

That man, who had been following the situation with growing alarm, was now compelled to act. But what could he do? Some thought he should take charge of the movement and, in so doing, take charge of the government. Power would be concentrated, and things would get done. But this man had different ideas.

◆   ◆   ◆

Of all the Founding Fathers, I've always had the hardest time relating to George Washington. I find Benjamin Franklin complex, even unknowable: a strange fusion of Puritan earnestness, sly wit and a whiff of moral laziness. It's a strange mix, but at least the components are recognizable. John Adams appeals to me in his very unattractiveness—fretful, humorless, vain—largely because he has the great virtue of honesty, including self-honesty, about faults I myself find all too familiar. I almost believe I know him. By contrast, the more I learn about Thomas Jefferson, the less I like him. He strikes me as a superficially graceful man who is incapable of being honest with himself or anyone else. His noble sentiments (such as the Declaration of Independence) more than offset by deplorable behavior, including his now-documented sexual relationship with his slave, Sally Hemings, and his two-faced relationship with John Adams, whose presidency he helped destroy amid professions of friendship. Even Alexander Hamilton, a brilliant creep, was more consistent, with more of a sense of loyalty, than Jefferson.

But Washington? A cipher. The traditional view, going back two centuries now, is Washington as The Great Man, the Father of His Country, the Man Who Would Never Tell a Lie (the whole cherry tree thing). For a long time I considered him a self-important real estate speculator, whose primary reason for hostility toward Britain was its let's-not-have-any-Indian-hassles ban on sales of western lands he and other rich Virginians desperately wanted to get their hands on. Certainly, the man we see in portraits always *looked* presidential. But he also looked more than a little stiff.

What none of these views clarifies, however, is whether there was anything beyond the impressive profile in those portraits that justified the faith so many people put in him. And trust him they did, over and over again—as commander-in-chief during the Revolution, as president of the Constitutional Convention, and again for two terms as president. He never seemed to actually *want* these jobs—a perception, of course, that's useful for a leader, even if it's almost never a reality. And yet, by the end of his life, at least, it apparently *was* a reality; old man Washington didn't want a third term that was his for the asking, and finally went home to his fabled estate at Mount Vernon in 1797, the one he kept claiming he wanted to return to, but kept leaving, for over two decades. But because he *did* go home, no man for the next 150 years felt like he could decently serve more than two terms as president. Franklin Roosevelt, who presided over the Great Depression and World War II, was elected four times; a few years after his death in 1945, a constitutional amendment made two terms the law. But Washington didn't need any such laws in order to give up power. However dull, I had to admit there was something shrewd about the way he managed his reputation (and it appears that managing his reputation was something that seemed very important to him).

Then I came across a brief reference to the Newburgh Conspiracy in a U.S. history textbook I was assigned to use in my first year as a high school teacher. Washington's behavior in that affair piqued my curiosity: Perhaps here I could get a clue about what all the fuss was about, and whether it was really justified. This chapter came about as much at least as much because of a desire to understand Washington generally as the Newburgh Conspiracy in particular.

Here's one of the first things I learned when I began checking into the matter: Washington was truly *provincial*, in the most literal sense of that term.[5] While it would be foolish to claim he had Lincolnesque beginnings in a log cabin deep in the woods, Washington was nevertheless born in 1732 as a subject at the outer edges of a global empire into circumstances that, while certainly comfortable, were not impressive by aristocratic standards. Insofar as he had anything going for him, it was that he did, in fact, know a little about life deep in the woods. Washington's father died when he was a child, and he was taken under the wing of his half-brother, Lawrence, who served briefly as an officer in the British army. As a young man, Washington himself hoped to get a commission as colonel, naïvely unaware that such a position was only open to British subjects with more distinguished backgrounds than he did—and who had much more money than he did to actually buy the job. He was fortunate enough, however, to befriend some members on the lower rung of the relatively influential Fairfax family. And so, when the governor of Virginia, Robert Dinwiddie, needed somebody in 1754 to hack his way west toward the Ohio River and tell the encroaching French to get lost, Washington, who had some experience mapping western lands, was chosen to lead a small detachment of soldiers, translators, and Indian guides to run the errand.

He was almost comically in over his head, having no idea his Indian companions had their own agenda. When his party came upon the French building a fort in what is now western Pennsylvania, Washington never got the chance to inform them they had to go, nor did they manage to convey to him that *he* had to go, because the Indians short-circuited any dialogue by murdering any Frenchmen they could get their hands on. The news literally triggered a world war between France and England, one that stretched from the Indian territories of North America, across Europe, and into the Indian subcontinent. When this conflict, the Seven Years War (or, as it was known in America, the French and Indian War), was finally over in 1763, Britain was supreme in North America. But the price tag was staggering, and in a series of attempts to recover the costs, Britain tried to make its colonies pay what His Majesty's government regarded as their fair share. The colonies resisted, and a series of moves and countermoves culminated in the outbreak of the Revolutionary War.

Washington made the most of his opportunities in these years. When the British sent regulars—what the government regarded as *real* soldiers—to Virginia in 1756, Washington's knowledge of the terrain allowed him to gain an appointment as an aide to General William Braddock, an arrogant commander who plunged his way to catastrophic defeat. In the ensuing campaign, Washington performed with valor despite illness, surviving four bullets through his coat and two horses shot from under him before managing to escape with his life. (Braddock did not.) Over the course of the next two years, Washington led the defense of Virginia as a colonel of colonial forces despite inadequate resources and the open contempt of regular British officers, who did not regard him as their equal. When the French finally withdrew from their best-defended position in western Pennsylvania, which the British renamed Fort Pitt, the Virginia frontier was secure, and Washington left the army at the end of 1758. The following year he was elected to the colony's legislature, the House of Burgesses (very much a part-time job), and settled down by marrying a wealthy widow, Martha Custis, and managing a growing estate.

The next fifteen years were relatively quiet and generally prosperous for Washington. If, hypothetically, this hearty outdoorsman had taken ill and died in, say, 1772 at age forty, it could have been said he lived an impressive life in which his ambition and talent had found an outlet, and in which he had experienced a perceptible degree of upward mobility. In fact, you might have said Washington was an authentic representative of an emerging American Dream, and as such was by no means unique, even in relatively hierarchical eighteenth-century Virginia. Like such men, Washington avidly embraced the role of gentleman, entertaining countless guests with legendary Southern hospitality. It was a role that also brought with it deeply traditional assumptions about the role of women and control over a large number of slaves. (The "self-made" man, especially the Southern self-made man, depended on "inferiors" of various kinds.) Like such men, too, he was an aggressive investor in land, and, as one prominent biographer has noted, "the type of real estate speculation Washington most enjoyed wasn't for the faint of heart."[6] Finally, like many of such people, Washington incurred deep and growing debts to London merchants and brokers, debts that belied their prized sense of autonomy and even mobility.

Yet by the middle of his life, Washington showed a striking independence of mind, an ability to think outside the social box in which he lived, even if he couldn't get outside that box entirely. Take, for example, the issue—or, to put it more accurately for many people in his time and place, the *non*-issue—of slavery. Simply put, Washington's lifestyle depended on it. And yet, despite the near-total absence of anything resembling an antislavery movement,[7] he clearly felt the "peculiar institution," as it was later called, was a real problem. One telling indication of this was an offhand remark in 1774 to a member of the Fairfax family, in which he complained the increasingly heavy-handed British rule threatened to "make us [colonists] as tame & abject Slaves, as the Blacks we Rule over with such arbitrary sway."[8] Washington himself strived to avoid such "arbitrary sway" in what he seemed to regard as a necessary evil. From the 1770s on, he adopted a financially onerous policy of refusing to sell any slave without that slave's permission—no slave of his ever gave it—and during his first term as president he secretly investigated the possibility of breaking up Mount Vernon into smaller farms, emancipating his slaves, and allowing them to work as tenant farmers so as "to liberate a certain species of property which I possess very repugnantly to my own feelings."[9] He was told by his financial advisers that the plan wouldn't work, and so put it aside. But when he left the presidency, he freed the slaves he brought to office so quietly that the act wasn't discovered until 170 years later. He also gave all his slaves their freedom in his will, to be provided by his executors "without evasion, neglect or delay."[10] None of this, of course, can remove the odiousness of Washington's participation in an evil system of labor. But it does seem worth pointing out that his actions were far more appropriate than most of his peers—notably Jefferson, who was so irresponsibly in debt that his slaves had to be sold off after his death—and that his concern for his slaves was in some ways more genuine than many Northern critics of slavery. His actions are also suggestive of a larger point: that even when exercising power illegitimately, Washington operated within self-imposed limits.

This sense of inner discipline was also important for Washington in achieving some freedom for himself. Here again, Jefferson furnishes a good counterexample. Washington was by no means unique in his unease toward the London merchants and brokers who held him in debt. But unlike Jefferson, who also chafed against indebtedness even as he bought more books and wine and tinkered with renovations to his Monticello estate, Washington had the will as well as the resources to extricate himself from financial exploitation. Realizing the generally accepted policy of cultivating a single crop—tobacco—had addictive consequences for those who subjected themselves to the whims of an unpredictable commodities market, Washington strived to make Mount Vernon a self-sufficient enterprise. By the late 1760s, he stopped growing tobacco entirely, focusing his resources on corn and wheat, which were much less labor-intensive. This, in turn, allowed him to diversify still further, not only in agriculture, but also in directing efforts toward weaving and milling, that is, proto-industrial enterprises. By the 1770s, with his dream of becoming a regular British officer behind him, Washington was psychologically, as well as economically, declaring his independence.

So by 1775, when, as one of the few revolutionaries who had real military experience, Washington was chosen to head the new Continental Army, he embodied some of the values they cherished most: competence, autonomy, mobility—qualities characteristic of a "natural" aristocracy of merit (as opposed to the corrupt, inherited aristocracy against which they were rebelling). To these qualities, Washington also went on to demonstrate another that also went to the heart of what was called a "Whig" philosophy: a deep concern about the inherent excesses of power. The right to lead had be earned, confirmed, and limited in order to be truly legitimate.

As a leader, Washington enjoyed substantial support, but his supremacy did not go unchallenged. This is because questioning authority was also part of the revolutionary Whig culture. John Adams of Massachusetts, who nominated Washington to lead the army, did so because he thought was Washington qualified for the job, and because he thought it was symbolically important that a Southerner lead what in 1775 were mostly New England troops. Yet Adams was skeptical of Washington for much of the war because he feared the despotic potential of *any* man with that much power. Horatio Gates, who, as the victor at Saratoga in 1777, briefly overshadowed a Washington who seemed to be continually retreating across New York, New Jersey, and Pennsylvania, was anxious to replace him and colluded with a number of officers to do so. When an irritated Washington threatened to resign if the Irish-born French general Thomas Conway was promoted against his wishes, the members of the so-called Conway Cabal attempted to maneuver him into doing so. Their maladroit efforts became known prematurely and fizzled out. But Washington was clearly rattled by the affair.[11]

Washington could also be prickly and defensive if he felt he wasn't getting his due. Perhaps the best illustration was his spat with his trusted aide, Alexander Hamilton. One morning in February 1781, Washington encountered Hamilton on a stairway in New Windsor, New York, and told him he wished to speak with him. Hamilton, on his way to deliver a letter, told Washington he would return as soon as he had done so. On his way back, Hamilton was apparently accosted by another Washington protégé, the Marquis de Lafayette, and the two conversed. When Hamilton returned, Washington was angry. "Colonel Hamilton you have kept me waiting at the head of the stairs these ten minutes. I must tell you sir, you treat me with disrespect." Hamilton, who was even haughtier than Washington, replied, "I'm not conscious of it, sir, but since you have thought it necessary to tell me, so we part." A surprised Washington retorted, "Very well, sir, if it be your choice." Yet it was the restless Hamilton, who admired Washington and yet chafed at what he regarded as his somewhat plodding style, who dwelled on the exchange, which at the urging of Hamilton's family and friends, the two put behind them.[12] Actually, one of the most striking things about Washington was his ability to tolerate and accept people who did not think the way he did. His lifelong mentoring of Hamilton, only twenty years old at the outbreak of the Revolution, is one indication of this. So was the mere presence of a rival like Gates, whose disastrous performance at the Battle of Camden in 1780 put his career in permanent eclipse, at Washington's headquarters in Newburgh at the end of the war.

In an important sense, however, the biggest challenge Washington faced wasn't in getting too little respect, but too much. In the spring of 1782, with tensions mounting in the Continental Army over the state of the army and congressional gridlock, one of his officers wrote him suggesting that "strong arguments might be produced for admitting the title of king," and that there had been some conversation about crowning him George I. Washington responded by saying "no occurrence in the War has given me more painful sensations than your information of there being such ideas existing in the Army as you have expressed, and I must view with abhorrence, and reprehend with severity. For the present, the communicatn. of them shall rest in my bosom, unless some further agitation of the matter shall make a disclosure necessary."[13]

Washington may have wished such subversive talk would go away, but he seemed fully aware it was intensifying in the months that followed. His correspondence with Congress in 1782–1783 was an anxious stream of complaints, demands, and laments about the lack of resources for his men. An October 1782 letter to Secretary of War Benjamin Lincoln shows his understanding of concrete realities as well as psychological imperatives that were apparent "universally throughout the Army":

> The Complaint of Evils which they [the soldiers] suppose almost remediless are, the total want of Money, or the means of existing from One day to another, the heavy debts they have already incurred, the loss of Credit, the distress of their families (i.e. such that are Married) at home, and the prospect of Poverty and Misery before them. It is vain Sir, to suppose that Military Men will acquiesce *contently* with bare rations when those in the Civil walk of life (unacquainted with the hardships they endure) are regularly paid the emoluments of Office.[14]

Despite the lack of action after the climactic Battle of Yorktown in October 1781, Washington declined to take time off and visit his family because he felt he needed to be "like a careful physician to prevent if possible the disorders getting to an incurable height."[15] By December, he was writing Virginia Congressman Joseph Jones saying, "the temper of the Army is much soured, and has become more irritable than at any time since the commencement of the War."[16] In early 1783, Jones himself wrote back that "reports are freely circulated here that there are dangerous combinations in the army" and that some of the conspirators were even trying to Blacken Washington's reputation.[17]

Though he knew there were people in and out of the army who were seeking redress of their grievances with Congress, Washington wasn't privy to the often-shadowy deliberations of General McDougall, Hamilton, and the Morrises. These people, however, considered his stance toward them to be pivotal to their plans, and they needed to sound him out. On February 13, 1783, the very day that news of the pending peace treaty with Britain was announced in Philadelphia, Hamilton wrote Washington an exquisitely calibrated letter that simultaneously managed to sidestep and invite treason. We all know, Hamilton told his mentor, that the situation is potentially explosive, and despite what all responsible people may want, it could quickly get out of hand. The challenge will be "to keep a *complaining* and *suffering army* within the bounds of moderation."

This, Hamilton told Washington, is where you come in.

> This [moderation] Your Excellency's influence must effect. In order to it, it will be advisable not to discountenance their endeavours to procure redress, but rather by the intervention of confidential and prudent persons, *to take direction of them.* This however must not appear: it is of moment of to the public tranquility that Your Excellency should preserve the confidence of the army without losing that of the people. This will enable you in case of extremity to guide the torrent, and bring order perhaps even good, out of confusion.[18]

Overthrow the government? Of course not! But it would not be a bad idea to be in charge once the insurrection gets underway. What you do is up to you. (However, you'll never be able to say that *I* recommended anything illegal.)

It's not known exactly when Washington received Hamilton's letter of February 13—it probably would have taken about a week to get from Newburgh to Philadelphia—but he apparently did not respond right away, whether because he didn't regard it as urgent, or because he felt he needed time to strike the right note in replying. That reply, written March 4, was relatively mild-mannered (though Washington did close by saying that their exchange was, and should remain, private). While he agreed with Hamilton that the situation with the army was indeed serious, "I shall pursue the same steady line of conduct which has governed me hitherto." Washington said he was under "no *great* apprehension of its exceeding the bounds of reason & moderation, notwithstanding the prevailing sentiment."[19]

Yet within a week of sending that letter, Washington *was* in great apprehension, because the first of the Newburgh addresses became public on March 10, calling for a meeting the next day. The vigilant but minimalist approach the commander-in-chief had adopted for the past year-and-a-half no longer seemed adequate: If he didn't do something, the train would leave the station without him. Now Washington acted with striking speed—and his first move was to freeze the conspiracy in its tracks. On Tuesday, March 11, he announced his awareness of an anonymous document and the call for a meeting. "Fully persuaded that the good sense of the officers would induce them to pay little attention to such an invitation," Washington made clear his "disapprobation of such disorderly proceedings." Instead, he told the men, there would be another meeting five days later, on Saturday, March 15, to be attended by senior officers and representatives from each army company "to devise what further measures ought to be adopted as the most rational and best calculated to attain the just and important object in view." The meeting was to be presided over by "a proper representative of the staff of the Army"—someone, apparently, that Washington would designate for the task.[20]

This was, by design, a confusing message. On the one hand, Washington was expressing disapproval for what the conspirators were up to. On the other, he was saying the meeting they were calling for *would* be held in order to obtain goals that were "just and important." And yet Washington himself apparently wasn't going to be there because he was putting someone else in charge—so he could deny any involvement even as he managed the movement, perhaps? Maybe the old man was craftier than they thought.

The conspirators were not, however, willing to surrender the initiative. The next day, March 12, a second Newburgh address appeared. Tuesday, Thursday, Saturday—whatever, it said. The important thing was that Washington, in his response, had "sanctified" their appeals. In any event, the soldiers were reminded any such meeting held under official auspices "cannot possibly lessen the *independence* of your sentiments."[21]

Washington, for his part, was also active that day. He reported to Elias Boudinot, the president of Congress, about what was happening. He reported as well to Jones, emphasizing to the congressman that however wrongheaded the conspirators may be, the surest way to resolve the problem was for Congress to act responsibly. Washington also fired off a letter to Hamilton, whose letter of February 13 he now seemed to see in a new light. "There is something very mysterious in this business," Washington wrote. "It appears, reports have been propagated in Philadelphia, that dangerous combinations were forming in the Army; and this at a time when there wasn't a syllable in Camp."

Only the return of Colonel Stewart (referred by Washington as "a certain gentleman") in early March seems to have triggered the unrest. Though not asked explicitly, a question seemed to hang in the air: You wouldn't have anything to do with this, now, would you, son?[22] In any case, a march on Philadelphia now would be a terrible idea, resulting in "a gulph of Civil horror from which there might be no receding."[23]

The next few days were quiet but tense. On the morning of the 15th, men gathered in the so-called New Building, which Washington had ordered built back in December to foster sociability among officers from different states. The presiding officer of the meeting was Horatio Gates—a man widely suspected then and since to have been involved in the conspiracy, though this has never been proved.[24] As presiding officer, however, his job was to direct the proceedings without participating in debate. As Gates opened the meeting, Washington suddenly appeared. He asked for permission to speak, which Gates could hardly refuse.[25]

Washington was in no mood to mince words. "Gentlemen: by an anonymous summons, an attempt has been made to convene you together," he began. "How inconsistent with the rules of propriety! How unmilitary!" He then moved on to the writer of the first address,[26] admiring his cleverness, though "I could wish he had as much credit for the rectitude of his heart." Washington reminded the men he was deeply sympathetic to their grievances—and shared them. But what did they see as the solution?

> The way is plain, says the anonymous Addresser. If War continues, remove into the unsettled country and there establish yourselves, and leave an ungrateful country to defend itself. But who are they to defend? Our Wives, our Children, our Farms, and other property which we leave behind us...If Peace takes place, never sheath your swords Says he until you have obtained full and ample justice; this dreadful alternative, of either deserting our Country in the extremest hour of her distress, or turning Arms against it, (which is the apparent object, unless Congress can be compelled into instant compliance) has something so shocking in it, that humanity revolts at the idea. My God! What can this writer have in view, by recommending such measures? Can he be a friend to the army? Can he be a friend to this Country? Rather, is he not an insidious foe?

Washington assured them he would do everything in his power to get them justice. But while he did so, "let me entreat you, Gentlemen, on your part, not to take any measures, which, viewed in the calm light of reason, will lessen the dignity, and sully the glory you have hitherto maintained."[27]

Accounts vary on the details of what happened next—Washington apparently had a letter from Congressman Jones he wished to read them—but all agreed he fumbled for his reading glasses, something only those close to him had ever seen him wear. "Gentlemen," he reputedly said, "you'll permit me to put on my spectacles, for I have not only grown gray but almost blind in the service of my country."[28]

Whether because of the accumulated impact of Washington's remarks, or the unexpected (and at least *seemingly* unrehearsed) display of vulnerability, the spectacles seemed to be the turning point. Grown men began to cry. Washington left the room. His trusted colleague, Knox, proposed motions that affirmed the army's "attachment to the rights and liberties of human nature" and its "unshaken confidence" in Congress. They passed unanimously.[29]

That's not quite to say everything ended happily ever after. Nationalists in Congress seized on the news emerging from Newburgh Conspiracy to press their case in Congress, and got a deal—of a sort. But it was so riddled with compromises and half-measures that Hamilton himself would not sign it. In the years that followed, many Revolutionary War veterans concluded they would never see the money they were owed and sold the promissory notes they had been issued, for pennies on the dollar, to speculators who bought them and then demanded they be paid at full value. (As Secretary of the Treasury, Hamilton successfully persuaded Congress to do so, which outraged former allies like Madison, but probably also put the nation on a safe financial footing. The rich, as they so often do, found a way to come out ahead.) Nor did Washington's Newburgh Address calm soldiers elsewhere in the country. Detachments of drunken soldiers in Lancaster, Pennsylvania, actually marched on the capital in June 1783, surrounding fifteen members of Congress, Hamilton included, in the Pennsylvania Statehouse. The members were allowed to leave, and the uprising petered out, but the prestige of Congress was damaged, and the body moved the nation's capital to Annapolis, Maryland.

Sounds like something out what we (North) Americans patronizingly call "a banana republic," doesn't it? Sullen soldiers, rumors of intrigue, renegade detachments that are by turns threatening and incompetent. And yet within a matter of a few years, it all seemed to be forgotten. The Treaty of Paris was signed in September 1783, the Constitution was framed four years later, the pension issue was resolved, however unfairly, in the 1790s, and the wobbly filly of a nation grew strong and became a thoroughbred. The Newburgh Conspiracy became little more than a footnote (or a few pages in the biographies of Washington and Hamilton).[30] In some sense, we've had the *luxury* of forgetting about it, living as we have in a society in which military takeover of the government has been a nightmare for fretful patriots, but not (yet) a reality.

So be on the lookout for dictators: Is that the point of all of this? Well, yes, sort of. But there's a bit more—or is it less?—to it than that.

◆   ◆   ◆

"Caesar rode into Annapolis on December 19, 1783," Robert Middlekauff writes toward the end of *The Glorious Cause*, a book many historians consider the standard textbook account of the Revolution.[31] Middlekauff is being ironic here; his point is that Washington wasn't a Roman general about to turn a republic into an empire, the way Julius Caesar did about 1,800 years earlier, and in fact was trying very hard to make that clear. He had come to what was now the capital of the United States to formally surrender his commission as commander-in-chief. As Middlekauff notes, he might have simply sent a letter to this effect, but Washington wanted to make a pointed and public statement about the subordination of military to civilian rule. This was to be a different kind of country.

To understand just how striking this act was, consider the following (far from complete) list of military leaders who chose not to make such a statement in the 220 years since:

- Napoleon Bonaparte (France)
- Simon Bolivar (Venezuela)
- Francisco Franco (Spain)
- Josip Tito (Yugoslavia)
- Mao Tse-Tung (China)
- Juan Peron (Argentina)
- Gamal Nasser (Egypt)
- Augusto Pinochet (Chile)
- Manuel Noriega (Panama)
- Saddam Hussein (Iraq)

Some of these people are more highly regarded than others, and some had more respect for the political process than others. (Note the last three were among many others who received significant military assistance from the United States.) Yet their record is mixed at best, particularly in Latin America, where "the man on horseback," to cite the famous phrase of novelist Gabriel Garcia Marquez, has all too often proved to be a destructive addiction.

Had Washington led, or failed to stop, the movement at Newburgh, could the United States have ended up like one of its Latin American brethren? Maybe not. As Richard Kohn, the historian who has looked more closely at the Newburgh Conspiracy than any other, believes the underlying social conditions simply weren't there. "Even though the Continental Congress was weak," Kohn notes, "there was no political vacuum in the country. State and local authorities were strong; the extremist groups or grinding class conflicts that precipitate chaos, revolution, and military interference were comparatively insignificant." I'm not sure Kohn is right—he himself describes the United States of 1783 as "extremely vulnerable"—but it is true the infant United States wasn't torn by ethnic strife, scarce resources, or persistent social disorder. [32]

As Kohn is suggesting, Washington himself wasn't really a decisive factor. Even if he *had* been a Napoleon or a Franco, much of the country would simply not have gone along with him. New England in particular was deeply suspicious of professional armies, which is why the crisis had emerged in the first place. Then again, this would hardly be the last time that a group of people brought about precisely what they were trying to avoid. Perhaps it's for the best, perhaps we're lucky, that we'll never know just how important Washington himself was to the outcome.

There is something we *do* know, however, and it's something that's not quite, or at least entirely, a matter of luck: George Washington *himself* was an "outcome": a product of the circumstances of his birth, yes, but also a product of his values. Those values included a belief that people ruling themselves through what we've come to know as the democratic process was a very, very attractive idea, and one he was willing to make considerable sacrifices for, including giving up home, family, and any income for eight years. It was also something he was willing to accept self-imposed limitations to achieve, so much so that by the mid-1790s he was desperate to leave the presidency so that he would not die in office and power would be transferred smoothly and constitutionally.

The values Washington lived by were instinctive, they were environmental, and they were learned. They have to be perpetrated in order to survive, and their survival is one of the things schools are supposed to do, and teachers are supposed to teach. You're being indoctrinated here, dear reader, with American propaganda—a certain *kind* of American propaganda. Can I *make* you accept my point of view? Nope, and I don't want to. But I hope you'll forgive me for trying to persuade you, and believing that *you* (me, sure, but you too) stand to benefit by taking the message I'm trying to get across seriously.

And what is that message? You're probably not going to find yourself at the head of a large army, and I hope you won't ever find yourself in the position of being afraid that one is about to take away your rights. But this notion of limits, even denial: That's something to consider right now. That the best way to actually gain your freedom is in giving it up—not to someone who asks for or seizes it, but as something you give, and can take back any time, and yet elect not to. That there might be something life-affirming, even joyful, about such a choice, whether in leading a revolutionary movement, raising a child, or simply deciding not to grab the spotlight at the next staff meeting. And that groups of individuals choosing to do this on an aggregate basis might really make a decisive difference in the way a place (a household, a school, a country) is run. That's what I've taken away from this story. What about you?

At the close of his Newburgh Address, Washington urged his soldiers to show their patriotism by reconciling themselves to the neglect and ingratitude of their fellow citizens. In so doing, he told them, "You will, by the dignity of your Conduct, afford occasion for Posterity to say, when speaking of the glorious example you have exhibited to Mankind, 'had this day been wanting, the World had never seen the last stage of perfection to which human nature is capable of attaining.'"

Lord knows, George Washington wasn't perfect. But at the end of the day (perhaps a day that will last about 250 years), I must say what he and his fellow Americans did show themselves capable of attaining really was quite impressive. We do them, and ourselves, a disservice to forget or minimize how important it can be to simply say: No (thank you).

2

Mr. Adams Stops Gagging

Son of a Founding Father. Harvard professor. Ambassador. Senator. Secretary of State. If anyone seemed destined for presidential greatness, it was John Quincy Adams. And yet, by most accounts, the second Adams presidency was a dismal failure. In an important sense, though, the most important phase of his life began after he left the White House. Even cynics will be amused, if not impressed, to learn about the scrappiness of a marginal congressman who took on defenders of slavery, and in the process became a legend worthy of his name. This is the story of a man even his opponents called "Old Man Eloquent."

CHAPTER 2:
CONGRESSMAN ADAMS STOPS GAGGING

in which we see that a privileged upbringing
need not handicap a (very) senior citizen

WHAT ARE YOU GOING TO DO when your plans don't work out?

Maybe that's not an especially useful question. After all, you don't make plans expecting them not to work out. Quite the contrary. That doesn't mean you take a best-case scenario for granted. In fact, I'm certain there have been many times when you began a sentence that begins the following way: "And if it [whatever *it* is] doesn't work out, I'll just _____" (go back to doing what I was doing before; do this other thing I don't particularly like but know I *can* do; and so on.) Such an approach may make sense for deciding to wait in line for concert tickets, hooking up with an acquaintance, or applying for a job that's clearly appealing, but which you're no shoo-in to get. Still, while you may predict what you're going to do if things don't work out, you're probably most likely to actually figure out what's next when you finally get there, which is one reason why asking what you're going to do may not be a great question.

Of course, there are plans, and then there are *plans*—like deciding what you're going to do with your life. But then not everybody formulates a discrete series of imagined steps that constitute what is commonly called a "plan." More often than not, you make a series of relatively open-ended choices (like, say, going to law school, the default option of many a recent college graduate) and then hope for the best. So you can't really ask someone what they're going to do if their plans don't work out if they don't really have plans in the first place—yet another reason why such a question may not be a particularly worthwhile one.

And yet I pose it anyway. Here's why: Even if you haven't explicitly formulated any particular plan, you have some general hope, even expectation, for any number of things you do—or don't—want to happen. How could you not? Such feelings are particularly honored in the United States, where formulating and executing plans, also known as "the pursuit of happiness," is an officially sanctioned way of life. This national license to dream—which, somewhere along the way, often becomes of a form of personal, if not social, pressure—is particularly potent when you come from a family that has high expectations for you, whether because your parents are themselves high achievers, or because they're living vicariously through you, or both. Under such circumstances, you may find yourself wondering *whose* plan you're working on, and *what*, in fact, success really means. So your plans, their realization (or lack thereof) may reveal a fair amount about who you really are and where you're really going.

Which brings us to the case of John Quincy Adams. Now here's a guy who began with a lot, and who did a lot—more, I can say with some confidence, than you or I ever will. But in his own eyes, and that of his contemporaries, Adams was a failure: a son who failed to achieve his father's eminence; a dour, even rigid personality who failed to overcome his faults; a tone-deaf politician almost hopelessly out of touch with his times. He did manage to become president of the United States, but he did so under a cloud of controversy, and even sympathetic biographers agree his presidency was a pathetic failure. Afterward, he did what some might consider an even more pathetic thing: He left the White House and, two years later, accepted a position as a member of the U.S. House of Representatives—not exactly a menial job, but hardly typical or even fitting for a former president. And then, in 1842, Adams found himself accused of one of the most serious of high crimes: treason. The House debated and voted as to whether he should be censured for advocating the United States be dissolved.

How on earth did something this marvelous come about?

◆   ◆   ◆

Although the United States is customarily viewed as a place where opportunity is open to all, it has always had an unofficial aristocracy. I say this less as a matter of pointing out national hypocrisy—you might think there would be no room for an aristocracy in a truly democratic republic—than as something that was actually part of the plan. You ask Founding Fathers like John Adams or Thomas Jefferson what the problem with European governments of their time was, and they would not say it was aristocracy per se, but the lack of what they called a *natural* aristocracy. George III was the King of England only because his father was (and his father before him). To the Founding Fathers, this was unnatural, which is to say it was arbitrary. A *natural* aristocracy, by contrast, is one in which people of demonstrated merit rise to power because of their achievements, not who their daddy was. All men may have been created equal in terms of their rights and their ability to tell right from wrong, but it was patently obvious that not all men were equal in their ability to, say, shoe a horse or write a constitution. That John Adams, a shoemaker's son, could rise to a position of prominence in which he would write a constitution (for Massachusetts, a model for the eventual federal one) is a sign the early republic was a place where there was room at the top for people who lacked pedigrees but had talent. Jefferson, for his part, wanted smart kids to be plucked out of the hands of their parents and placed in special academies, where they would be trained as leaders. Two centuries later, policies like affirmative action are similarly designed to open space in the elite for people who might not be able to otherwise join it, because they lack the advantages (from home tutors to crime-free neighborhoods) of those from more privileged backgrounds. How *"natural"* any of this is can be—is—questioned, but no one disputes there is now, and always has been, a certain group of people, almost never actually *called* an aristocracy, but who nevertheless enjoy many of the perks, from wealth to deference, that have always gone along with one.

But what about the children of such people? Theoretically, they should enjoy no special advantages—the lack of heredity privilege is the typical reason *why* we say we don't have an aristocracy—though they often do. (As anyone who takes even a cursory look into affirmative action knows, the most sure-fire way of getting into an Ivy League college rests not on the color of your skin, but whether your parents attended the school in question. Our current president, an indifferent student at best, is a case in point.) On the other hand, coming from an esteemed family shouldn't *disqualify* you from enjoying the fruits of your talents, and it's pretty clear that many (though not all) children of the successful are talented themselves, whether because of their genes, environment, or good fortune.

This assertion certainly applies to John Quincy Adams. The second child and oldest son of the formidable John and Abigail Adams, JQA, as he was known, was something of a child prodigy. It didn't hurt he had parents who had high expectations for him and provided him with the resources to meet them. Nor was the fact that he literally had a front-row seat for some of the defining moments in American history. JQA was seven years old when his mother took him to Bunker Hill in June 1775 (Dad was in Philadelphia as a member of the Continental Congress) to witness a pivotal early battle in the American Revolution. He was ten years old when his father took him along to Paris as part of an American delegation seeking aid and recognition from France. (The ship the two traveled on was chased more than once by British naval vessels, though bad weather proved even scarier.)[33] From there, JQA savored the best the civilized world had to offer, from tutors to theaters. He wasn't to the manor *born,* but he certainly was to the manor *raised.*

Still, there was no mistaking the boy was talented. His French was so good that JQA was appointed, at the age of fourteen, to be the interpreter for the U.S. minister to Russia, a mission he took unaccompanied by his father. He toured the continent before returning to the senior Adams in 1783, who promptly made the sixteen-year-old his private secretary. Unlike George Washington or even Adams himself, JQA's parents feared their cosmopolitan boy wasn't provincial *enough*, and so sent him home to Harvard, which he entered as a junior. Upon his graduation in 1787, he went on to study law, a subject he didn't have much feeling for but which he felt might prove useful. (Some things never change.)

JQA wasn't an especially effective young lawyer, perhaps because his heart wasn't in it (he liked writing and translating poetry more than arguing cases). He also wrote a highly publicized series of essays defending the Washington administration's foreign policy. A pleased president appointed Adams as a U.S. minister to the Netherlands in 1794. Adams Sr., then vice president of the United States, swore he had nothing to do with it. I'll let you be the judge of that one.

Over the course of the next thirty years, Adams lived an exceptionally busy life that included marriage, the birth of four children (including a daughter who died in infancy), stints in the Massachusetts legislature and the U.S. Senate, a professorship at Harvard, and appointment to the U.S. Supreme Court—an honor he declined. He did so in large measure because the real focus in his life in these years was diplomacy. At one point or another Adams not only represented the United States at The Hague, but also Berlin, London, and St. Petersburg, where he became a walking companion of the tsar of Russia. He saw the rise and fall of Napoleon Bonaparte firsthand, as French armies invaded countries where he was posted. And he participated in negotiating treaties with Napoleon's rival, Great Britain, in agreements that stretched from Jay's Treaty in 1795 to the Treaty of Ghent, which ended the War of 1812 three years later. From there he went on to become Secretary of State for eight years in the Monroe administration (1817–1825). Adams conceived and wrote the Monroe Doctrine, whereby the United States would view European intervention in the Western as an unfriendly act (a policy Britain, with the naval muscle to support it, was happy to endorse for its own reasons). As its name suggests, Adams was also a pivotal figure behind the Adams-Onis Treaty, which made Florida part of the United States. To a great degree, this happened because Adams strongly supported the highly controversial actions of an American general, Andrew Jackson, who chased hostile Seminole Indians into Spanish Florida, convincing the Spanish government that it should sell the territory for cash before losing it in battle.

Reading the previous paragraph, can't you just feel the momentum propelling Adams? How could the guy *not* become president? Not only had he held or been offered just about every important job in the U.S. government, but every other Secretary of State (Jefferson, Madison, and Monroe) had gone on to become the Chief Executive. And, of course, dear old dad, who was still around and would be until 1826, had been president. Adams Sr. had only served one term in what had proven to be a stormy tenure (no thanks to Hamilton or Jefferson, who both schemed behind his back). Maybe the son could do one better and, like every *other* president, serve two full terms. After all, had there ever been anyone who was so well-groomed and so obviously qualified for the job?

There were, however, two big obstacles in the way. The first was Adams himself. No one ever denied the man was smart, but in politics as in much else, being smart isn't enough. Let's just say Adams wasn't Mr. Congeniality. "The tendency to dissipation at Paris seems to be irresistible," he wrote in his diary in 1815, a somewhat typical sentiment from a child of the Puritans. That diary, by the way, is something Adams kept for over fifty years, a document in which the *edited* version ultimately ran twelve volumes, and in which he ritualistically berated himself for his laziness. The entry I just quoted goes on, "There is a moral incapacity for industry and application, a 'mollesse,' [debilitating form of laziness] against which I'm as ill guarded as I was from the age of twenty."

You have to wonder—well, no, you don't have to wonder at all—about how Adams felt about his fellow negotiators at Ghent, non-workaholics who stayed up playing cards until 4:00 AM, the hour in which he typically got up. Adams was kind of guy you would be very happy to have at the negotiating table, but unless you liked to read the Bible in Hebrew, perhaps not the kind of guy you would be comfortable with at the dinner table. Actually, he irritated his partners during the peace talks by eating alone because he didn't like the cigars they smoked and bad wine they drank. His future ally and rival, Henry Clay, showed some of his legendary aplomb by coaxing JQA back to join them.[34]

Adams may have also been a little too principled for his own good. The classic example is his behavior as U.S. Senator during the presidency of Thomas Jefferson, a man JQA, like his father, regarded with some ambivalence. In the global tension between England and France that dominated American foreign policy for the first forty years of the nation's existence, Jefferson adopted a "pox on both houses" approach in the form of an embargo on foreign trade that delighted the South but crippled New England's commercial interests. Ever a strong nationalist, JQA infuriated his usual allies by backing the Jefferson administration. They were so mad at him, in fact, that a special meeting of the Massachusetts legislature named his successor before JQA's term was even up.[35] He responded by resigning so that he could better defend the man who had defeated his father for reelection. A century-and-a-half later, another Massachusetts senator, John F. Kennedy (or, I should say, his ghostwriter, Ted Sorensen) made this episode of six "profiles in courage" in the Pulitzer-prize winning book about politicians who took brave stands.[36] It should be noted, however, that JQA's stance wasn't without benefits; a grateful Jefferson named him minister to Russia, and his political career survived in ways that many of his former friends, the Federalists, did not. In this case, then, JQA doing what he considered the right thing also turned out to be a shrewd recognition of a generational shift in American politics.

But this success only underscores a larger failure and the other big obstacle Adams faced as he reached—well, maybe "reach" isn't the right word, because it implies the kind of electioneering Adams always said he disdained—for the presidency in 1824. At the very moment his attainment of the prize might have seemed like a foregone conclusion, the American political system was undergoing one of the most decisive transformations in its history. And Adams, to put it simply, was yesterday's man. Ever since his father had lost his job, the presidency had been passed down in a fairly orderly procession by consensus. Now, though, a number of people were contending for the job, people who were not inclined to defer to JQA's obvious qualifications, among them William Crawford, Monroe's Secretary of the Treasury; Henry Clay, now a senator from Kentucky; and Andrew Jackson, a man whose conduct Adams once defended, but who now competed with him for the position. Clay and Jackson in particular had a much better feel for the emerging democratic climate, in which the word "aristocracy" would only be used in negative tones (albeit by a new elite of increasingly slick politicians, many of them rich and many of them slaveholders). Adams's dilemma—wanting the job but not wanting to want it; wishing to avoid campaigning when only campaigning would make victory possible—is evocatively suggested by a diary entry in the spring of 1824:

> We know so little of what in futurity is best for ourselves, that whether I ought to wish for success is among the greatest uncertainties of the election…when I consider that to me alone, of all the candidates before the nation, failure of success would be equivalent to a vote of censure by the nation upon my past service, I cannot dissemble that I have more at stake upon the result than any other individual in the Union. Yet a man qualified for the elective Chief Magistracy of ten millions of people should be a man proof alike to prosperous and adverse fortune. If I am able to bear success, I must be tempered to endure defeat.[37]

The presidential election of 1824 was one of the more convoluted ones in American history. Andrew Jackson won both the electoral and popular vote, but he failed to get a majority of either, throwing the election into the House of Representatives, where each state would get one vote. After a protracted struggle, Adams emerged as the winner in February 1825, largely because Clay threw his support to him. When Adams then appointed Clay as Secretary of State (there's a legendary silence in JQA's diary about whether the two cut a deal), charges of a "corrupt bargain" began that dogged Adams for the next four years. If indeed he could have known what the future would bring, he might well have chosen not to "bear success" after all.

The "corrupt bargain" was only part of the problem. (Actually, even if was true that JQA and Clay struck one, there wasn't anything particularly insidious about this, and any back-scratching between the two was mild compared to what followed.) A newly mobilized group of small-government Jeffersonians—what came to be known as the Democratic Party[38]—dedicated itself to making Adams and his supporters miserable. Even when supporting things Adams wanted, such as high taxes to support manufacturers, they did so in lopsided ways that would enrage the voters in the South and West (such as the so-called "Tariff of Abominations").[39] But Adams didn't help his own cause, either. Policies he supported, like strong cooperation with the new nations of Latin America, were widely scoffed at, particularly by white North Americans who deemed South and Central Americans as their inferiors. Relative moderation in dealings with Native American peoples was also fiercely resisted. When Adams proposed things such as federal government support for a national university, or the founding of an astronomical laboratory, his call for "lighthouses *of* the sky" was lampooned as "lighthouses *in* the sky." (Can you imagine anything more ridiculous than using taxpayer dollars to support research and higher education?)[40] However far-seeing such ideas might have seemed in retrospect, Adams was hopelessly out of touch with his times, even in the eyes of his supporters. By 1828, he was a political joke. In that presidential election, Jackson demolished him at the polls, inaugurating a period of white male egalitarianism that has come to be known as the "Age of Jackson."

By this point, you won't be surprised to learn, Adams loathed Jackson. He could not bring himself to attend Jackson's inauguration—the only other president who failed to be present for the transfer of power was his father, when Jefferson took office—and was appalled when he learned in 1833 his beloved Harvard was going to give an honorary degree to a man Adams termed "a barbarian who could not write a sentence of grammar and hardly could spell his own name."[41] Jackson and his cronies, after all, consigned Adams to political oblivion; they had accelerated his transformation from a wonder boy into an irrelevant old man.

Adams had other woes as well. His oldest son, George Washington Adams, committed suicide in 1829; his second son, John Quincy Adams II, died of alcoholism in 1834. It would be too simplistic to say JQA was responsible for disorders that probably had a large genetic component (he had two brothers, for example, who were also alcoholics), but his relatively severe parenting style and frequent separation from his children probably didn't help matters much. Some old-line Federalists still held a grudge about his alliance with Jefferson, but friends did manage to procure him a congressional seat in his hometown of Quincy, which he was able to win in 1830 without campaigning and by a large margin. Still, like the retired executive who takes on consulting work to keep the proverbial hand in play, this seemed to be a minor consolation at best.

But as that first term in Congress became a second and then a third (he would be reelected eight times, serving from 1831 to 1848), it became increasingly clear this final errand in governance would offer him a deeply ironic form of redemption.

◆   ◆   ◆

Though they may not seem especially relevant now—which, if you'll bear with me, is part of my point—here are some of the matters Congress eagerly debated during JQA's early years as a member of the House of Representatives in Washington, DC:

- **Nullification.** While the so-called "Tariff of Abominations" that crippled the Adams administration was a stage-managed fiasco, taxation of foreign goods represented a major economic and political divide in the 1830s. Southern politicians under the leadership of Vice President (and then Senator) John Calhoun argued states had the right to ignore federal laws (notably tariffs) they considered damaging to their interests. Nullification was fiercely resisted by President Jackson, who threatened to use force if South Carolina, which led the Nullification charge, did not back down. It did—but the notion that the South could, and maybe even should, leave the Union lingered for decades to come.

- **Indian Removal.** The state of Georgia, growing rapidly and hungry for land, encroached on territory guaranteed by treaty to belong to the Cherokee Indians. The Constitution clearly spelled out that Indian policy was a federal matter, and when the Cherokee Indians appealed to the federal government, their case went all the way to Supreme Court, which upheld their rights. Yet Jackson, for all his nationalism in the Nullification controversy, took a states' rights stand on this issue, refusing to intervene as the Cherokees were forcibly removed to what is now Oklahoma (which was itself later taken away from the Indians). In this approach Jackson had substantial, though not complete, congressional support, especially in the South.

- **The Bank of the United States.** Created by Alexander Hamilton in 1796, the Bank of the United States anchored the nation's commercial development for the next twenty years, and its charter was renewed without controversy by President Madison in 1816. But Jacksonian Democrats were hostile to the Bank, feeling it tended to support elite Northeastern interests at the expense of small farmers and entrepreneurs. When Henry Clay, leader of the newly formed Whig opposition party, tried to make the Bank an issue in 1832, four years before its charter would expire, Jackson acted decisively and announced he would destroy it by refusing to renew the charter. The move was widely celebrated at the time, but it also helped precipitate the Panic of 1837, one of the major economic depressions in American History, and one that dominated national affairs well into the 1840s.[42]

So if you were to pick up a random newspaper in the 1830s (and, by the way, the 1830s were the golden age of newspapers, the dawn of the mass media age), these are the kinds of national issues you would be reading about.

Now here's an issue that Congress wasn't at all eager to take up in the 1830s: slavery. This was a topic virtually no one wanted to talk about—and hadn't wanted to talk about for decades. The Constitution never mentions the word at all, tap-dancing around it with phrases like "three-fifths of all other persons" in the so-called Three-fifths Compromise or "person held to Service or Labour" in the fugitive slave clause, which required escaped slaves to be returned to their owners. In 1790, a group of Quakers had presented Congress with an antislavery petition, which James Madison, then Speaker of the House, skillfully channeled into parliamentary oblivion.[43] The subject burst onto the floors of Congress in 1819–1820 during the exceptionally bitter debates that culminated in the so-called Missouri Compromise that admitted Missouri as a slave state and Maine as a free state. The rancor of that debate convinced many politicians that like religion at Thanksgiving dinner, the less said the better. Certainly, there were plenty of other issues awaiting resolution that hadn't anything to do with slavery.

Or were there? One of the things that people who make such assertions—like the common one where people say the Civil War wasn't really over slavery—seem to have a hard time understanding is that slavery laced through all kinds of subjects that seemed to have nothing to do with it. Take Nullification, for example.

Powerful South Carolinians really didn't like those tariffs. And why was that? Because tariffs make goods, especially foreign goods, more expensive. In fact, tariffs are *designed* to make foreign goods more expensive so that consumers will be more inclined to buy domestic products and in so doing foster industrial economy of workers and investors who make jobs and money—and, who in turn, can buy more stuff. The United States government promotes free trade now, but back when the nation was starting out, capitalists were tireless about seeking protection to build their industries. But South Carolinian voters weren't especially interested in developing an industrial economy like this; they just wanted to buy their products from the cheapest source, foreign or domestic, and sell their products, notably cotton, with minimal government interference. And why didn't they care about developing an industrial economy? Because they were largely happy with an agrarian economy they already had, one whose foundation wasn't wage-earning workers, but slaves. While free states invested their money by buying labor-saving machines (in large measure because such machines were cheaper than hiring wage-earning workers) slave states invested their money by buying people (which, like real estate, tended to appreciate in value without any exertion at all). Nullification hadn't anything to do with slavery, and yet it had everything to do with slavery. So did the Bank of the United States, which was much more of a tool for capitalists than slave owners (though the slave trade could operate with ruthless capitalist efficiency). Even Cherokee removal, a matter of race relations generally, had a slavery component in particular. One of the issues in the debate was how civilized the Cherokees were: If they were just savages, then they had no real rights that white men were bound to respect. Cherokee advocates responded by saying these Indians were indeed civilized, as was evidenced by their written language—and their enslavement of African-Americans.

It's clear, however, that such complexities could be finessed by Congress. The problem was that events outside Washington were making the subject harder to avoid. In August 1831, four months before Adams took his seat in the House, the notorious slave insurrection of Nat Turner struck terror into the heart of the South. Turner's rebellion was put down swiftly, as all previous slave revolts had been. Yet the potential for mayhem was always there, and in response, the Virginia legislature actually considered abolishing slavery in 1832. The idea was debated, rejected, and then swept under the rug. That's why some Southerners felt a new Northern movement that was growing in strength, known as abolitionism, was even more threatening than sporadic slave revolts. Before the 1830s, many slaveholders themselves, among them Jefferson and Clay, had been advocates of relatively mild measure like colonization, whereby philanthropists bought slaves their freedom and sent them back to Africa (notably Liberia, which was created by the U.S. government for this purpose). Now, though, a new generation of activists was led by William Lloyd Garrison, who launched a militant abolitionist newspaper, *The Liberator*, right around the time Turner was planning his revolt. These abolitionists explicitly invoked moral justifications for ending slavery, and took a wide-ranging offensive whose tactics included the publication of pamphlets and abetting the escape of slaves via an emerging network known as the Underground Railroad.

In the short term, these abolitionists posed little threat to slave owners (nor, for that matter, the New England companies that financed and insured them), because virtually all Americans regarded abolitionists as a lunatic fringe. Moreover, slave interests were deeply entrenched in the U.S. government: With the exception of the Adamses, every president through Jackson had been a slaveholder, and even subsequent ones who weren't (like Jackson's handpicked successor, Martin Van Buren) cooperated with them. The Chief Justice of the Supreme Court from the mid-1830s to the mid-1860s was Roger Taney, whose majority opinion in the Dred Scott case of 1857 ruled that slaves had no rights. The admission of new slave states from Kentucky (1792) through Texas (1845), each of which acquired two senators and an artificial sixty percent boost in House representation because slaves were counted as three-fifths of a person even though they weren't considered citizens, guaranteed that slaveholders would exert significant, if not decisive, power on the direction of race relations for the foreseeable future. Far from shrinking, or even holding its own, the slave interest of JQA's lifetime—and his congressional career in particular—was growing in power.

Nevertheless, the Slave Power was spooked by the rise of abolitionism, and had every intention of stamping it out by any means necessary. No one could call William Lloyd Garrison—who burned the American flag at Boston's Fanueil Hall in 1844 and called the Constitution "a covenant with death"—a mild-mannered man. But neither were some of his opponents. Take, for example, these comments on the House floor by South Carolina Congressman James Henry Hammond in February 1836:

> And I warn the abolitionists, ignorant, infatuated, barbarians that they are, that if chance shall throw any of them into our hands he may expect a felon's death. No human law, no human influence, can arrest his fate. The superhuman instinct of self-preservation, the indignant feelings of an outraged people, to whose hearth-stones he is seeking to carry death and desolation, pronounce his doom; and if we failed to accord it to him we would be unworthy of the

forms we wear, unworthy of the beings whom it our duty to protect, and we would merit and expect that indignation of offended Heaven.[44]

God himself hates abolitionists, Hammond claims, and God help any we get our hands on. This threat was more than a rhetorical flourish. The following year, abolitionist Elijah Lovejoy of Illinois—a *non*-slave state—was told to stop publishing an abolitionist newspaper. He refused repeatedly, and his press was destroyed repeatedly. When he still insisted on condemning slavery, he was murdered. So much for free speech.

Which brings us to the heart of the matter. By the mid-1830s, defenders of slavery and their sympathizers decided the best way to preserve their power was simply to shut down discussion. It had long been a tradition to devote the opening of every congressional session, and some segment of time during the months that followed, to receive petitions from ordinary citizens. By this point, however, more and more of these petitions concerned slavery—and more and more of them were not necessarily coming from kooks like Quakers and abolitionists (who in many cases were one and the same). In particular, many of these petitions called for the abolition of the slave trade in the nation's capital—the Constitution protected slavery in much of the South, but there was no law against ending it in Washington, DC.) For a long time, such petitions were ceremoniously ignored through a standard procedure of tabling them or referring them to a committee that would end of up producing the legislative equivalent of a form letter (for example, thank you for your concern, there's nothing we can do, and so on).

Now, though, slavery's defenders would take two further steps. The first was to stop talking about slavery as some regrettably necessary evil, the way Thomas Jefferson did, and begin asserting it was a positive good. So, for example, in the same speech I just quoted, James Henry Hammond described slavery as "the greatest of all great blessings which a kind Providence has bestowed upon our glorious region" and that it "produces the highest toned, the purest, best organization of society that has ever existed on the face of the earth."[45] This strategy would become a fixture of the debate for the next quarter-century.

The second, more important step, which was the culmination of Hammond's remarks, was a proposal to *automatically* table such petitions, removing them from any consideration whatsoever. On May 25, 1836, this proposal was packaged with two others by Hammond's fellow South Carolinian Henry Laurens Pinckney: one affirming the denial that Congress could do anything about slavery in states where it already existed, and another saying it would be "unwise" and "impolitic" to change the status quo in the District of Columbia.[46]

At this point, sixty-nine-year-old John Quincy Adams stood and signaled the Speaker of the House (and future president) James Polk that he wished to speak. Polk, however, ignored Adams—he already had a reputation as one of those people who introduced far too many of these petitions—and instead recognized Georgia Congressman George Owens, who sought to have the proposals voted on without debate. Adams tried to stop this from happening, but congressmen from Virginia, Kentucky, and Indiana repeatedly cut him off, with some help from Polk. Finally, in exasperation, Adams asked, "Am I gagged or not?" Polk replied the proposals in question were not debatable—in other words, yes. It's time, Mr. Polk and a large majority of House members was silently saying, for Mr. Adams to shut up.[47]

But Mr. Adams would not.

◆   ◆   ◆

Was John Quincy Adams an abolitionist? As with many such questions, it depends on how you define "abolitionist," a word whose definition, you won't be surprised to hear, was the subject of intense argument in the middle third of the nineteenth century. The short answer is no.[48] It would be more accurate to call JQA antislavery, but this distinction, implying a willingness to work within the political system to end bondage, wasn't quite as clear as it would be later (if in fact it's clear to students even now). No serious historian argues JQA was a chip off the Garrisonian block, but there is disagreement about just where he fits on the racial map.[49]

I've tried to show that in many ways, John Quincy was a pretty singular figure in American life—his upbringing alone testifies to that. However, in other ways, he was a thoroughly conventional man of his time. Like many of his contemporaries, JQA had little appetite before 1836 in speaking out about slavery, and tended to look skeptically on the new abolitionist movement, whose aims and methods he regarded as impractical, if not downright counterproductive.

This isn't to say he lacked convictions on the issue. After all, he was an Adams. His father had always been opposed to slavery; his mother perhaps even more so. "I sometimes think that the passion for liberty cannot be equally strong in the breasts of those who have been accustomed to deprive their fellow creatures of theirs," she wrote to her husband in 1776—the same letter in which she fruitlessly urged him to "remember the ladies" as he worked toward independence.[50]

As a United States Senator, JQA complained about the Three-fifths Compromise, advocated for hearing (another) Quaker petition for restraining the spread of slavery, and unsuccessfully promoted a tax on imported slaves. For the most part, however, Adams kept his views to himself; remember that for most of his career, he was a professional diplomat. So, for example, he did not oppose, as many New England Federalists did, the acquisition of the Louisiana territory, which permitted slavery. As Secretary of State, he subordinated his distaste for the slavery to the principle that foreign powers (like England, which outlawed it) had no right to board American vessels in its attempt to enforce British policy. As president, he declined to recognize the new Haitian government, created as a result of a slave insurrection, because he believed (undoubtedly correctly) doing so would cause a political firestorm.[51]

In his post-presidential congressional career, Adams was very much his own man, supporting his archrival Jackson in matters like Nullification, while opposing him on others like the Bank of the United States. (The Whigs he was loosely affiliated with, like the Federalists before them, could find themselves exasperated with him.) But while he was willing to work with slaveholders as he deemed the circumstances warranted, his bedrock hostility toward slavery became increasingly relevant as it began to intersect with other issues. During the Missouri furor of 1820, when he was Secretary of State and thus officially silent on domestic issues, Adams described slavery as "the great and foul stain upon the North American Union, and it is a contemplation worthy of the most exalted soul whether its total abolition is or isn't practicable." He speculated that "a dissolution, at least temporary, of the Union, as now constituted, would be certainly necessary…The Union might then be reorganized on the fundamental principle of emancipation. This object is vast in its compass, awful in its prospects, sublime and beautiful in its issue."[52] But Adams, for all his high-mindedness, was nevertheless a politician in what habitually compromising contemporary Americans call "the real world," and did not pick up an antislavery banner, because he had other fish to fry.

By the time of James Henry Hammond's speech in 1836, however, he was beginning to see that Southerners were making it increasingly impossible for him to fry anything. You could view JQA's behavior in ensuing years as a late, feisty counterattack on the people who made him miserable while president. You could also see the fight he went on to lead as a passionate struggle for civil rights, specifically free speech. Yet it's finally impossible to separate either of these imperatives from the way slavery was entwining so many aspects of national life as a toxic weed, something Adams himself was among the first to recognize…

And speak out on.

Even before the gag rule became a formal proposal, floating as a trial balloon that House Speaker Polk could not give unequivocal backing, JQA identified what was at stake in refusing to even hear what ordinary citizens had to say in their petitions, even those he disliked himself. "You suppress the right of petition; you suppress freedom of the press; you suppress freedom of religion," he told these congressmen in December 1835. The best way to prevent a protracted debate, he said, was to let these people have their say, and then "we will hear no more about this exciting subject." The following month, discussing the prayer of 107 women to end slavery in the District, he argued it was important "to let error be tolerated," as he had "no sort of doubt but that a committee could furnish reasons why the prayer of these petitions should not be granted." The best way to deal with people with whom you disagree is to have a dialogue, not to ignore them. And the best way to keep a disagreeable subject *alive* is to insist that you *can't* talk about it.[53]

But as the gag order took formal form and gathered political momentum, it became clear that dialogue wasn't going to be easy or even possible. Despite his attempt to debate the gag rule proposal of May 1836, Adams was firmly told the matter would not be discussed, only voted on. So he was going to have to try a different approach, and he did. It was time to get tough with these people.

Remember that the gag rule was only one of three proposals in a package to be voted on that spring. The first, and presumably least objectionable, was affirmation of a commonsense statement: "Congress possesses no constitutional authority to interfere in any way with the institution of slavery in any of the states." Certainly the Constitution said nothing about limiting slavery where it already existed, or prevented it from spreading elsewhere. And there are provisions, however oblique, that are unmistakable in support of it. Yet when it came time for Adams to verbally record his vote, he asked whether he could have five minutes to explain why this resolution was "false and utterly untrue." Proslavery House members who weren't shocked—even most *antislavery* members took the resolution for granted—shouted to call Adams to order. Tired of wrangling, and perhaps getting ensnared in an argument that could get out of control, the House dropped the subject to consider other business. (After all, these petitions were supposed to be something to get out of the way so that Congress could get on with the *real* business of governing.)

The subject shifted to a resolution to provide relief to refugees in Alabama and Georgia, who had been displaced in American conflicts with Seminole Indians. Adams got the floor again, and taking advantage of a parliamentary technicality that would allow him to connect this topic to a previous one, launched into an explanation of a scenario whereby Congress *could*, completely constitutionally, interfere in slavery where it already existed: in wartime. "From the instant that your slaveholding states become the theatre of war, civil, servile, or foreign, from that instant the war powers of Congress extend to interference with the institution of slavery in every way by which it can be interfered with," he explained. An astonished Pennsylvanian asked Adams if he had heard correctly: Was JQA saying that in the event of a slave insurrection, for example, the Constitution would end? (Some of these people could not believe what they were hearing; this one apparently could not actually hear what he was hearing.) No, Adams replied; The *Constitution* wouldn't end, but *slavery* might.

> The very fact of the people of a free portion of the Union marching to the support of the masters would [*itself*] be an interference with those institutions; and that, in the event of a war, the result of which no man could tell, the treaty-making power [something the federal government very explicitly reserves to itself and *not* the states] would come to be equivalent to universal emancipation.

Twenty-five years later, one of JQA's protégés, the abolitionist senator Charles Sumner (who would be beaten within inches of his life on the floor of the Senate in 1856 for his own speeches on slavery) visited a newly elected president and outlined this theory for him, which he had first heard from Adams. The following year, that president issued the Emancipation Proclamation ending slavery in the South as a wartime measure, using powers granted to him as such in the Constitution.[54]

In 1836, however, most members of the House considered JQA's reasoning absurdly theoretical, and the resolution passed by the crushing margin of 182–9. So did the other two, also by wide margins (though the margins were not that wide; the gag rule passed 117–68). JQA's assertion that the gag order resolution was "a direct violation of the Constitution of United States, the rules of this House, and the rights of my constituents" was shouted down by other members, and for the rest of the congressional session, the subject of slavery was forbidden.[55]

But what about the next session? As soon as it convened in 1837, Adams introduced a petition praying for the end of the slave trade in Washington. Can he even do that, his opponents asked? Yes, replied Speaker Polk—the gag expired with the last Congress. So they tabled the petition. On his next chance, Adams did it again, this time with the petition of 150 women. Proslavery members tried to stop it cold, but failed, and Adams introduced yet another. A series of maneuvers followed, culminating in a *new* gag rule, which passed by a decisive 115–57 margin.

Well, asked Adams, what about the petitions that were brought up *before* this new gag took effect? Could *they* be discussed? After more wrangling, the answer was no. Hmmm, he replied; I have here some petitions that sort of fall into a gray area. Take this one, from nine ladies of Fredericksburg, Virginia—Adams didn't want to name them for their own safety—praying for the end of the slave trade in Washington. He wasn't even sure if it was legitimate. Didn't matter: The petition was immediately tabled. But there was bait at the end of this line. Later in the day, JQA's colleague, John Patton of Virginia, who had grown up in Fredericksburg, had a look at the petition. There are no *ladies* who signed this petition, he said on the House floor, and if the gentleman from Massachusetts had only asked him, he could have made that clear. Patton only recognized one of the names, and that was from a free mulatto woman, and she was "of infamous character."

Oh really? "How does the gentleman know it?" Adams asked.

"I did not say I knew the woman personally," Patton responded.

Well, that's good, said Adams.

> I'm glad the gentleman now says he does not know these women, for if he did not disclaim that knowledge, I might have asked who it was that made these women infamous—whether it was those of their own color or their masters. I have understood that there are those among the coloured portion of the slave-holding states, who bear the image of their masters.

Whoa! According to the transcript from the *Congressional Globe*, a "great sensation" followed this rapier-sharp sexual allusion.[56]

Adams wasn't done tweaking his adversaries that day. He had another petition, too. This one was also complicated, because it happened to come from slaves, some of whom could not write and only made their mark. He would submit to the rules of the House as they pertain to petitions from U.S. citizens, but how do the rules of the House apply to those that the House who *aren't* full citizens?

Speaker Polk described himself as "baffled." Some of his colleagues, however, knew exactly what *they* thought. One member suggested that Southern congressmen should walk out in protest. Another suggested the slave petition be set on fire right there on the House floor. Multiple members cried out: "Expel him!" Cooler heads prevailed: a resolution was drafted merely censuring Adams for "extending to slaves a privilege only belonging to freemen, directly incit[ing] the slave population to insurrection."

There's only one problem, Adams observed when things quieted down enough for him to reply. No one was talking about an insurrection. These slaves were asking that slavery be *preserved* in the District of Columbia. (In fact, this petition was probably a hoax, which Adams then turned to his advantage.) A whole new uproar then broke out: Adams should be censured for playing tricks on Congress! The House debated a resolution for the next few days, but it could come to no definitive resolution...except, perhaps, an informal one that John Quincy Adams was a crazy loon bent on making a mockery of the U.S. government.

Even those who presumably supported Adams paid him only the most backhanded of compliments. "It would be unjust to believe that, in the prime and vigor of manhood, the honorable member would have adopted the course of action which, at this late stage of his life, seems to control him," said Abijah Mann of New York, the first free state member of the House to get the floor amid the raucous debate about JQA's behavior. "The high noontide of his life has long since passed with him, and its wane is no doubt upon him, before he is either aware or sensible of it." (The less than senile Adams, sitting right there, was no doubt wondering whether friends like these made enemies unnecessary.)[57]

But he didn't care. Every year, from 1836 to 1840, he tried to introduce petitions to end slavery, and every year the gag rule was invoked or renewed. Nor did the invective or threats stop him from making modest proposals like an 1838 one suggesting the creation of a "committee of color" to make sure all members and office holders in Congress be pure Anglo-Saxon, and to expel any member with one drop of colored blood in his veins. Or stop him from giving speeches like the one making clear that he wasn't going to talk about slavery, much in the way I'm going to tell you right now not to think about an elephant. (That's right, an elephant. *Don't* picture one. No trunk, no tusks, no peanuts. Not even representations of an elephant. Go away, Dumbo.) Or he would ask those congressmen who described slavery as a positive good to please explain in some detail to somewhat obtuse Northerners like himself just why that is. He would be fascinated to hear the logic whereby the peculiar institution could be justified as a blessing for slave and master alike. It's absolutely fascinating. Really.[58]

In some sense, of course, JQA's campaign did little good. Sure, it irritated proslavery advocates in ways that even their Northern allies found secretly amusing, but it didn't change the gag rule, which became permanent in 1840, literally written into the rulebook governing the House of Representatives and no longer requiring regular renewal. On the other hand, it was becoming increasingly clear the gag rule was having precisely the opposite effect that was intended. Indeed, at times it was difficult to discuss matters Congress really *did* want to take up. A good example is the status of Texas, which rebelled against Mexico and became an autonomous republic in 1836. Many Americans and Texans alike wanted Texas to join the Union, and indeed JQA himself had explored such a possibility when he was president. But by the 1830s everybody knew Texas would join the Union as a slave state. Mexicans had originally welcomed American settlers into poorly populated areas as long as they *didn't* bring their slaves, one rule among many that settlers simply ignored. Bringing Texas into the Union now was going to raise all kinds of sticky questions the Jackson and Van Buren administrations would rather avoid. Nor were the Whigs, the party to which Adams presumably belonged, eager to engage the issue, which polarized the electorate. They were just as happy to have slavery taken off the table altogether when they took control of Congress after the election of 1840.

Yet still JQA still prattled on. When he tried to bring up a petition from yet more abolitionist women in 1838, Adams responded to those who asserted that females had no place in politics with a long speech about their importance in history from the time of the Old Testament (including "Esther, who by a *PETITION* saved her people and her country"), culminating in a discussion of the role of South Carolinian women in the American Revolution. When, during the uproar over his attempt to introduce a petition by slaves, one of his colleagues complained he would just as soon hear a petition from a horse or dog, Adams assured the congressman that if a horse or dog ever did send him a petition, he would be sure to try and introduce it. When slaveholders tested how far he would go by sending him what they considered outrageous petitions, he called their bluff, presenting one asking that all free blacks be enslaved, and another that Adams be expelled from Congress altogether as a public enemy. He was subject to ridicule and even death threats. But still the man would not shut up about the damned subject.[59]

And then, in January 1842, John Quincy Adams went too far. The immediate context was yet another petition, again introduced by Adams himself, calling for his removal from the chairmanship of the foreign relations committee because he was "possessed of a species of monomania on all subjects connected with people as dark as a Mexican" and therefore could not be trusted to deal with important issues like U.S. policy toward that country. Proslavery advocates claimed this petition was a hoax and just another pretext for bringing up slavery, but Adams responded by supplying evidence that House members themselves had been discussing the idea of removing him in their own correspondence with constituents. The gag aside, Adams said, his personal and professional competence was being called into question. As such, he had a right under House rules to defend himself, and Polk reluctantly agreed. This defense required him to address a series of petitions he had received, an opportunity Adams made the most of, resulting in repeated cries from his colleagues: "I demand Mr. Speaker that you *put him down*"; "What, are we here to sit here and endure these insults?"; "I demand that you shut the mouth of that old harlequin!" One of the petitions Adams referred to came from his own constituents, a group of women from Haverhill, Massachusetts. They were concerned that "a vast proportion of the resources of one section of the Union is annually drained to sustain the views and course of another section." (Though the "s" word is never mentioned, you can see where this is headed: think smokers or motorcycle riders whose recklessness ends up costing taxpayers money). And so they asked the Union be dissolved.

"This is a petition for the dissolution of the Union," an incredulous congressman from the land of Nullification observed. Adams replied by suggesting the petition be referred to a committee that would draft an answer to the petitioners explaining why their hopes should not be realized. Congressman Henry Wise of Virginia countered by suggesting Adams be censured for violating the gag rule. "Good!" said Adams. Some Southerners had their doubts about going ahead with such a resolution, which would allow the old man to keep talking, but the vote to proceed narrowly passed. Adams was finally going to be subject to a censure vote. He was thrilled; in fact, he had heartily voted with those who wanted to censure him. This was going to be interesting—and interesting to many people who lived far from Washington, DC.

The man designated to make the initial case against Adams was Thomas Marshall of Kentucky. His father, John Marshall, the legendary Chief Justice of the Supreme Court, was appointed to the Supreme Court by JQA's father. More in sorrow than in anger, Marshall said that if his own father had taken seriously a petition to end the Union, his son would be obligated to do what he now did to Adams: accuse him of treason.

The charge against him was now ratcheted up, and it was JQA's turn to respond. But rather than give a speech, he asked the clerk of the House to read the first paragraph of the Declaration of Independence. Pausing, a bit uncertain, Adams exhorted the clerk on ("Proceed! Proceed!") until he reached this passage: "But when a long train of abuses and usurpations, pursuing invariably the same object, evinced a design to reduce them under absolute despotism, it is their right, their duty, to throw off such government."

This is the point, Adams told the House. The people have a right to seek to seek changes. I myself don't believe we've reached the point we need to dissolve the Union. But I should be able to discuss the views of those who feel we *have* reached that point.

At *this* point, Henry Wise stood up and asked the clerk to go find Washington's famous "Farewell Address." Adams asked for a pause so that Marshall's treason charge could be printed and he have time to prepare a formal answer, but Wise plunged ahead with a speech that invoked Washington's address in order to compare the abolitionists of the 1830s to the Tories who supported England in the American Revolution and their New England successors who painted Jefferson as a wild pro-French radical during the French Revolution. When another member asked what this somewhat less than obvious argument had to do with printing Marshall's charges and postponing the hearing, Adams himself expressed a wish that Wise "be permitted to go on" (give him plenty of rope). Wise did go on, making this assertion: "The principle of slavery is a leveling principle; it is friendly to equality. Break down slavery and you would with the same blow break down the great democratic principle of equality among men."

A *Congressional Globe* reporter noted laughter was heard in the House.

In fact, there is a kind of logic to this: Senator John Calhoun, in highly legalistic and philosophic language, had been making this case for many years: Freedom is a relative concept that depends on a consciousness of slavery; equality draws its meaning from an awareness of inequality. But in this context, as in many since, Wise just sounded ridiculous. The Declaration of Independence did not say *some* men are created equal, it said *all,* and if that was more a wish than a reality, the desire of some proslavery advocates to make slavery an *ideal* seemed, well, un-American.

In any case, no one in that room was going to win a pissing contest over the Founding Fathers with John Quincy Adams. George Washington had given him his first job in the government. Jefferson had been a frequent dinner guest in his home. He had held important positions in the Madison and Monroe administrations. All these men were Virginians—southerners and slaveholders. But they never argued that slavery was a *good* thing. Necessary, perhaps…*perhaps*…but not desirable. If anything had changed in JQA's relationship with the South, it wasn't John Quincy Adams. Instead, it was the men of the South.

> "It was unexpected, most perfectly unexpected to him [here Adams is speaking in the third person] when he knew what these great men of Revolutionary times, who were Virginians, thought of slavery—of the institution to which

now everything was to be sacrificed—when he now saw members from that State, endeavoring to destroy him and his character, for the sole purpose of presenting a petition. He should have hoped better things of Virginians."

By early February, it was clear the censure proceeding against John Quincy Adams was becoming an embarrassment. The proposer of the first, non-treasonous measure suggested he would withdraw his resolution if Adams would withdraw the Haverhill petition. Nothing doing, replied Adams. I'm just getting started. And as he did, over a period of days, petitions poured into Congress. At one point, someone objected that during his defense Adams had violated the gag rule, but Speaker Polk ruled in JQA's favor. When *Polk's* ruling was contested, a vote was taken and it was affirmed—the first time Adams had ever prevailed in a gagging contest. After a week of this, a Virginia Whig proposed surrender by tabling the motion against Adams. By a vote of 106–93, the resolution was tabled. Adams had won.

Not that his victory was complete. In fact, the gag rule remained on the books for almost three more years. But this was a turning point, and often the complex procedural attempts to affirm it prevailed by gradually smaller margins until it was finally overturned for good in December 1844. There are multiple explanations for this development. Certainly, antislavery, if not abolitionist, sentiment was rising. And, this being politics, there must have been some mutual backscratching (I'll stick it to your gag-supporting rival by voting against him, if you vote for that big railroad project in my district for me). But one can also sense reasoning that went like this: I'm no nigger-loving abolitionist, and I regard John Quincy Adams as a crotchety relic. But the old man does have a point: That proslavery gang really is trying to ram this slavery thing down our throats, and it just isn't right. Northern Democrats who had been collaborating with Southern Democrats began to see that, for better or worse, their regional identity was more decisive than their party identity. (Southern Whigs, for their part, began disappearing entirely, soon to be followed by Northern Whigs. From their ashes would emerge a Republican Party that was decisively Northern.)

This increasing sectionalism reflected the emergence of a new common sense shared even among antagonists: Slavery wasn't just a sideshow, an annoying nuisance. Instead, it was the core issue in the nation's future. That's why, with war with Mexico looming in 1846, Congressman David Wilmot of Pennsylvania made a modest proposal: a "proviso" that no territory the United States took from Mexico would allow slavery. (Imagine the reaction of Pennsylvania Congressman offering a resolution that no American would be allowed to make money from oil after the invasion of Iraq in 2003, and you have an idea how Wilmot's proviso was received.)

These developments illuminate another important point: Adams was never completely alone in his fight. William Slade of Vermont and Joshua Giddings of Michigan, for example, were stalwarts in the fight against slavery. Giddings, in fact, resigned his seat in disgust after a particularly hostile gagging in 1842, upon which he was reelected by the voters. Others, like Caleb Cushing of Massachusetts, were fellow travelers, even if their racial attitudes were not exactly what we would call enlightened. But from the beginning, Adams was the leader in the struggle. Only "Old Man Eloquent," as he was called with increasing fondness by his growing number of supporters, had the stature and cleverness to stand up consistently to his opponents. He also, again with collaboration (notably that of abolitionist Theodore Weld), articulated the most powerful rationales for fighting the gag and slavery alike. Adams was an instrumental figure in using the very states' rights logic of proslavery theorists against them. If indeed slavery was strictly a local affair, as they claimed, then freedom was, in effect, the default setting: Only with special intervention by law could slavery be created and sustained—special intervention which in many cases would require the approval and resources of non-slave states. And, as he suggested in his famous speech on the Mexican question or in the petition of those Haverhill women, such approval and resources might not always be there on demand.[60]

Above all, there was that legendary Adams will, a will all the more impressive because it wasn't superhuman. In the aftermath of *Amistad* case of 1839–1841, in which Adams, making a rare appearance before the Supreme Court, won the freedom of slaves who overpowered their Spanish captors only to be captured off Long Island Sound (a case made famous in the Steven Spielberg movie of the same name, in which Anthony Hopkins does a marvelous turn as JQA), made the following observation in his diary:

> The world, the flesh, and all the devils in hell are arrayed against any man who now in this North American Union shall dare to join the standard of Almighty God to put down the African slave-trade; and what can I, upon the verge of my seventy-fourth birthday, with a shaking hand, a darkening eye, a drowsy brain, and with all my faculties dropping by me one by one, as teeth are dropping from my head—what can I do for the cause of God and man, for the progress of human emancipation, for the suppression of the African slave trade? Yet my conscience presses me on; let me die upon the breach.[61]

He did. Adams collapsed on the floor of the House in February 1848 while protesting the reading of a tribute commending Mexican War veterans, because he felt the war, begun under false pretenses by the Polk administration, had been illegal and immoral.[62] He died, still in the Capitol, two days later. Twenty-eight years earlier, during the debates over the Missouri Compromise, Adams had written, "Oh, but if one man could arise with a genius capable of comprehending, a heart capable of supporting, and an utterance capable of communicating those eternal truths that belong to this question...such a man would perform the duties of an angel upon the earth."[63]

That man was in the House the day Adams collapsed. He was a one-term congressman who also thought the Mexican War was illegal and immoral, and he would be punished by the voters back home by saying so on the record (not that anyone in the House was paying much attention to *him*). But he had more of a common touch than Adams did, and in the end that would make all the difference. His name—you know who I'm talking about, don't you?—was Abraham Lincoln.

◆   ◆   ◆

As I suggested at the beginning of this chapter, to be an American is to live in a country where the idea that you can achieve your dreams is a national birthright (or something you acquire along with your citizenship). This is true whether you're the child of an immigrant or the child of a president, and as such is just about the only truly shared aspect of our national identity. While having, pursuing, and achieving dreams are universal human experiences, nowhere else do they receive the kind of collective affirmation they do in the United States. Of course, not everyone here *does* believe you can achieve your dreams, but those that don't can't help but be conscious of the governing perception, which for better and worse is just about inescapable. And it's been that way for hundreds of years.

But dreams are a tricky business. For one thing, we don't exactly choose them, either because they're pressed upon us by peers or loved ones, or because they come to us unbidden—indeed, we might well wish we *didn't* want what we in fact do. Dreams motivate and even sustain us, but they also haunt us, particularly when they go unrealized, as they very often do. Even successfully realized dreams can be problematic, because they raise surprisingly slippery questions about what success really means. We often find they amount to less than expected, as any lonely movie star or bored millionaire will tell you. I've often wondered why our

Creator saw fit to wire us with this seemingly unavoidable, yet perverse, human ache.

John Quincy Adams has given me an answer to that question. Here's a man who was born with great expectations and who, by just about any reasonable standard, fulfilled those expectations. He was a dutiful son, a good student, and a devoted husband. Some of his children would no doubt raise objections about his parenting, but clearly, he was human (and what children don't have objections?). He often claimed he wanted to be an artist or poet, wishes which, however sincere, were not borne out by his choices, almost all of them in government service. The pinnacle of government service in the United States is the presidency, and Adams attained it. How much more could one man ask?

Alas, much more. From its awkward beginning to its embarrassing end, the Adams presidency was a bust, as he knew as well as anyone. However distinguished his record, he isn't as vividly remembered as his father (who also had a lousy presidency) or Abraham Lincoln, who, for all his trials, nevertheless represents the gold standard in this regard. By such measures—tough, but realistic—you'd have to say that Adams was a failure. When's the last time you heard about an exhibit on John Quincy Adams at the Smithsonian, an institution he deserves more credit than he gets for creating?

But in another, more important sense, failure was the beginning, not the end, for John Quincy Adams. The truest measure of a person in American life isn't whether she succeeds, but rather *how she fails.* As I've suggested, a bunch of motives can explain Adams' behavior in Congress, not all of them good. But if there isn't something deeply honorable in the way the man finished his life, then I'm not sure what that word—a word that seems to have fallen out of common usage, but one which we desperately need—means.

So keep John Quincy Adams in mind when your plans don't work out. You never know how good failure can be.

3

Mrs. Stowe Writes Wrongs

"The pen is mightier than the sword," we're often told. But as truisms go, this one seems dubious at best. Swords (and bullets, and bombs) seem to have been primary force for change in human history in general, and American history in particular. John Quincy Adams, profiled in the last chapter, was certainly a clever man, but cleverness didn't end slavery. War did.

And yet this isn't the whole story. Even those who wield swords recognize that pens (and presses, and word processors) move brains in ways that finally move bodies. More than one American war has been described in terms of winning "hearts and minds," and this is better done with words than weapons. But not just any words—or even words as weapons. Sometimes, it seems, people can be persuaded to think and act differently, through means that range from reason to emotion. Few people are more aware of this than mothers. And when it comes to writers who really seem to have made a difference, the mother of all persuaders in the United States was Harriet Beecher Stowe. Here's the story of how she wrote the most famous novel in American history.

CHAPTER 3:
MRS. STOWE WRITES WRONGS

in which we see a housewife and mother
think about someone else for a change (in society)

THERE ARE FEW TASKS IN ACADEMIC LIFE more difficult than writing. Many a weekend has been blighted by writing an essay, a process that often goes well into evenings, if not ensuing mornings. This is true even for good writers—indeed, new or uncertain ones often have a mistaken idea that experienced inkslingers sit down at a computer keyboards and play them like concert pianists. Sloppy Oscar Madison, the sportswriter character the 1970s sitcom *The Odd Couple,* speaks for many such professionals when he says, "I hate writing—I love having written."

I must say, though, that there is something worse than writing academic papers, and that's reading them: many a weekend has been blighted by *that* chore as well. Many teachers, shameless performers that they are, would happily teach classes for free; salaries are for grading papers. If not for a reluctant belief that writing, a strenuously labor-intensive process for everyone involved, is nevertheless at the core of real learning—something more than mere regurgitation of facts, the core of what it means for a student to actually *make sense* of something—most teachers would gratefully stop giving out writing assignments.

The question, in any case, remains: Why, taken as a group, are student essays so bad? Part of the answer is that they *are* taken as group: there are few things more deadening than forty different versions, only about half of them vaguely grammatical and even fewer properly footnoted, on why Shakespeare was such a genius when he wrote *Macbeth.* Mentioning grammar and footnotes brings up another issue: Writing papers means learning to conform to a series of rules, ranging from spelling to more subjective matters, like tight introductions and clearly sign-posted topic sentences, that signal a reader where you're going. And it takes practice, often mind-numbing practice, to master the formula of the standard academic essay.

Of course, any time you're talking about a formula, you're getting into something that's not only inherently boring (real excitement comes in purposely breaking formulas, not purposefully mastering them), but also raising a legitimate question about how relevant a formula really *is.* How interesting can *any* academic essay on *Macbeth* really be? Being able to explain why Shakespeare was such a genius doesn't necessarily mean you're going to be any more capable of selling a Honda to a soccer mom. On the other hand, as any math teacher will tell you, the ability to master one kind of formula really can make it easier to master others, if only from the sense of confidence that experience brings. That's why teachers who know very few of their students will ever end up as Shakespearean scholars nevertheless try to teach them to write like one: you have to start somewhere (and teachers typically know more about reading Shakespeare than selling cars).

But the real problem with most student essays has less to do with technique than imagination. Too few writers think hard enough about who they're writing *for,* that a real person reads their work. That's why one often reads disembodied prose that seems to unspool aimlessly from the writer's word processing software. "One of the most blah blah blahs of any blah blah blah is blah blah blah," is the general spirit of such essays. "But of course your stance toward blah blah blah depends on your perspective." Someone who writes like this isn't thinking very hard, and doesn't exactly make a reader want to think very hard, either. Indeed, a teacher often resents assessing this kind of work, because she's going to have to put in more work explaining what's wrong with it than the student ever did in producing it in the first place.

Though not always posed bluntly, there's a question a reader brings to any piece of writing, and that is, "Why should I care?" Teachers are paid to care, but if they're doing their job correctly, they're nudging their students toward producing work that people will want to read on its own merit. And the chief merit of any piece of writing is this: persuasiveness. Good writing brings a reader around to a writer's point of view, whether in the belief that *Macbeth* is a really good play for a particular reason or in a particular way.

Of course, in order to persuade anybody of anything, you have to know what you yourself think about a given subject. Not everybody does. But that's less of a problem than it may appear to be, at least in the early going. (And as any serious writer will tell you, writing is *re*writing.) Far worse are those students who know all too well what they think and barrel ahead with a series of bald assertions that alienate rather than persuade. A really good piece of writing will demonstrate an awareness of other points of view, and will address them in one form or another. And while coming to a sense of resolution isn't always easy, engaging imagined skeptics is an important part of drawing useful conclusions for yourself as well as somebody else. The noun "essay" is also a verb; it means "to try out." And trying, to return to an earlier point, is to a great degree a matter of imagination: If I were a person who thought differently than me, what would I think? Like many things, doing this successfully takes practice. But that, after all, is what school is for.

Which brings us to our next subject, Harriet Beecher Stowe and her internationally famous novel, *Uncle Tom's Cabin* (1851). You might think the work of a nineteenth-century novelist would have little relevance for the matter at hand. After all, fiction is governed by a different set of rules than nonfiction; a novel is a very different thing than an academic essay. And yet in an important sense, novels and essays—and, for that matter, movies, songs, and advertisements—are all engaged in an effort to say the same thing: "This is the way the world really works." ("Not *that* way," some may go on to say. "*This* way.") In the words of one writing textbook, "Everything's an argument."[64] So, for example, we are told that people who will do anything to achieve power get destroyed by it (Shakespeare, *Macbeth*, 1606), and that there is a circle of life in which even uncertain heirs can nevertheless achieve their destiny (Disney, *The Lion King*, 1994). Sometimes such arguments, any number of which may be made in a single document, are implicit. Other times, they're relatively direct.

Actually, Stowe has been taken to task by later generations of critics for being a little *too* direct, of writing propaganda rather than real art—which, according to some literary critics, isn't supposed to have an explicit political agenda. It's certainly true that Stowe's characters, for example, lack the psychological ambiguity of some of her contemporaries, such as Nathaniel Hawthorne. Yet I would argue that even the least argumentative writers, determined as they may be to avoid any definitive conclusions, are still trying to persuade readers of *something*, if only of the essential ambiguity of the world. (This was Hawthorne's stock in trade.) But I'll leave the question of Stowe's value as an artist to literary critics. I'm more interested in telling you about what she did in her time, and how it might inform the way you think, write, and act in yours.

In many ways, Stowe can be compared with John Quincy Adams, who died when she was thirty-six years old. Like Adams, Stowe came from flinty New England stock. (I've seen no evidence the two ever met.) As with Adams, Stowe opposed slavery, yet her opposition, like his, did not become decisive until relatively late in life. Like Adams, too, Stowe became a high-profile figure who rubbed a great many people, pro-and antislavery, the wrong way. In both cases, their impact was less a matter of leading diehards to change their minds than in appealing to indifferent or ambivalent ordinary citizens and showing them they really had a stake in issues that may not have affected them directly.

There are also some significant differences. Adams was a statesman whose legitimate interest in the great issues of the day was unquestioned even by his fiercest opponents. Stowe, by contrast, was a wife and mother, whose gender was widely regarded as a disqualification for weighing in on political debates. A ruthless logician, Adams used irony, sarcasm and invective to embarrass and even humiliate his opponents. Stowe, who could also be quite logical, went out of her way to balance her arguments, even if she didn't typically convince her opponents she really was playing fair. But Stowe also relied on sentiment to make her case. She didn't only try to convince people to *think* the way she did; she also hoped they would *feel* the way she did, too. She was literally up-front about that, writing in the preface of *Uncle Tom's Cabin* that "the object of these sketches is to awaken sympathy and feeling for the African race, as they exist among us."[65]

Sympathy and feeling, however, are tricky matters. Appeals to emotion, even when welcome, are not always effective in novels. And feelings are often viewed particularly unwelcome at all in academic essays. But here too there may be less of difference than one might think. Bloodless prose in any form is usually hard to take. If appeals to feelings don't always work, they still may be worth a try, if only to make clear to yourself just what your feelings *are* in a first draft, like the letter you write, but wisely choose not to send, to that person who has just pissed you off. Again, the real measure of success will not be in the choice or mix of reason and/or passion, but rather your use of them to reach your imagined reader.

This is something that Harriet Beecher Stowe was very good at. Her prose is hardly a handbook of style for contemporary writers. But it's worth exploring, not only as a case study in the particular rhetorical skill known as counterargument, but also as a vivid demonstration of how big, often remote issues can be made immediate and relevant in the lives of ordinary citizens. Taking a page out of her book—more specifically, examining the way she tried to challenge the thinking of skeptics—might be of some use not only for structuring an essay on *Macbeth*, but also for selling Hondas or succeeding as a soccer mom (a job in which most skeptics are under five feet tall).

◆   ◆   ◆

As has often been noted, Harriet Beecher Stowe was the daughter, sister, and wife of ministers. She was also a mother, a housekeeper, and a beloved friend. But here's something else you should know about her: She was a dedicated student. She spent a lot of her life in schools of all kinds.

Her first school, naturally, was home. Born on June 14, 1811, in Litchfield, Connecticut, Harriet Beecher was the seventh of ten children born to her mother, who died in 1816 (Harriet went on to have four more stepsiblings). Her father, Lyman Beecher, was a prominent New England minister of the old school, a man who adamantly resisted more liberal varieties of Protestantism that flourished in his lifetime, and yet promoted Puritan tradition with his children and others in a notably flexible way. Harriet later described a revealing childhood scene:

> Occasionally he would raise a point of theology…and ask the opinion of one of his boys, and run a sort of tilt with him, taking up the wrong side of the question; for the sake of seeing how the youngster would practice his logic. If the party on the other side did not make a fair hit at him, however, he would stop and explain to him what he ought to have said. 'The argument lies so, my son; do that, and you'll trip me up.' Much of his teaching to his children was done in this informal way.[66]

There are two points worth making here. First, note that Beecher is talking with his *sons*. In the nineteenth century, they were the ones who were supposed to get educations. Second, note that it is *Harriet* who is recording this scene—she's the one who clearly absorbed the lesson.

In fact, Lyman Beecher wasn't notably progressive in his approach to female education. In 1819, at the age of eight, Harriet was enrolled four years early at the Litchfield Female Academy, whose purpose, according to its founder, was to "vindicate the equality of the female intellect." At age eleven, an essay she wrote was anonymously selected for the Academy's annual exhibition. Her father was among the dignitaries who visited that day, and listened with avid interest. Afterward, he asked the head teacher who wrote the essay. He replied, "Your daughter, sir!" Harriet described this as "the proudest moment" of her life.[67]

She wasn't the only star in her family. Her younger brother, Henry Ward Beecher, became one of the most famous ministers of the nineteenth century (and, after an adultery trial in the 1870s, the most notorious one). Her older sister, Catherine, who helped raise her, founded the Hartford Female Seminary, in which the adolescent Harriet was enlisted as a teacher. Harriet spent eight years in this female-run institution, where she gained her first sustained experience as a writer working on the school newspaper. She also produced a sheaf of letters on religion that suggest a more egalitarian approach from that of her father—a temperament that would have important consequences in her later work.[68]

In 1832, a pivotal event in Harriet's life occurred: Her family relocated to Cincinnati, Ohio, so her father could head the newly founded Lane Theological Seminary. She would remain there for eighteen years. During this time, she met and married her husband, Calvin Stowe, a nationally prominent minister in his own right. She also gave birth to six of her seven children, worked as a school-teacher in the Western Female Institute founded by Catherine, and participated in the Semi-Colon Club, a coed writing and discussion group. This club fostered the writing of, and conversation about, what Stowe biographer Joan Hedrick has dubbed "parlour literature," defined as writing for entertainment and amusement. "Meant to be read aloud," Hedrick explains, "these domestic literary productions were an integral part of polite society in antebellum America and were as accessible to women as to men."[69] Hedrick believes the encouragement and stimulation provided by the Semi-Colon Club was crucial to Stowe's emergence as a writer in the 1830s, as she began writing short stories for women's magazines and published her first book, *Primary Geography for Children* (1833). A collection of her pieces, *The Mayflower, or Sketches and Scenes of Characters among Descendants of the Pilgrims*, was published in 1843.

Stowe's heightened sense of place made her long sojourn in Cincinnati particularly significant. Situated at a key point on the Ohio River, the city, which was in its golden age economically, was a regional juncture between East and West and (especially) North and South. Ohio generally has always been something of a bellwether state politically. In this period, it had a significant abolitionist presence. In fact, abolitionists were particularly militant at Lane, much to the chagrin of the moderate Lyman Beecher, who was caught between them and more conservative donors as well as vocal anti-abolitionists. Cincinnati, with its strong commercial ties to the South, had a clear proslavery tilt. Stowe's brother, Edward, president of Illinois College, was among the defenders of Elijah Lovejoy, who was ultimately murdered for publishing an abolitionist newspaper. Stowe herself, writing under a male pseudonym for the *Cincinnati Journal* in 1836, wrote in defense of Ohio abolitionist (and future presidential candidate) James Birney, who also published abolitionist writings. Tellingly, she did so in the form of a conversation between two men:

> "But you must allow that it is undesirable to have that Birney here sending out these inflammatory things."
>
> "Why? What harm to do they do?"
>
> "Why? They inflame the community."
>
> "Well, and what harm is there in inflaming the community?"
>
> "Why it makes men furious, gives rise to popular commotions and disturbances, and *mobs,* and so forth.
>
> "Now my friend, do you think liberty of the press is a good thing?"
>
> "Certainly, to be sure."
>
> "...Well, then, as Mr. Birney is a man, I suppose you think it's right to allow him to do it [publish a newspaper] in particular?"

"But Mr. Birney's opinions are so dangerous!"[70]

Stowe is a bit heavy-handed here, ending with a sermon in favor of free speech, but there can be little doubt she accurately expressed the reservations of Birney's critics. In her 1845 story "Immediate Emancipation," a master sends a well-cared-for slave on an errand and is dismayed when he does not return. The master learns the slave has run away, aided by a Cincinnati Quaker, who successfully convinces the master that while an owner may be decent, the slave is nevertheless vulnerable to resale if the master dies or finds himself in debt. The ending, in which the master frees the slave, may not be altogether convincing (though Stowe claimed the story was based on a true incident), but its emphasis on the evils of the slave *system*, combined with a sharp ear for dialect, suggests real sophistication in making her case.[71]

As the nine years between these two documents suggests, however, slavery wasn't exactly high on Stowe's agenda. The truth is that she had very limited experience with the institution and very little experience with African-Americans in particular. The Beecher family did have black indentured servants, whom Stowe remembered fondly, and she hired black household help when she was in Cincinnati, including one woman she later learned was an escaped slave (and who her husband and brother Edward aided in going safely further North).[72] Nevertheless, her direct contact with slavery seems limited to a single visit to Kentucky. Like many people of her time, place, and class, slavery was something she cared about, but only one thing she cared about. In art and life, Stowe showed herself to be highly attuned to the cultural currents of her time, following, and often commenting upon, movements that included temperance, the theological movement of perfectionism, health fads like the water cure, and early consumer culture. (Later she would be part of a leading edge of travel literature and regionalism and a pioneer of wintering in Florida.)

Above all, Stowe was deeply immersed in what was once known as women's work. A letter she wrote to a friend during this phase of her life is deeply suggestive of the balls she was juggling.

> Since I began this note, I have been called off at least a dozen times; once for the fish man, to buy a codfish; once to see a man who had brought me barrels of apples; once to see a book-man; then to Mrs. Upham, to see about a drawing I made for her; then to nurse the baby; then into the kitchen to make chowder for dinner; and now I'm at it again, for nothing but deadly determination enables me ever to write; it is rowing against wind and tide.[73]

In reading about Stowe's career, one can't help but think her household must have been deeply chaotic. It's remarkable she ever wrote anything, and many observers then and since must wonder how she did it all (or, more darkly, if she *could* have done it all). Yet writing was more than just a distracting hobby for Stowe. It was also an increasingly important source of income in a household in which Calvin's breadwinning never quite seemed adequate for his large family. By the late 1840s, Stowe seemed to regard writing a short story as something akin to baking a pie, a domestic skill that offered sustenance for her family—and personal satisfaction to boot.

Two events seem to have set her on the road toward fame, fortune, and historic significance. The first was the death of Charles, her son of eighteen months. While the loss of a child was all too common in the nineteenth century, this seems to have been a particularly crushing blow—and one that seemed to open a window of imaginative projection. As Stowe later explained, "It was at *his* dying bed, and at *his* grave, that I learnt what a poor slave mother may feel when her child is torn away from her."[74] One possible reason for this imaginative identification was the intensification of the slavery debate, in anecdotal stories that Stowe herself noted, of slave women who put their children to death rather than have them live in slavery.[75]

This intensifying interest points toward the other major factor in the transformation of Stowe's life and work. The ending of the gag rule, a controversial war with Mexico, and increasing sectionalism in the political parties in the 1840s led many politicians to try to address the slavery issue once and for all. The result was the famous Compromise of 1850, a complex and multifaceted series of deals. One key provision of the Compromise was the much-hated Fugitive Slave Act, which made it a crime to aid—and, crucially for many Northerners who were previously indifferent to slavery, to ignore—escaped slaves. For many Northerners, Stowe included, the Fugitive Act was a crucial event in the coming of the Civil War, an act that intensified rather than lessened sectional tension. In fact, Stowe turned to the issue once again in 1850, publishing a story, "The Freeman's Dream: A Parable," in which a generally decent man refuses to help escaped slaves for fear of prosecution, only to face the wrath of God ("the sky grew dark, and the earth rocked to and fro, and the heavens flashed with a strange light"—this wasn't Stowe's most subtle hour).[76]

By this point, Stowe had left Cincinnati for Brunswick, Maine, where Calvin was hired to teach at Bowdoin College. It was here, back among native New Englanders, that her die was cast. In late 1850, Stowe's sister-in-law wrote her a letter saying, "If I could use a pen as you can, I would write something that would make this whole nation feel what an accursed thing slavery is."[77] Upon reading the letter aloud to her family (as letters were often read in those days), Stowe rose from her chair and said, "I'll write something. I'll if I live." She did. The story goes that she had a vision during a chapel service at Bowdoin of a black man being beaten by his master[78]—and what she wrote took on a life of its own.

◆   ◆   ◆

In the century-and-a-half since its publication, *Uncle Tom's Cabin* has been considered so many things—an indirect cause of the Civil War; a classic example of sentimental literature; Exhibit A in a long history of white racism all the more damning for being unintentional—that it takes some effort to remember what it was written to be: an extended response to those who believed it was impossible to end slavery. It took the form it did for a number of reasons: Fiction was the mode in which Stowe herself felt most comfortable; novels were one of the few media in which women were allowed to speak in the public sphere; and storytelling could be appreciated by young and old, male and female, literate and illiterate alike (no doubt the book was read aloud to children and slaves). These were the days, more than those before or since, when a woman's place was in the home. But the core of Stowe's point was that events in the public life were encroaching on private life. Women could not do their jobs as wives and mothers properly when bad laws, including the Fugitive Slave Act, were corrupting notions of right and wrong (in which "right" means treating human beings like things). In such a world, the political was personal.[79]

Uncle Tom's Cabin, which was published in serial form each week in the abolitionist newspaper *The National Era* from June 1851 to April 1852, and in book form in March 1852, is a novel with two (only tenuously connected) plots. The first is the story of the enslaved Harris family: George, Eliza, and little Harry. George, a talented mechanic, is slave of a Mr. Harris. Eliza and Harry are the property of a Mr. Shelby. George's master is a thoughtless and cruel man, so he runs away to Canada, planning to earn the money to buy the freedom of his wife and son. But although Mr. Shelby is largely a decent individual (and his wife is a *very* decent individual), financial considerations force him to sell Harry, who Eliza spirits away rather than be separated from him. Much of the novel concerns the family's quest to reunite in freedom.

The other main plot of the novel concerns another one of Mr. Shelby's slaves, Uncle Tom. Tom is part of the same sale as Harry, but he submits to his removal from his loved ones (including the Shelby's young son) in a spirit of Christian stoicism and, perhaps, in a realization that a refusal to go would endanger those loved ones further. He initially has the good fortune of being sold to a New Orleans slaveholder named Augustine St. Clare, who is the most fully realized person in the novel—more passive than he should be, but witty, wise, and generous. St. Clare has a saintly young daughter, Eva; a selfish wife, Marie; and a well-intentioned but morally complacent visiting New England cousin, Ophelia. Unfortunately for Tom, this living arrangement isn't permanent, and he finds himself the property of the evil Simon Legree, who demands he abandon his principles and inform on two escaped slaves. This sets up the climax of the novel and a denouement that links the two plots back together.

Though it seems a little pedestrian now, and is generally only read by scholars and (a few) students in its entirety, *Uncle Tom's Cabin* was a phenomenally successful novel. Key incidents from the book, such as Eliza and Harry hopping across ice floes on the Ohio River, went on to become staples of stage and screen adaptations. The death of Little Eva, heavily foreshadowed from virtually the moment we meet her, became the quintessential tearjerker scene, rivaled only by that of Amy in Louisa May Alcott's *Little Women* (1868). Yet threaded through the moments of high drama and humor is a sustained critique of slavery that, while not necessarily central to every reader, nevertheless holds the book together and gives it its durable power. That critique works to the considerable extent that it does because Stowe takes seriously—and makes a real effort to represent—the arguments of her opponents. They're worth examining in some detail.

Slaves as animals/children. As we saw in struggle over the gag rule, one crucial development in the slavery debate was an increasing insistence that far from a necessary evil, slavery was a positive good. One of the most common arguments made by proslavery theorists were two seemingly contradictory assertions that stemmed from a shared belief that slaves were not quite fully realized human beings. On the one hand, slaves were animals who were a threat to themselves and others, requiring ruthless discipline. On the other, slaves were immature children who needed the kindly ministrations of paternalistic owners. Jefferson Davis, the senator from Mississippi who would later become president of the Southern Confederacy, suggested both when he said in 1861 that "in moral and social condition they [slaves] had been elevated from brutal savages into docile, intelligent, and civilized agricultural laborers, and supplied not only with bodily comforts, but careful religious instruction."[80]

Uncle Tom's Cabin does feature slaves who indeed could be described as brutal savages or incorrigible children. Indeed, one of the great strengths of the book is that it has *many* kinds of slaves (and non-slaves).[81] Tom's tormentors Quimbo and Sambo, for example, take glee in flogging field hands. The amorality of Topsy, a child slave, would also seem to fit the bill, though, like many children, she has deceptively sophisticated antennae. And we also see some enlightened slave owners as well, St. Clare principal among them (though he isn't particularly interested in religious instruction). But what we also see—what we're reminded of, in fictional stories that mirror factual ones—are slaves who behave in ways that are decidedly not savage *or* childlike. "I'm a man as much as he is," notes a bitter George Harris, who works for wages that are paid to his master, much in the way of the young Frederick Douglass. Harris, much like Douglass, will run away.[82]

True, runaway slaves, like children and animals, show waywardness, stealth, and an instinct to flee, but animals nor children typically seek advice, express gratitude, or agonize about whether they're doing the right thing, as Eliza does on the eve of her flight with her son. And insofar as slaves do behave like animals, perhaps the same can be said of their owners. "If it were *your* Harry, mother, or your Willie, that were going to be torn from you by a brutal trader, tomorrow morning...how fast could *you* walk?" the narrator asks.[83] Ironically, the most brutalized characters in the novel are slave traders, completely inured to the anguish and despair of the property they buy and sell. "You can get used to such things too, my friend," the narrator taunts her reader. "It is the great object of recent efforts to make our whole northern community used to them [via the Fugitive Slave Act], for the glory of our Union."[84]

Stowe intends for the greatest refutation of the animals/children argument to be Tom himself, a deeply committed Christian who reads the Bible, albeit with some difficulty. (He was taught by the Shelby's son.) Many readers of *Uncle Tom's Cabin* find Tom to be an unrealistic figure in his saintliness, and they may be right. Yet the rigor of his nonviolent resistance to Legree was later a hallmark of the twentieth-century Civil Rights movement, and religious commitment often seems unrealistic to those that lack it. As Flannery O'Connor, a Southern writer, put it in a novel published exactly a century after *Uncle Tom's Cabin*, "That belief in Christ is a matter of life and death has been a stumbling block for readers who would prefer to think it is a matter of no great consequence."[85] That people like Tom were uncommon in the nineteenth-century South may be safely taken for granted. That there were *no* slaves who were intelligent, complex, mature human beings may not.

The Bible sanctions slavery. This argument was common in the nineteenth century, and one can still hear it today if you talk for any length of time with an apologist for the Old South. The usual justification comes from the Book of

Genesis, when a drunk, naked Noah is seen by his son, Ham. Noah curses Ham by declaring, "A servant of servants/He shall be to his brethren" (Genesis 9:25). Proslavery theorists also used New Testament justifications, such as St. Paul's injunction for the slave Onesimus to return to his master, Philemon (Phil 1:10).

Stowe, who knew these verses as well as anyone, does not try to refute them as much as she does note their self-serving quality. So, for example, she includes this exchange between Marie and Augustine St. Clare, after Marie comes home gushing over a sermon she heard at church:

> "The text was, 'He hath made everything beautiful in its season;' and he showed how all the orders and distinctions in society came from God; and that it was so appropriate, you know, that some should be high, and some low, and that some were born to rule and some to serve, and all that, you know; and he applied it so well to all this ridiculous fuss that's made about slavery, and he proved distinctly that the Bible was on our side, and supported all our institutions so convincingly. I only wish you'd heard him."
>
> "Oh, I didn't need it," said St. Clare. "I can learn what does me as much good as that from the *Picayune* [a New Orleans newspaper] any time, and smoke a cigar besides, which I can't do, you know, in a church."[86]

Stowe's other approach involves countering one biblical verse with another. "It's undoubtedly the intention of Providence that the African race should be servants—kept in a low condition," says a clergyman on a Mississippi riverboat in *Uncle Tom's Cabin*. To which another responds, "'All things whatsoever ye would that men should do unto you, do ye even unto them.'" Significantly, it's this man, who is *not* a minister, who invokes the injunction of Jesus Christ that has come to be known as the Golden Rule.

In the final analysis, of course, the Bible is a limited tool at best for arguing human beings shouldn't be slaves. But then, it's not a particularly good tool for arguing they *should* be slaves either, particularly if one thinks of Christianity as something more as a means for excusing present arrangements. This point is made most vividly by St. Clare, who does not consider himself religious. "My view of Christianity is such," he tells his cousin Ophelia, "that I think no man can consistently profess it without throwing the whole weight of his being against this monstrous injustice that lies at the foundation of our society...I confess that the apathy of religious people on this subject, their want of perception of wrongs that fill me with horror, have engendered in me more scepticism than any other thing."[87]

With Tom's help, St. Clare eventually does find a Christian God in time to find his redemption in the next world, but while he makes some effort to act, he loses the chance he had to really make a difference. In this, of course, he is far from alone with many of his fellow citizens, regardless of what part of the country they come from.

The North is just as bad, if not worse (and certainly more hypocritical). The evils of the world, proslavery advocates would often argue, are not limited to slavery or the South. The hypocrisy of slavery's critics is particularly apparent when one compares the ravages of slave labor with those of the emerging factory system. Sometimes this critique professed concern for exploited Northern factory workers, many of them immigrants. More often, it took the form at a more generalized revulsion. "Let the North enjoy their hireling labor, with all its...pauperism, rowdyism, mobism, and anti-rentism," said a customs collector in Charleston in 1854. "We are satisfied with our slave labor...We like old things—old wine, old books, old friends, old and fixed relations between employer and employed." An 1856 newspaper article in Georgia was even blunter: "Free society! We sicken at the name. What is it but a conglomeration of greasy mechanics, filthy operatives, and moon-struck theorists?"[88]

Stowe's response to this line of argument is, to a great degree, to adopt it. She doesn't do much with the critique of factory labor (few abolitionists, ignorant and even hostile toward the life conditions of many working-class people, did), which may be the novel's greatest weakness. But she goes very far in granting Southerners an idealized version of plantation life, particularly as represented by St. Clare. At his estate and elsewhere, slaves really *are* well taken care of, and really *do* take comfort from their surroundings. And, in what may be the shrewdest move in novel, Stowe makes what may be the most instinctively racist character an uptight New Englander: Miss Ophelia, an obvious stand-in for Stowe herself. Ophelia can't hide her revulsion at Topsy (as Topsy well knows), and reacts with alarm when she sees Eva sitting on Tom's lap. This gives St. Clare a chance to land a gentle but unmistakable punch on his cousin and abolitionists generally:

> "You loathe them as you would a snake or a toad, yet you're indignant at their wrongs. You would not have them abused; but you don't want to have anything to do with themselves. You would send them to Africa, out of your sight and smell, and then send a missionary or two to do up all the self-denial of elevating them compendiously. Isn't that it?"
>
> "Well, cousin," said Miss Ophelia thoughtfully, "there may be some truth in this."

Stowe's implicit response to the "North is bad" argument is a largely implicit suggestion that two wrongs don't make a right. She also argues for (well, it's more like she asserts) a deeply human instinct human instinct for freedom. This is no incidental matter when one considers the novel is set in a nation resting on the proposition of liberty as a self-evident truth. "Well, anyway, thar's wrong about it *somewhar*," says Tom's wife, Aunt Chloe, who is described as having a "stubborn sense of justice" about her husband's forced removal. "I can't jest make out whar 'tis, thar's a wrong somewhar, I'm *clar* o' that."

The value of freedom is made most vividly by Tom himself, who, for the entire novel, acquiesces to almost every condition of slave life. St. Clare is surprised—and a little hurt—when he sees Tom express joy upon learning that St. Clare is drawing up the paperwork to emancipate him. "You haven't such very bad times here that you need to be in such a rapture Tom," he notes dryly." Tom nevertheless explains he would rather have the most meager food and shelter than be a slave in finery. "I suppose so, Tom," St. Clare resignedly concludes, though Tom insists he will stay with St. Clare as long as he's needed (which, Tom explains, means he'll stay until St. Clare has finally converted to Christianity).[89]

Tom keeps up his end of the bargain, but things don't go as planned—a point that goes to the heart of Stowe's general critique: Slavery is about more than good intentions or even acts; it's a system that enmeshes everyone. And in this system, even things that are right all too often go wrong: People die, lose their fortunes, and are subject to forces beyond their control. "I thought I could gild it over—I thought that by kindness, and care, and instruction, I could make the condition of mine better than that of freedom—fool that I was," a disgusted Mrs. Shelby says of her slaves when she learns her husband has sold Tom and Harry. "Why, wife, you're getting to be an abolitionist," he notes sardonically. "Abolitionist! If they knew all I know about slavery, they might talk," she replies. When Shelby points out their minister had recently given a sermon defending slavery, she answers by saying, "Ministers can't help the evil, perhaps—can't cure it, any more than we can—but defend it!—indeed, it always went against my common sense."[90]

Indeed, as Stowe tries to show, common sense isn't always what you might think it is.

It's only a few bad apples/It's illogical to damage your property. Perhaps the strongest of proslavery arguments rests on making concessions: Yes, bad things do happen, and there are cruel or stupid slave owners who do evil things. But they are the exception rather than the rule. Slave owners have the most potent motivation of all—self-interest—to treat their property well, for damaged goods simply don't perform as well as properly maintained ones. And while slave trading is distasteful, owners typically turn to it as a last resort.

The problem with this theory, Stowe responds, is that there are more bad apples than you might think, and that self-interest can be calculated in different ways. "I used to, when I fust begun, have considerable trouble...tryin' to keep 'em sort 'o decent and comfortable," Simon Legree tells some fellow passengers on a boat on Louisiana's Red River. "Law 'twasn't no use; I lost money on 'em, and 'twas heaps o' trouble. Now, you see, I just put 'em straight through, sick or well. When one nigger's dead, I buy another; and I find it comes cheaper and easier, every way."[91] Significantly, Legree is from Vermont—that is, he's a transplanted New Englander—and his evil has a distinctly capitalist flavor. (He's a consumer in the most literal sense.) But even less vicious slave traders don't inspire much in the way of confidence. "I b'lieve in religion, and one of these days, when I've got matters tight and snug, I calculates to tend my soul and them ar matters; and so what' the use of doin' any more wickedness than's re'lly necessary?" slave trader Dan Haley tells a bounty hunter he's hired to track down Harry. "It don't seem to me it's t'all prudent."[92]

Yet even the most prudent and calculating of men have impulses that are less than wholly rational. Legree, whatever his financial imperatives, is in the thrall of passions that Stowe only hints at in her novel. "You see, Mrs. Stowe did not hit the softest spot," the famed Southern diarist Mary Chesnut, no fan of Yankees, noted in 1861. "She makes Legree a bachelor."[93] Besides his lust for the quadroon Cassy, love of alcohol, and fear of the dark (he's afraid of the ghost of a slave woman he murdered), Legree also finds himself increasingly obsessed with breaking Tom's will, a desire that ultimately proves counterproductive. He's viewed with repulsion by just about everyone, black and white. "Well," a riverboat passenger who observes Legree notes, "there are also many considerate and humane men among planters." "Granted," a companion traveler replies, "but in my opinion, it is you considerate, humane men, that are responsible for all the brutality and outrage wrought by these wretches; because if not for your sanction and influence, the whole system could not foothold for an hour."[94] Slave trading would be impossible if good men didn't turn over the slaves to bad ones. "I hope you'll remember that you promised, on your honor, you wouldn't sell Tom, without knowing what kind of hands he's going into," Mr. Shelby tells Haley. "Why you've just done it, sir," Haley responds. "Circumstances, you well know, *obliged* me," Shelby retorts. "Wal, you know, they may 'blige *me*, too," Haley answers, his assertion that he's "never noways cruel" ringing more than a little hollow.[95]

Yet even if one considers Haley and Legree isolated figures in their viciousness, the assumption that people operate out of a largely rational sense of self-interest, that doesn't mean they always know what their self-interest really *is*. Shelby, Haley, and Legree all make miscalculations about the tractability of the people they buy, sell, and own. Ten years after Stowe's novel appeared, Southern politicians decided the best way to save slavery was to leave the Union. Subsequent events seem to suggest they were incorrect.

Yes, it may be wrong. But it's too hard to do anything about it now. This may be the most powerful argument of all, one that sidesteps ideals or morality altogether in the name of realism. Let's assume slavery really is evil, this line of thinking runs. There are nevertheless billions of dollars tied up in that evil, and laws to protect those billions, and all the lectures, sermons, or novels in the world will never lead the people invested in that evil to give it up. "Your feelings are all quite right, dear, and interesting, and I love you for them," Senator John Bird tells his wife, "but, then, dear, we musn't suffer our feelings to run away with our judgment; you must consider it's not a matter of private feeling—there are great public interests involved." George Harris' owner puts the matter more succinctly: "It's a free country, sir; the man's *mine* and I do what I please with him—that's it!"[96]

Ever the voice of reason, St. Clare sees the issue with more clarity than anyone in the book. "If I was to say anything on the slavery matter, I would say out, fair and square, 'We're in for it; we've got 'em, and mean to keep 'em—that's the whole of what all this sanctified stuff amounts to, after all.'" He also questions whether *Northerners* are really capable of facing the consequences of a slave-free nation:

> Suppose we should rise up tomorrow and emancipate, who would educate these millions, and teach them how to use their freedom? The fact is, we [Southerners] are too lazy and unpractical, ourselves, ever to give them much of an idea of that industry and energy which is necessary to form them into men. They will have to go north, where labor is the fashion—the universal custom; and tell me, now, is there enough Christian philanthropy, among your Northerners, to bear with the process of their education and elevation?

How many families would take in freed slaves, he asks? How many employers would train them? Given subsequent Northern race relations, these are very good questions.[97]

And yet, for all his clarity on the difficulties involved in change, St. Clare is also skeptical the status quo is tenable. "I don't think my feelings about slavery are peculiar," he tells Ophelia. "I find many men, who in, their hearts, think of it just as I do. The land groans under it; and bad as it is for the slave, it is worse, if anything, for the master. It takes no spectacles to see that a great class of vicious, improvident, degraded people, among us, are an evil to us, as well as themselves." "And what do you think will be the end of this?" Ophelia asks. "I don't know," St. Clare answers. "One thing is certain—that there is a mustering among the masses, the world over; and there is a *dies irae* [funeral dirge] coming on, sooner or later."

He continues this line of argument with his twin brother, Alfred, who takes a much harder position on this question (among others). "That's one of your red humbugs, Augustine!" Alfred retorts to his brother's apocalyptic (and curiously proto-Marxist) predictions of revolution. "I hope I shall be dead before this greasy millennium of your greasy masses comes on." (With that millennium having arrived, I think one can say that the greasy masses really *have* taken over as far as Alfred, or, for that matter, John Calhoun, would be concerned.) When St. Clare insists the day of the greasy masses is coming, Alfred insists, "The Anglo-Saxon is the dominant race of the world, and *is to be so.*" His brother retorts "there is a pretty fair infusion of Anglo-Saxon blood among our slaves now"—another reminder of the interracial sexuality that belied so many premises of purity and patriarchy that governed Southern life. The heirs of the planters might well run the country—and they might be found in Uncle Tom's great-granddaughter's cabin, too. Just ask the heirs of Tom Jefferson.[98]

Although they were vague and even incorrect about the details, St. Clare (and, of course, Stowe) was right that the status quo wasn't ultimately tenable. But that would not be clear until later, and it is apparent that for all her attempts to engage with her proslavery opponents, she clearly failed to persuade all or even many of them. Indeed, it's telling that every single proslavery argument I've cited in this chapter (for example, Jefferson Davis or that Charleston customs collector) was made *after* the book was published, though always drawing on ideas that were in circulation before. "To you, generous, noble-minded men and women, of the South—you, whose virtue, and magnamity, and purity of character are greater for the severer for the trail it has encountered—to you is her appeal," the author writes in her final chapter.[99] Since the argument raged on after the book was published, and thousands of Southerners ultimately decided they would rather die than give up slavery, it appears her appeal fell on deaf ears. By this standard, you could say, *Uncle Tom's Cabin* was a failure.

You could, yes. But in the realm of persuasion, failure, like success, is almost always relative.

◆   ◆   ◆

There's a lot not to like about Harriet Beecher Stowe. The most obvious thing that strikes any modern reader is Stowe's grating, even embarrassing, racism. The opening sentence of the book is a case in point: "The scenes of this story, as its title indicates, lie among a race hitherto ignored by the associations of polite and refined society; an exotic race, whose ancestors, born beneath a tropic sun, brought with them, and perpetuated to their descendants, a character so essentially unlike the hard and dominant Anglo-Saxon race, as for many years to have won from it only misunderstanding and contempt."[100] Repeatedly in the story that follows, Stowe defends slaves by emphasizing their innocence, decency, and even childlike character. In effect, she simply turned negative stereotypes on their head. No one better typifies this tendency than the title character, who would eventually become a symbol of black subservience. "The Uncle Tom Nigger has got to go," Marcus Garvey told the United Negro Improvement Association in 1920, coining a term that has prevailed long after most Americans, black or white, know anything about its fictional origin.[101]

Stowe's lack of insight about black people extended to an inability to really imagine a credible future for African-Americans in the United States. Like a lot of antislavery activists—a damn moderate one, in the eyes of some abolitionists—the best she could do was promote the old colonizationist idea of the idea of slaves returning to Africa, specifically Liberia, a notion that was logistically dubious at best. And for all the variety and even complexity *among* her characters, she was unable to represent variety and complexity *within* them—Eva is never anything *but* a saintly little girl; Tom never expresses the anger than any fully rendered human being would seemingly have to in one way or another in order to be fully believable.[102] Heavy-handed in some ways, oblivious in others, one can plausibly wonder just what kind of world the woman was calling for—and why she thought she could get it.

In the short term, at least, *Uncle Tom's Cabin* did not have any obvious impact on the political process that inspired it. The presidential election of 1852 brought Franklin Pierce, a New Englander sympathetic to Southern interests, to the White House. (He was a graduate of Bowdoin, where Stowe's husband taught.) No obvious party realignment occurred in Congress. Even abolitionism seemed to be waning as militant members of James Birney's Liberty Party drifted back into the antislavery ("Barnburner") wing of the Democrats. And though Stowe "sincerely disclaim[ed] any invidious feeling toward those individuals who, often without any fault of their own, are involved in the trials and embarrassments of slavery,"[103] she seems to have succeeded only in enraging them.

And yet this in itself is an indication of something valuable and important. In a March 1851 letter, Stowe told her editor at the *National Era* she had, with some trepidation, decided to write a story about "the patriarchal institution" in which she would show "the *best side* of the thing, and something *faintly approaching the worst*." Toward the end of the letter, she described what she understood to be the heart of her method: "My vocation is simply that of *painter*, and my object will be to hold up in the most lifelike and graphic manner possible Slavery, its reverses, changes, and the negro character, which I have had ample opportunities for studying. There is no arguing with *pictures*, and everybody is impressed by them, whether they mean to be or not."[104]

Stowe was either exaggerating or naïve when she asserted, "there is no arguing with pictures," for that's precisely what happened—precisely because virtually everybody *was* impressed by them. The power of those pictures, carefully framed by a sharp awareness of how they would be perceived, made *Uncle Tom's Cabin* a phenomenon of the kind the world had never seen. Within days of its publication in book form, the novel sold 10,000 copies. Within a year, it was 300,000, more than any book in the United States other than the Bible. In Great Britain, over a million copies were sold in the first year, and there were another million-and-a-half in English or in translation all over the world. In good capitalist fashion, the novel generated countless tie-ins, including figurines, candles, toys, and games. By 1853, over 300 infants in Boston had been named Eva. "No age, or sex is spared, men and women and children of all ages confess to its power," a critical reviewer in the *New York World* noted. "No condition is exempt; lords and ladies; flunkies and kitchen maids are equally infected with the rage." No less a personage than Ralph Waldo Emerson, the leading American intellectual of the day, acclaimed it for appealing to "the universal heart." Think Harry Potter with a political edge.[105]

Tracking the reception of the novel in the slave South is impossible, partly because it was banned in much of the region—itself a telling fact. "Mrs. Stowe betrays a malignity so remarkable," the leading Southern novelist of the day, William Gilmore Simms, wrote in a review, "that the petticoat lifts of itself and we see the hoof of the beast under the table."[106] But the most impressive demonstration of the book's impact is the entire genre of "anti-Tom" novels it spawned: *Aunt Phillis's Cabin* (1852); *The Cabin and the Parlor* (1852); *Uncle Robin in His Cabin in Virginia* (1853); *The Planter's Northern Bride* (1854); and so on. There were dozens, each trying to refute various aspects of Stowe's depiction of slavery, all (often unwillingly) flattering her through imitation. Stowe, for her part, replied with *A Key to Uncle Tom's Cabin* (1853), a collection of documents meant to show her depiction of slavery was actually on the mild side.[107] Yet it was the original novel that continued to be the focus of almost obsessive fury in the South, a decisive indication of the power of her fusion of thought and feeling.

Ironically, what proved to be the most effective way of subverting Stowe's message came not from books or reviews attacking her, but rather stage productions of *Uncle Tom's Cabin*, particularly minstrel shows in which white actors in blackface caricatured people and scenes from the book. These proved to be so popular, so durable, and so racist that over time they influenced the perception of the novel, which was increasingly remembered—and forgotten—as sentimental pap. The pictures lost their frames and became cartoons. (Martin Scorsese includes a comically anachronistic one in his film, *Gangs of New York* [2002], in which the character of Abraham Lincoln makes an appearance.)

Uncle Tom's Cabin fall from grace wasn't rapid, but it was steady. Sales fell sharply after the Civil War. For much of the twentieth century, the novel was out of print, and, when referred to at all, was usually in terms of condemnation, such as James Baldwin's scathing attack in his famous 1949 essay, "Everybody's Protest Novel," in which he charges that Tom, the only real black man in the novel, "has been robbed of his humanity and divested of his sex."[108]

Yet, by the time of the Civil Rights movement, at least some readers were discovering a book of surprising power. In his celebrated literary history of the Civil War, *Patriotic Gore* (1962), the famed essayist Edmund Wilson described reading *Uncle Tom's Cabin* as "a startling experience. It is a much more impressive work than one has ever been allowed to suspect." Wilson noted, "The farther one reads in *Uncle Tom*, the more one is aware that a critical mind is at work, which has the complex situation in a very firm grip." He concluded, "Mrs. Stowe was a very observant and essentially realistic woman."[109] Even some African-American writers, among them Langston Hughes and Gerald Early, have pronounced themselves impressed with the book. "Stowe knows from her experience with the abolitionist movement in Ohio and from suffering the death of one of her children that to rid this world of evil will not be simply the act of good asserting itself, of saying that evil is impossible, but the act of the shedding of the blood of virtue," Early wrote in 1989.[110] What strikes him isn't the sentiment, but a tough-minded assessment of the world missing from self-affirming contemporary writers such as Alice Walker—and what it takes to change it.

But did *Uncle Tom's Cabin* really change the world? It's impossible to say. Abraham Lincoln was probably (half) joking when, upon greeting Stowe on January 1, 1863—the day his Emancipation Proclamation took effect—he reputedly pronounced her as "the little lady who made this great war." Stowe may not have succeeded in convincing the South to abandon slavery, but she made the subject, which had been largely taboo both inside and outside the capital, a subject for household discussion in a way that John Quincy Adams could only envy. She also seemed to frame the debate in a durable way. Not until the publication of *Gone with the Wind* in 1936 was the dominant picture of the South changed in the collective imagination.[111]

To go back to my original point, this was possible because Stowe thought long and hard about her fellow citizens, and she had faith in the power of persuasion (variously pursued). In the end, such faith can be little more than just that—a belief. There are some people you can't persuade of anything: Slavery only ended after a Civil War. (Hell, there are surely some things no one can convince *you* of either.) But education, as you're currently experiencing it, rests on the confidence that words can make a difference—not only in school, but also in your home, at work, and in the polling booth. And it's always possible that in the act of writing you may be able to change at least one mind: your own. So the next time you find yourself staring at a blank screen (or, for that matter, standing in a Honda dealership, or sitting in your room alone trying to decide whether you're ready to get married) ask yourself: What would someone who's *not* me say in this situation? The answer just might be surprising—and useful.

4

Miss Wells Mocks Terrorists

An important part of our shared Anglo-American heritage is the often-expressed notion that we "are a nation of laws, not men." Among other things, this means that not only that no person is above the law, but that every person is entitled to certain basic rights, among them the presumption of innocence until proven guilty, a trial by one's peers, and so forth. Yet these principles have sometimes been violated in American history, as in the detention of Asian-Americans during World War II or in the detention of Americans by the Bush administration in the War on Terror. They were also violated in the American South in the decades after the Civil War through a brutal cultural practice known as lynching, that is, murdering people for crimes—or what an angry community considers a crime—without due process.

Despite the dangers involved, a few brave people have always been willing to speak out against those who commit acts of lynching and call attention to their violation of what we like to consider "the American way of life." This is the story of a young woman who spoke out against what a famous Billie Holiday song of the 1930s called "Strange Fruit"—black men swinging from poplar trees.

CHAPTER 4:
MISS WELLS MOCKS TERRORISTS

in which we see a young journalist
make some "respectable" people very, very angry

YOU MIGHT SAY it began as child's play, but the principal players were not children, and the final result was deadly serious. On or about Wednesday, March 2, 1892, in a racially mixed Memphis, Tennessee, neighborhood known as the Curve, a group of boys was playing marbles. A disagreement between them led to a fight between a group of white boys and another group of black ones. After it appeared the white boys had lost, the father of one, Cornelius Hurst, intervened by whipping one of the black victors. This, in turn, led a group of enraged black fathers to gather near Hurst's home. Someone called the police, but by the time they arrived at the scene (twice), the scene was quiet.[112]

Though the precise circumstances were disputed, it's reasonably clear it was at this point that a white man named W.H. Barrett got involved. Barrett owned a grocery store in the Curve (so named because it was where a streetcar line turned). It had been the only such establishment until 1889, when a group of locally prominent African-Americans invested in a store known the People's Grocery, under the leadership of Calvin McDowell, Henry Stewart, and Thomas Moss, the president of the corporation whose wide contacts made even white neighbors patrons of their store. Barrett claimed he intervened in the fight to aid Hurst, his fellow white man. But McDowell, who worked as a clerk at the People's Grocery, claimed Barrett entered the store and pistol-whipped him. In any event, Barrett and Hurst convinced a judge to issue a warrant for McDowell, who was arrested, posted bond, and released the next day.

Barrett also succeeded in convincing the judge to indict the other two owners of People's Grocery for maintaining a public nuisance. The charges would be settled with nominal fines, but before that happened, a meeting of African-Americans had resulted in the expression of anger that included suggestions that dynamite would be a good remedy for "damned white trash." Taking these remarks literally, Barrett then persuaded the judge to issue warrants against two of the men for conspiracy. He also spread a story that a white mob was going to raid the People's Grocery as part of the arrest.

To prepare for the anticipated raid, the store's owners consulted an attorney, who told them that because the store was technically outside city limits and thus beyond police protection, they were justified in defending themselves. They therefore stationed armed guards outside on the evening of Saturday, March 5. At about 10:00 PM that night, as McDowell was serving a final round of customers, shots rang out: the guards were shooting at the approaching white men. Three of the men, police deputies dressed in civilian clothes, were wounded before the patrons and guards fled. The remaining deputies, aided by reinforcements, arrested a dozen men, including McDowell and Stewart. The third owner, Moss, wasn't arrested and was apparently not even at the store that night. But he was subsequently described as the ringleader who had shot the most seriously wounded deputy. In the aftermath of the confrontation, as whites looted the store and broke into black homes, thirty more "co-conspirators" were arrested, among them Moss.

Tensions rose still further in the days that followed, as press accounts described "a bloody riot" and "war." The arrested men were held without bond and not allowed any visitors. Some were beaten. The African-American community, for its part, mobilized their local militia, the Tennessee Rifles, which guarded the jail until the judge issued an order to disarm all black citizens.

By the evening of Monday, March 8, tensions were ebbing. Newspapers reported the wounded deputies would recover, and the (now unarmed) black men guarding the jail went home.

At about 3:00 AM on the morning of March 9, however, a group of about ten white men was admitted to the jail. They took McDowell, Stewart, and Moss out of their cells. They were loaded on a railroad engine, which ran behind the jail, and carried north of city limits. Aware they were about to be lynched, Moss begged for his life for the sake of his wife, daughter, and unborn child. When it was clear his appeal had fallen on deaf ears and was asked if he had any last words, he reportedly replied, "Tell my people to go West—there is no justice for them here." McDowell, for his part, managed to grab one of the mob's guns, and when they failed to pry it loose, they shot him in the fist. When the bodies of the three men were found, McDowell's right hand had been shot to pieces and his eyes were gouged out.

In the days following the lynchings, some white newspapers described the event as regrettable. Others, however, reported on the evident with evident admiration. "The vengeance was sharp, swift, and sure, but administered with due regard to the fact that people were asleep all around the jail, and that it isn't good form to arouse people from their slumbers at 3 o'clock in the morning," opined The *Memphis Appeal-Avalanche*, which ran a drawing of the murdered men. None of the perpetrators was ever found, much less tried.

The black community of Memphis was infuriated by the murders, and galvanized by them. Hundreds gathered around the bodies of the three men in the morning after the murders until the judge in the case sent armed whites to "preserve order." The funerals were large, though peaceful. In the weeks that followed, however, systematic efforts were made to respond to the lynching. A meeting held two weeks after drew over a thousand people, who agreed on a series of resolutions ranging from denunciations of the white press to calls for boycotts. In the days that followed thousands of African-Americans also acted on Moss's admonition: They went west to Oklahoma. The white business community grew increasingly alarmed. One prominent citizen noted that valuable labor was leaving the city and urged a biracial mass meeting.

Among the most vocal voices in the aftermath of the lynching was a Memphis African-American newspaper, the *Free-Speech*. Its editor had been out of town on the night of the lynchings. But in the days and weeks that followed, the paper published a string of blistering editorials supporting a strong, activist response to the murders. "There is only one thing left we can do," read one, advising readers to "save our money and leave a town which will neither protect our lives and property, nor give us a fair trial in the courts, but takes us out and murders us in cold blood when accused by white persons."

Six weeks after the lynchings, the superintendent and treasurer of the City Railway Company came to the offices of the *Free-Speech*, hoping to convince the paper to soften its line and relieve the painful decline in business. The editor refused—in fact, the paper told its readers to keep up the good work. For the *Free Speech*, there was more at stake here than a boycott, or even the deaths of these three men. The murders of March 9 were part of an epidemic of lynching all over the South in the 1890s. The May 21 edition of the paper noted that eight more people had been lynched since the paper last appeared. And, in an unsigned editorial, it responded to the oft-cited justification for such acts—one not cited in the Memphis case, but in many others—in a notably provocative way:

> Nobody in this section of the country believes the old thread-bare lie that Negro men rape white women. If Southern men are not careful, they will over-reach themselves and public sentiment will have a reaction; a conclusion will be reached which will be very damaging to the moral reputation of their women.[113]

This was waving a red flag in front of a bull. The conventional wisdom of the time among whites held that the only conceivable way a white woman would have sex with a black man is if she was forced to against her will. Here, by contrast, is a suggestion that such women might indeed have consensual sex, out of sheer lust, with black men. (The horror!) But there are other implications lurking in this editorial as well. One is that white women may hide their desires for black men from the wrath of white men by falsely claiming to be raped. More subtle is a challenge to white manhood itself: Some white women might actually *prefer* to sleep with black men, and they consider the widely invoked and celebrated Southern white manhood to be a pathetic fraud on the part of insecure men who can't deal with their (penis) envy. Wouldn't it be awful if white women thought that!

Not surprisingly, the reaction to this editorial was one of widespread outrage. "The fact that a black scoundrel is allowed to live and utter such loathsome and repulsive calumnies is a volume of evidence as to the wonderful patience of Southern whites," declared the *Memphis Commercial*. However, another Memphis paper, the *Evening Scimitar*, apparently did not believe such a scoundrel should be allowed to live, reproducing the *Commercial* editorial a few days later and going on to call for a lynching of the editor of the *Free Speech*: "Patience under such circumstances isn't a virtue. If the negroes themselves don't apply the remedy without delay, it will be the duty of those whom he has attacked to tie the wretch to a stake at the intersection of Main and Madison Sts, brand him in the forehead with a hot iron, and perform on him a surgical operation with a pair of tailor's shears." That evening, a mob descended on the offices of the *Free Speech* and tore it to pieces. Creditors later took possession of it, and the paper never appeared again.[114]

In the end, there were at least two reasons why the operation with the tailor shears would not be performed, however. The first is that the editor had left town—permanently.[115] The other is that the operation advocated here could never occur as imagined, because "he" wasn't a man: "His" name was Ida Wells. And "his" career was only beginning.

◆   ◆   ◆

Literally and figuratively, Ida Bell Wells was a child of slavery.[116] She was born, in bondage, on July 16, 1862, in Holly Springs, Mississippi, six months before the Emancipation Proclamation of Abraham Lincoln theoretically ended slavery. Its effect was theoretical because the Emancipation Proclamation, issued in the middle of the Civil War, was issued as an emergency military measure that asserted the freedom slaves in the seceded South, where the Lincoln administration generally lacked effective authority to enforce it (though Holly Springs passed back and forth between Union and Confederate control throughout the war). Yet even after the war was over and slavery was formally abolished because of the Thirteenth Amendment to the Constitution, the question still remained of what practical meaning freedom would actually have for former slaves. For many determined former slave owners, adamant about resisting the Reconstruction efforts of the 1860s and 1870s, the answer would be: as little as humanly possible.

But the Wells family was among those that actively sought to make the most of their limited opportunities. Jim and Elizabeth Wells, who had married before the war, did so legally after it was over, as many wedded slaves did at the time. The couple had eight children, of whom Ida was the oldest (two died in childhood). Elizabeth, a cook in the household of slave owner James Bolling, was born in Virginia and sold with two of her sisters (trying in vain to reconnect with her family after the war was over). Jim Wells, also owned by Bolling, was trained as a carpenter, and enjoyed a measure of independence before emancipation, continuing working for Bolling in the years immediately following the war. But when Wells refused to vote for the Democratic ticket in local elections, Bolling locked him out of his workshop. Wells responded by demonstrating his freedom: buying a new set of tools and renting a new house.

This sense of self-assertion was passed on to their children in a household that valued religion (the family was Methodist, though Ida had a thoroughly ecumenical bent, often attending a variety of Protestant services on Sundays) and, especially, education. The Freedmen's Aid Society established a public school in Holly Springs in 1866, which the Wells children attended, and Ida enrolled in Rust College, later renamed Shaw University. Though she never finished her undergraduate degree—she was expelled from the school for obscure reasons sometime around 1880—it's clear the education she did receive provided her with an impressive intellectual foundation (and that the fiery temper she exhibited throughout her life had something to do with her departure).[117]

But an interrupted education wasn't the biggest problem for the adolescent Wells. Rather, it was the death of her parents and brother in the devastating yellow fever epidemic that struck the South in 1878. Jim Wells had been a member of the Masons, who arranged to divide the family. But sixteen-year-old Ida insisted she could raise her five siblings as the head of household, and they consented. With the help of family and friends to watch the children, she got a job as a schoolteacher. In 1880, she accepted an invitation to relocate to nearby Memphis with two of her sisters, leaving her other siblings behind in the care of relatives. Except for stints in Kansas and California, she spent most of the next twelve years there as a teacher and, increasingly, as a writer for church and other publications for which she received nominal or no pay.

This brief sketch of her early life calls attention to some notable traits in the young Wells, among them a sense of duty that combined (and, perhaps, competed) with an active quest for upward mobility. But most striking of all was an often fierce commitment to justice for herself and others. That commitment was both admirable and a source of much trouble in her life.

One good example of this involved a train ride the twenty-one-year-old Wells took in September 1883.[118] She had bought a ticket for, and was sitting in, the first-class car when a conductor told her she would have to move to the second-class car. The incremental measures of racial segregation that would culminate with the Supreme Court case of *Plessy vs. Ferguson* (1896) were being enacted throughout the South and were well underway. Wells, the child of proud parents and the product of a Reconstruction era in which African-Americans had at least some rights and electoral representation, ignored the conductor. He went on to collect other tickets and returned to remove her luggage and umbrella, telling Wells he would "treat her like a lady" if she acted like one. Wells replied that, if he wished to treat her like a lady, he would leave her alone. When he responded by trying to drag her out of the car by grabbing her arms, Wells did the distinctly unladylike thing of biting his hand and drawing blood. He went to get help, and as a group of passengers cheered on, Wells was ejected from the car. But because the train had stopped at a station, Wells chose to leave the train entirely rather than move to the second-class car.

This wasn't the end of it. Wells secured the services of a lawyer and sued the railroad company over that incident and another the following year. The company tried to get Wells to settle out of court, but she adamantly refused. The judge, an ex-Union soldier from Minnesota, dismissed charges of assault and awarded Wells $500 in damages for discrimination in December 1884. But in the spring of 1887 the Tennessee Supreme Court ultimately ruled that Wells' suit "wasn't in good faith" and reversed the verdict, requiring her to pay court costs of about $200. All through this period she had resisted any efforts to sit herself in inferior accommodations on trains, asserting a sense of pride in herself and her race, but the outcome of the case was inevitably depressing. "I had hoped such great things from my suit for my people generally," she noted in her diary. "I have firmly believed all along that the law was on our side and would, when we appealed to it, would give us justice. I feel shorn of that belief and utterly discouraged."[119]

But it wasn't in Wells' character, then or later, to remain so, and she remained committed to speaking truth to power. By 1891, her journalism career was beginning to take off—pieces for local Memphis publications, written under the pseudonym of "Iola," were widely reprinted in black newspapers around the country—even as she continued working in her better-paying, but less satisfying, job as a schoolteacher. In an 1891 article for the *Memphis Free Speech and Headlight*, Wells decried teaching conditions (racially separate and unequal ones were already the norm) and criticized those teachers, by name, whom she found professionally deficient. She asked the owner of the paper to put his name on the piece, but when he refused, she decided to run it anyway in her name. The following year her contract wasn't renewed, and the article was explicitly given as the reason why. Out of a job, Wells nevertheless scraped together the money to buy a share in the *Free Speech and Headlight*, soon to simply become the *Free Speech*, and work full-time as a journalist. What appalled Wells most about the incident wasn't her firing per se ("Of course I feared that might be the result," she later remembered), but the failure of black parents who failed to seek the best for their children. "Up to that time I felt that any fight made in the interest of the race would have its support. I learned then I could not count on that," she concluded.[120]

Nevertheless, she would continue to fight for her race—and she would continue to fight *with* her race when she considered it necessary. When, shortly after her firing, a local minister she knew expressed suspicion her firing may have had something to do with bad character, she tracked him down and, with a witness present, demanded an explanation. When he confessed he had made disparaging remarks, she told him she would accept an apology she wrote for him to be read from his pulpit during church services. He complied. A girl's reputation—particularly a black girl's reputation, and even more particularly, an activist black girl's reputation—required the most vigilant protection in a society where words like "troublemaker" very quickly translated into others like "whore."[121]

No issue, however, was finally as powerful to Wells as the crime of lynching. An 1886 diary entry makes clear how viscerally such crimes affected her even before the events of March 1892: "A colored woman accused of poisoning a white one was taken from the county jail and stripped naked and hung up on the courthouse yard and her body riddled with bullets and exposed to view. O my God! can such thing be and no justice for it?...It may be unwise to express myself so strongly but I cannot help it & I know not if capital may not be made of it against me but I trust in God."[122]

By the time of this entry, the rate of lynchings of African-Americans had more than doubled in the previous five years, and would continue to rise rapidly in ensuing ones.[123] But the murders of the three men of the People's Grocery literally came closer to home than any others in her life. She was a close friend of the Moss family, and the godmother of the couple's eldest daughter. These crimes changed Wells' life by giving it a new sense of purpose. She had made a number of fights close to home in the years before this event. Now she was ready to take on the biggest one of all: an open confrontation with the murderous mobs of Jim Crow rule.

◆   ◆   ◆

Terrorism n. The unlawful use or threatened use of force or violence by a person or organized group against people or property with the intention of intimidating or coercing societies or governments, often for ideological or political reasons.

—*American Heritage Dictionary of the English Language* (2000)

For Americans of the twenty-first century, the word "terrorist" often conjures up images of young foreign men (Muslim/Arab/Middle Eastern—they all run together in many minds) blowing themselves and others up in busy public settings. There are good reasons for that, of course. What we sometimes forget is we have the homegrown variety as well—not simply modern examples, such as Timothy McVeigh, who worked with a group of conspirators to blow up a federal building in Oklahoma City in 1995, but also a long tradition of fanatics, from presidential assassins to union-breaking corporate thugs, who have committed violent acts to cow their opponents into accepting their demands. But in terms of sheer numbers (and in terms of mass appeal), by far the most common kind of terrorist in American history was anonymous figures who committed lynching, that is, taking the law into their own hands to murder people. This form of terrorism is different than, say, an insurgency against the government in that violence is ostensibly committed in the name of upholding rather than overthrowing the established order.

The term "lynching" has indeterminate origins. According to the Oxford English Dictionary, its earliest documented use in any form was in 1817, though it has also been associated with the so-called Regulators who intimidated Tories during the era of the American Revolution; they met at Lynche's Creek in South

Carolina. One recent historian claims to have found the term invoked in seventeenth-century Ireland.[124] Wells herself attributed it to Colonel William Lynch, who organized a group of citizens in 1780 to apprehend a cabal of horse thieves and counterfeiters.[125]

For much of American history, lynching was associated with frontier justice, carried across the continent via westward migration in which legal institutions like courts did not keep pace with American territorial expansion. It wasn't particularly racial in orientation or linked with the slaveholding South. As slaveholders frequently told abolitionists, abusing slaves, much less murdering them, was widely regarded in terms of foolish destruction of personal property (it was better to sell what you yourself couldn't use).[126] Certainly extralegal violence against slaves and others was common enough—and other practices, such as dueling, operated outside legal sanctions and *were* strongly associated with the South. But the sheer power of white over black generally made lynching itself unnecessary.

Southern white defeat in the Civil War and the abolition of slavery were an important economic, political, and psychological blow for slaveholding Southerners and their allies, one that generated widespread resentment and even violence. (Memphis, for example, was the site of a major race riot in 1866.) The destruction of traditional society wrought by the war, and the imposition of federal troops in many parts of the South during Reconstruction, made it relatively difficult to exact revenge, much less replace the old order with a new one more to their liking. But the gradual ebbing of Northern will, combined with Southern "redemption" of state governments, gave white Southerners growing power to limit the rights and privileges of African-Americans. Through a series of tactics that included segregationist laws, regressive taxation, and politically savvy appeals to Northern racism—*post*war segregation laws in the South used language from *pre*war segregation laws in the North, for example—an increasingly "solid" South was in many cases able to re-create slavery through another name in tenant farming, convict labor, and various forms of intimidation. In this context, lynching, as practiced by the Klu Klux Klan and more impromptu groups, was part of a political spectrum that ran from time-honored democratic practices like elections to bare-knuckled terrorism.

Almost by definition, lynching was an extremist practice, often conducted under shadowy circumstances. But that wasn't always the case. In fact, lynching was sometimes a community-wide celebration. One good example was the case of Henry Smith of Paris, Texas, accused of the murder of a child in February 1893. Smith had remained in the vicinity in the aftermath of the crime, but when it became clear he was a suspect, he fled into the countryside, where a posse of

2,000 men combed the area until he was found. Smith was brought back to Paris by train, brought to a platform in an open field and tied to a chair. About 10,000 people had gathered, some brought by special trains chartered for the occasion. The father of the murdered child then mounted the platform and asked for quiet. A contemporary account of the time explained what happened next:

> A tinner's furnace was brought on filled with irons heated white. Taking one [the father] thrust it under first one than the other side of the victim's feet, who helpless, writhed, and the flesh seared and peeled from the bones...By turns Smith screamed, prayed, begged, and cursed his torturer. When his face was reached, his tongue was silenced by fire, and henceforth he only moaned, or gave a cry that echoed over the prairie like the wail of a wild animal. Then his eyes were put out, and not a finger's breath of his body being unscathed, his executioners [the man's son and brothers in law also participated] gave way.

At this point, "combustibles" were placed on the platform, while Smith was soaked with oil. They were then set on fire. A photographer recorded the event, and it was said a sound recording, which included the cries of the victim, was made. The next day the ashes were raked as people took buttons, bones, and teeth for souvenirs.[127]

While accurate statistics are hard to come by, there is general agreement that lynching increased sharply in the 1890s. In 1882, according to the *Chicago Tribune*, there were fifty-two lynchings in the United States. By 1892, there were 241, two-thirds of them against African-Americans. In the half-century between 1882 and 1931 (the year of Wells' death), there were 3,318 recorded lynchings of African-American men, women, and children.[128] The numbers gradually receded from their peak in the 1890s. (Though, as late as 1954, the black adolescent Emmett Till was lynched for allegedly looking the wrong way at a white woman.) In a way, 3,318 lynchings may not seem like a lot—about as many people died on a single day because of the terrorist attacks of September 11, 2001—but mere numbers is hardly the whole story here. The deaths of these people had ripple effects in multiple directions over a long period of time. Perhaps more importantly, the *threat* of lynching no doubt shaped the behavior of people who might have otherwise resisted white supremacy, given the danger of their being deemed rapists, agitators, or simply "uppity niggers." Though largely submerged and not always widely talked about, lynching was a crucial component of the Southern way of life from the end of Reconstruction to the advent of the Civil Rights Movement. Under such circumstances, African-

Americans might well wonder just what "freedom" meant in the land of the free and the home of the brave.

This was the context for the antilynching campaign that became the life work of Ida Wells once she left Memphis in the spring of 1892. She left behind friends, family, home, and work because her press was destroyed and there were threats on her life once her identity became known.[129] Yet these facts alone gave her a compelling story to tell, and Wells set about telling that story (and others) in person and in her new pen name: "Exiled."

She began with the *New York Age*, an African-American newspaper that published her account of the Memphis lynchings and other pieces. This brought her to the attention of leaders in the African-American community, notably Frederick Douglass, who, in turn, referred her to other movers and shakers. Wells also began lecturing widely to enthusiastic audiences in the Northeast, which led to two invitations to give speeches in Great Britain, which Wells toured in 1893 and 1894. The publicity these tours generated gave international attention to the issue of lynching. Before this, lynching was often treated in a cavalier manner, even in the Northern press. (An 1891 *New York Times* editorial, for example, gave an account of the pursuit of an Alabama black man, suggesting he would be lynched if caught, but such an outcome would not "add to the prevailing excitement" over the more "serious" problem of illegal alcohol production.)[130] Yet by the turn of the century, even apologists for the practice often felt compelled to at least pay lip service to the idea that vigilante justice of the kind invoked by lynchers and their sympathizers was at least problematic.

Wells' public speaking appearances were augmented by her continuing journalism career, an important facet of which were a series of pamphlets she published in the years following the Memphis lynchings. The first of these, *Southern Horrors: Lynch Law in All Its Phases*, was published in late 1892, paid for with funds raised from a testimonial dinner given in her honor. It was followed in 1895 by *A Red Record: Lynchings in the United States 1892-1893-1894.* These two works were of particular importance in raising awareness of the problem and crystallizing her approach to it.

That approach involved a series of interlocking strategies. One was careful reporting of specific incidents. While she often did editorialize on events about she narrated (describing the lynching of Henry Smith, for example, in terms "shocking brutality and indescribable barbarism"),[131] Wells' writing and speaking were notable for their relative restraint and attempts to address counterarguments, such as the likelihood a particular lynching victim was guilty of the crime he was accused of committing. In *A Red Record* and other pamphlets, such tightly

focused narrated factual accounts were combined with lists and charts from reputable (namely white) sources, through which Wells sought to provide a broader
context for the stories she told. Wells also spelled out specific steps she wanted
her readers to take, ranging from support for antilynching legislation to invoking
black self-reliance—and black self-defense. Wells bought a gun after her friend
Moss was lynched, "determined to sell my life as dearly as possible if attacked,"
and once told an interviewer that a "Winchester rifle should have a place of honor
in every black home."[132]

Other strategies were more self-consciously polemical. Wells loved to have racist whites rhetorically hang themselves by quoting their own words, whether editorials attacking her personally (one can imagine her relish in quoting the
"surgical operation with tailor shears" threat in *Southern Horrors*) or a letter from
a Southern sheriff frankly admitting that no one has ever been arrested for a
lynching and that no one who knows anything will say anything.[133] Her use of
such accounts, combined with visual documentation like photographs, gave her
work credibility and authority.

Of particular importance to her was using white people's estimation of themselves against them. Again and again, she invoked the hallowed concept of "civilization," the widely prevalent late-nineteenth-century idea that white people
generally and Anglo-Saxons in particular ruled the world because they had
restrained their savagery and channeled their energies into high-minded pursuits.
Yet, as she often noted, lynching gave the lie that white people had any moral
superiority over any of those they considered beneath them. As she noted of a
five-person lynching that occurred in Mississippi in 1892:

> Had it occurred in the wilds of interior Africa, there would have been an out-
> cry from which human people of this country against the savagery which so
> mercilessly put men and women to death. But [here] it was an evidence of
> American civilization to be passed by unnoticed, to be denied or condoned as
> the requirements of any future emergency might determine.

As historian Gail Bederman has noted, one reason why Wells chose to give
speaking tours in England was her knowledge that white Americans wanted the
British to admire the United States' advanced civilization, and that publicizing
these hate crimes would give British opinion makers reasons to look dimly, even
patronizingly, on such claims, as indeed they did.[134]

Finally, Wells paid particular attention to the hypocrisies surrounding gender
roles in the nineteenth century. She documented the confession of a white
woman who had consensual sex with black man, only to falsely accuse him of

rape and have him spend fifteen years in jail because she was afraid of her husband's wrath. She gave factual accounts of white women who bore mulatto children of black lovers. And she pointed out that while it was apparently fine for white men to have sex with black women—this was, after all, an open secret for hundreds of years in the slaveholding South—the notion of black men having sex with white women was somehow revolting. Moreover, while white men proclaimed the necessity of lynching to avenge any assault to white womanhood, there did not seem to be any similar imperative to protect *black* women. As she pointed out, "Virtue knows know color line, and the chivalry which depends on the complexion of skin and texture of hair can command no respect." Instead, the real knights in shining armor of the South were the Northern women missionaries who flocked to the South after the Civil War to give black children an education. Wells observed that *they* never complained about rape, and that "no mob was ever called to avenge crimes against *them.*"[135]

Southern Horrors and *A Red Record* were the twin pillars of the edifice Ida Wells constructed to fight lynching. In addition to these two pamphlets, Wells also collaborated with Frederick Douglass and others on *The Reason Why the Colored American Isn't in the World's Columbian Exposition* in 1893 (the answer: racism), and a vigorous defense of a black man who resisted arrest and in so doing triggered race riots in *Mob Rule in New Orleans* (1900). She also continued to write and speak regularly in a variety of forums, and was an active participant in the women's club movement that promoted social reform across the United States. (In fact, one such club in Chicago, which met for decades, was named after Wells herself.) Her activism was particularly important in a 1909 Illinois lynching in which Wells' organizing proved instrumental in the removal of a local sheriff from his job for failing to protect the man in his custody, as well as reporting information in the aftermath of race riots in East St. Louis in 1917, Chicago in 1919, and rural Arkansas in 1920.

All this said, Wells' fame and influence diminished after about 1900. She remained a prominent figure in Chicago, where she married a black attorney named Ferdinand Barnett in 1895. (They had collaborated on *Why the Colored American*, and she had hired him in a libel case she ultimately dropped.) She went on to bear four children. This fact alone could be construed as reason enough to explain her lower public profile. But the reasons are a bit more complicated, in ways that reflect changing social conditions, Wells' personality, and the specific dilemmas that rise from being a woman—especially an African-American woman—in the United States.

◆   ◆   ◆

Did Ida Wells make a difference? It's impossible to say with any certainty. The number of lynchings did fall steadily after she launched her campaign, but not even she would take sole credit for that fact, and much of the drop was among white victims, making lynching an even more racial crime.[136] In any event, the practice certainly did not cease, even though there wasn't another lynching in Memphis for twenty-five years, and even the *Memphis Evening Scimitar*, which had called for her castration, later admitted "Every one of us is touched with blood-guiltiness" in the crimes of 1892.[137] Nor is it clear even how widely she was known among the white people at whom she hurled some of her most passionate invective, though her circle of associates included people like fellow Chicagoan Jane Addams and suffragist Susan B. Anthony. At the end of her life, Wells herself despaired at her impact, believing "I hadn't anything to show for all those years of toil and labor."[138]

Part of Wells' problem as the 1890s gave way to the new century was changes in the nature of leadership among African-Americans. She was friendly with old lions of the abolition movement, including poet and novelist Frances Ellen Watkins Harper and (especially) Douglass, who opened key doors for her. Douglass' death in 1895 was a professional as well as personal blow; Wells never really had a mentor again. His place of leadership among African-Americans passed to Booker T. Washington, a man with whom Wells had some general affinities—both, for example, emphasized the importance of self-help—but more decisive personal as well as ideological differences. As historian Thomas Holt has noted, for example, while Washington saw black economic power as the reward of working within the status quo, Wells viewed it as a weapon to be used against it (such as boycotts). Wells dismissed Washington's "gospel of work" as "slavery practice in a new dress." Such frankness not only alienated the increasingly powerful Washington, but even former allies who themselves accommodated to Washington's ascent as the primary spokesperson for African-Americans. T. Thomas Fortune, who published Wells' work in the *New York Age*, was himself stung by Wells' criticism, and described her as "a bull in a china shop" in an 1899 letter to Washington.[139]

Washington's influence did not go unchallenged, of course. The standard history of African-Americans considers his primary challenger at the turn of the century to be W.E.B. DuBois, who rejected Washington's emphasis on accommodation to segregation in favor of integration and the cultivation of a black leadership elite. Yet Wells' relations with DuBois were hardly any better. Wells was present at the creation at the 1909 conference that led to the creation of the National Association for the Advancement of Colored People (NAACP), but she was omitted from membership in a crucial committee, which led her to walk out in protest. The cool, professional, legalistic approach of DuBois and the other Progressives for whom the NAACP was an archetypal organization was in marked contrast to that of Wells, who relied on passion and moral energy. DuBois and company had more of a top-down approach than the increasingly bottom-up one of Wells, who founded her own organization, the Negro Fellowship League (NFL), in 1910 as a settlement house for black men in Chicago. It was ultimately supplanted by the Chicago chapter of the better-financed, national Urban League in 1920.[140]

There can be little question that Wells' candor, which was one of her greatest professional assets, could also be a serious professional distraction and even a liability, even when what she said was plainly true. The classic example is her well-publicized wrangle with suffragist and temperance activist Francis Willard. In an 1890 interview, Willard had denounced the prevalence of liquor in the South, where "the colored race multiplies like the locusts of Egypt" (in part because drinking fostered wanton reproduction), and asserted "the safety of women, of children, of home" was threatened by black rapists. On her 1893 tour in England, where Willard was also visiting at the time, Wells was asked about Willard's position on lynching and correctly pointed out that Willard believed the rape of white women justified it. This led to a highly public spat that dogged both women, as Wells quoted Willard's own words in subsequent settings, and Willard denied Wells' suggestion that white women would ever want to have sex with black men.[141] Not that Wells couldn't take criticism herself. In one fascinating exchange in her autobiography, she neutrally notes that Susan B. Anthony, a woman who herself has been frequently criticized for her racism in promoting suffrage, told Wells that she made a mistake in getting married and having children instead of carrying on the work of promoting women's rights. Wells described the remark as "a well-merited rebuke," but she also pointed out she lacked the institutional support people like her enjoyed to do such work.[142]

This is an important point. Many of Wells' allies had resources—financial and otherwise—that she simply did not. Men had careers; many of the women she worked with were either independently wealthy or at least solidly middle-class, while Wells was self-supporting for much of her life. Not that she let institutional obstacles stand in her way. In the summer of 1894, while making a pitch for funding from a Philadelphia church, a clergyman objected that the congregation did not know her well enough to endorse her work. Initially stunned into silence, Wells collected herself and replied, "Why gentlemen, I cannot see why I need your endorsement. Under God I have done work without endorsement from my own people. And when I think that I have been able to do the work with his assistance that you could not do, if you would, and would not do, if you could, I think I have a right to feeling of strong indignation. I feel very deeply the insult which you have offered and I have the honor to wish you a very good morning." With that, she walked out.[143] A satisfying response in some ways, though one can't help but wonder if it was the best one.

But beyond issues of organization and temperament, Wells had to contend with the fact that she was a woman—a black woman—in a society that sometimes acted as if people like her should be neither seen nor heard. And that if they transgressed such unspoken rules, they deserved what they got. Such just desserts ranged from racist or sexist remarks to the assault she endured on a Brooklyn ferryboat during the summer of 1894 by a pair of white men who had heard about her activities.[144]

And yet, through it all and right up to the end of her life, she persisted. She made an unsuccessful run for the Illinois State Senate in 1930 and joined the United Clubs Emergency Relief movement to alleviate the effects of the Great Depression in 1931, months before her death in March of that year. Though widely mourned in Chicago, her funeral services were, at her husband's direction, low-key. The Ida Wells Club, which had hosted her wedding reception over thirty-five years earlier, presented the only memorial.[145]

For a long time, Wells' work receded in collective memory. By the turn of the century, many of her important writings were being used, but uncredited, by a younger generation of activists.[146] A public housing project was named after her in Chicago in 1940, and, after a decades-long effort to find a publisher, her daughter Alfreda shepherded her meticulously edited autobiography (unfinished at the time of her death) into print in 1970.[147] It wasn't really until the late 1980s, however, that a new wave of black feminist scholarship recovered Wells, whose works were reprinted and whose career became the subject of a lively discourse.[148] This discussion was part of a larger effort to recover the voices of women in history, as well as a more specific interest in black militancy that included the rediscovery of other figures, notably Malcolm X, about whom there was something of an intellectual renaissance at the time.

Yet perhaps the most striking echo in Wells' life came from a somewhat different direction. She closed an 1892 article on lynching by arguing the quest to end it required the same kind of sustained efforts that had been made by abolitionists a half century earlier. "Then," she concluded:

> No longer will our national hymn be sounding brass and tinkling cymbal, but every member of this great composite nation will be a living, harmonious celebration of the words, and all can honestly and gladly join in singing
> My country! 'tis of thee,
> Sweet land of liberty
> Of thee I sing
> Land where our fathers died
> Land of the Pilgrim's pride
> From every mountain side
> Freedom does ring.[149]

Now you know: She, too, had a dream.[150]

5

Mr. Debs Goes to Jail (Again)

Many times, we understand the meaning of a word by trying to define what it isn't—what, in fact, may constitute its opposite. The word "left," for example, becomes meaningful when juxtaposed against "right." For most of the twentieth century, the word "American" was measured by what was un-American, even anti-American. And for many people in the United States, that meant any number of ideas under the (often imprecise) umbrella concept of socialism: anarchism, communism, even trade unionism. The American way was a capitalist way.

But from the end of the Civil War to the end of the First World War, the answer to the so-called Labor Question wasn't always capitalism. Indeed, a wide variety of Americans—native-born and immigrant; skilled and unskilled; urban and rural—viewed industrialization and the rise of the corporation with unease, even alarm. They responded to the challenges it posed by invoking a heritage of liberty and equality to counter the challenges of monopolistic businessmen who used Darwinian logic to justify their practices. No one invoked this heritage with more appeal than Eugene Debs, a man who simultaneously championed the cause of workers of the world even as he embodied traditional American values. It was a combination that could make a patriot even out of a cynic.

CHAPTER 5:
MR. DEBS GETS ARRESTED (AGAIN)

*in which we see an antiwar protester
demonstrate how radical socialism is really conservative patriotism*

GENE DEBS WAS STARTING TO THINK he couldn't get arrested.

It wasn't for a lack of trying. Though he'd been sick for much of the last few years—years in which a terrible World War was raging, and, simultaneously, opposition to that war also raged—Debs was now back on his feet and eager to join the fray. Most of the newspapers he had written for were now censored or suppressed by the government under the provisions of the newly passed Espionage (1917) and Sedition (1918) acts, which made it a crime to use "disloyal, profane or scurrilous" language about the United States. In wartime, apparently constitutional protections for free speech no longer applied.

But if Debs had a hard time getting his words read, he could still have his voice heard. In the first two weeks of June 1918 he had given a dozen speeches in Indiana and Illinois against the war and, in particular, to protest the imprisonment of many friends and colleagues, among them the labor organizer Katie Richards O'Hare and draft resister Emma Goldman (who would be deported from the country when she finished her jail term). Now, on June 16, he was going to try his luck in Canton, Ohio. Upon his arrival in that city, Debs paid a visit to the county workhouse to visit three friends serving time there. He returned to his hotel, where a reporter asked him if agreed with the official antiwar Socialist position on the war—he said yes—and then proceeded to Nimisilla Park, where over 1,000 spectators had gathered to hear him speak. The speaker's stand had been constructed in such a way that the prisoners could see Debs from their cells.[151]

It was hot that day in Nimisilla Park, but Debs, wearing a three-piece suit, neither took off his jacket nor unbuttoned his vest. The wooden bandstand lacked an American flag, which represented a pointed statement. Despite the severity of this backdrop, and the focused anger that Debs brought to his address, there was something lively and even inviting about him, even when he was at his most critical. People chuckled as he expressed his bemusement about the situation in which he found himself. "I realize that in speaking to you this afternoon, there are certain limitations placed upon the right of free speech. I must be exceedingly careful, prudent, as to what I say, and even more careful and prudent as to how I say it," he told the crowd. "I may not be able to say all I think [laugh-ter and applause]; but I'm not going to say anything I don't think" [applause].[152]

And what did Debs think? That supporting American involvement in the war was a terrible mistake. That while he hadn't anything good to say about Imperial Germany, the governments of its opponents, among them the United States, also put the corporate profits before personal welfare. That the arrest and imprison-ment of people like his friends made a travesty of the very democratic traditions the war was presumably being fought to protect. Above all, the Socialist Party, of which he was a proud member, was the most thoughtful, responsible, and, yes, patriotic, place to take a stand right now. Socialism represented the future, Debs asserted; all else was an effort to distract the masses from their true interest, which lay in a political revolution of the kind now occurring in Russia (though the one over here would have to reflect more specific American conditions and tradi-tions).

One man in the crowd was particularly attentive to what Debs had to say: the U.S. Attorney General for northern Ohio. He directed stenographers to record the speech, and sent a copy to the Justice Department in Washington, seeking an opinion as to whether Debs had violated the Espionage Act. Their finding was that Debs was "close to, if not over the line, though the case is by no means a clear one. All in all, the Department does not feel strongly convinced that a pros-ecution is advisable." Disregarding this advice, the prosecutor obtained an indict-ment and had Debs arrested in Cleveland four days later. Following the example of other political prisoners, he refused to contest the charges. During his trial in September 1918, a parade of prosecution witnesses could do little more than con-firm that Debs had indeed given the speech in that park on that day. Debs' defense consisted of an address to the jury in which he situated his actions as part of a long American tradition. "Washington, Jefferson, Franklin, Paine and their compeers were the rebels of their day," he told the jurors. "When they began to chafe under the rule of a foreign king and to sow the seed of resistance among the colonists they were opposed by the people and denounced by the press…But they had the moral courage to be true to their convictions, to stand erect and defy all the forces of reaction and detraction; and that's why their names shine in history, and why the great respectable majority of their day sleep in forgotten graves."[153]

"I'm not on trial here," he continued. "There is an infinitely greater issue that's being tried today in this court, though you may not be conscious of it. American institutions are on trial here before a court of American citizens. The future will render a final verdict."[154] Debs' fellow citizens were unmoved, how-ever, and he was found guilty. "I ask no mercy and I plead for no immunity," he told the judge at his sentencing.[155] He got neither, sentenced to ten years in prison. After his appeal was rejected, Debs began his term in April 1919. He had a relatively mild stint at a penitentiary in West Virginia, but was then transferred to a maximum-security facility in Atlanta. The following year, he was nominated for president for the fifth time by the Socialist Party and got almost a million votes despite (or perhaps because of) his incarceration. After Theodore Roosevelt (1912) and Ross Perot (1992), Debs was the most popular third-party candidate in American history.[156]

From the standpoint of the early twenty-first century, there are a number of odd things about this story, which is meant to suggest the appeal of Eugene Debs. First, his opposition to the war, while not unique, wasn't that of a typical American. To be sure, there was a lot of skepticism about the conflict before the United States got involved, but once President Woodrow Wilson asked Congress to declare war in April 1917, the consensus favoring it was solid.

That said, the war's validity in the eyes of subsequent generations is by no means clear. Indeed, by the 1930s, many of those who lived through the war regarded it as if it was stupid, if not criminal. Unlike World War II, where the moral issues posed by the Nazi regime have long since justified fighting it, the legitimacy of the First World War is far from clear. Whatever his crimes, most historians agree the German kaiser was no Adolf Hitler—and the kaiser's defeat in fact made Hitler's victories possible. Seen in this light, Debs' stance toward the First World War was both plausible and, in the context of his times, a little weird.

Second, Debs' embrace of socialism, an ideology "in which the means of producing and distributing good is owned collectively or by a centralized government that often plans or controls the economy,"[157] has never been fashionable in a land where private enterprise has been not only dominant, but widely celebrated, for hundreds of years. In fact, it has often been the case that to argue for anything else has been widely viewed as un-American. That Debs would have a relatively large national following for challenging this widely held view is also a little weird.

Third, virtually all accounts of the time and since have testified to the enormous personal appeal Debs had for millions of Americans. Repeatedly, in reading about his life, one comes across acknowledgments of his kindness, warmth, and instinctive generosity. And, most of all, a tremendous personal charisma that drew him generations of attentive listeners. "Is that Debs?" a working-class Irish woman reputedly once asked of a speaker during a Socialist Party rally during the presidential campaign of 1908. "Oh no, that ain't Debs," another Irishwoman replied. "When Debs comes out you'll think it's Jesus Christ."[158]

This is true even of those who rejected his ideas. "While the overwhelming majority of the people here are opposed to the social and economic theories of Mr. Debs, there isn't perhaps a single man in this city who enjoys to a greater degree than Mr. Debs the affection, love and profound respect of the entire community," James Lyons, the mayor of Debs' hometown of Terre Haute, Indiana wrote in 1907. Out-of-towners were similarly impressed. "I'm told that even those speeches of his which seem to any reader indifferent stuff, took on a vitality from his presence," journalist Heywood Broun reported in the 1920s. As one observer told Broun, "That old man with the burning eyes actually believes that there can be such a thing as the brotherhood of man. And that's not the funniest part of it. As long as he's around I believe it myself." Upon his death in 1926, an editorial in the *Chicago Evening Post* said, "We did not agree with him, but we could not help admiring him. Into our strong disapproval of his views entered a feeling of affection for the man who held them."[159]

Perhaps this last point explains the other two. Personality plays a big role in politics, as it does in much else. But Debs' significance, as he would be the first to say, rests less on his unique appeal than on a powerful sense that his concerns about the times in which he lived (we're talking here about a man whose public career spanned from the 1870s to the 1920s) were widely shared. To be sure, there were disagreements on how those issues were perceived and dealt with, and his opinions were always those of a minority. Yet those opinions had clarity and relevance to American society at large because Debs cherished many of the same values his opponents did. Debs has generally been perceived, for a number of good reasons, as a radical figure. And yet it has always been true—and it may now be more useful to see him this way than ever before—that in a fundamental respect, Debs was deeply conservative. As always, the question is just what it is that the conservative is trying to conserve.

◆　　◆　　◆

The late John Higham, one of the finest historians the academy ever produced, once said the two great symbols of the nineteenth-century United States were the covered wagon and the Statue of Liberty.[160] Strictly speaking, neither of these directly apply to the life of Eugene Victor Debs, whose first and middle names honor Eugene Sue and Victor Hugo, two European novelists. But the two phenomena embodied by these icons, western expansion and immigration, were intertwined in his origins. Debs' parents came from Alsace, a region in eastern France that would later become part of Germany. In 1851, they joined a relatively large French community in the Indiana town of Terre Haute, located on the banks of the Wabash River (it was a flatboat rather than a covered wagon that brought them there).

Founded in 1818, Terre Haute became a quintessential Midwestern example of what Debs biographer Nick Salvatore has called "deferential democracy," an ethos that combined Protestant morality, communitarian values, and an abiding belief in upward mobility. In the mythology of such Midwestern communities, people deferred to their betters because "better" was defined not in terms of birth or even wealth, but in esteem earned through character and achievement. Because this presumption wasn't always in fact accurate, it could produce friction and finally rebellion for many a native son or daughter. The famed iconoclast Clarence Darrow, who would later represent Debs in court, came out of a similar environment in small-town Ohio. For Debs though, his hometown engendered a durable affection that continued long after Terre Haute had become an industrial city. For much of his life, his mentors included people like William McKeen and Herman Hulman, entrepreneurs who got rich and saw in Debs the kinds of qualities (intelligence, earnestness, ambition) that made them successful.[161]

Perhaps no figure embodies the world of Debs' youth more vividly than Abraham Lincoln, himself a child Hoosier who had made the transition from backwoods youth to wealthy railroad lawyer by the times Debs was born in 1855.[162] In some notes to himself he wrote around the time of his election for his one term in Congress in 1846, young Mr. Lincoln sounds a lot like the future Mr. Debs:

> ...As most things are produced by labor, it follows that all such things of right belong to those whose labour has produced them. But it has so happened in all ages of the world, that *some* have laboured, and *others* have, without labour, enjoyed a large proportion of the fruits. This is wrong, and should not continue. To secure to each labourer the whole product of his labour, or as nearly as possible, is a most worthy objective of good government.[163]

According to Lincoln, the great thing about the United States is that it was, by and large, a country in which people really *did* enjoy the fruits of their own labor. [Lincoln's hatred of slavery grew out the way it contradicted this ideal for black people and corrupted it for those white ones who could not—or would not—try to get ahead on their own. If he couldn't actually abolish slavery, he wanted the government to at least bracket it, as I've literally done here.]

A decade later, in the aftermath of his defeat at the hands of Stephen Douglas for the U.S. Senate, Lincoln elaborated on his vision with his customary clarity:

> My understanding of the hired laborer is this: A young man finds himself dis-
> missed from parental control; he has for his capital nothing save two strong
> hands that God has given him, a heart willing to labor, and a He is benefited
> by availing himself of that privilege. He works industriously, he behaves
> soberly, and the result of a year or two's labor is a surplus capital. Now he buys
> land on his own hook; he settles; marries, begets sons and daughters, and in
> course of time he too has capital enough to hire some new beginner.[164]

This is the world—or, perhaps, this was the dream—into which Eugene Debs
was born. His father Daniel had married for love rather than money; indeed, he
walked away from a prosperous family in Alsace because his Protestant parents
refused to accept his working-class and Catholic fiancée. Once in America, the
disinherited family was saved from penury when his now-wife Marguerite, preg-
nant with Debs (who would ultimately be the oldest son of ten children) opened
a grocery store in the front room of their home. Debs enjoyed a secure and loving
childhood (his younger brother Theodore in particular would be a particularly
cherished collaborator) before striking out on his own.

Debs' first job upon his graduation from high school was working as a paint
scraper for a local railroad. He later became a railroad fireman in Terre Haute
before taking another such job in East St. Louis. (He also attended business
school in these years.) When he lost his job in the aftermath of the Panic of 1873,
Debs returned home and went into the grocery business. But his attachment to
the fraternal world of railroad workers led him to join the Brotherhood of Locomotive Firemen, a labor union, in 1875, in which he was quickly appointed secretary as well as treasurer. Even as he took on more responsibility at work and for
the Brotherhood (he became editor of the Brotherhood's magazine, a post he
held into the 1890s), Debs also found time to dabble in politics, winning an election to a city clerk position and later becoming a member of the Indiana legislator
as a Democrat in the late 1870s and early 1880s. He married Katherine Metzel
1885. The two, who were often separated by Debs' incessant travels, had no children.[165]

By the age of thirty, Debs seemed positively Lincolnian in his embrace of hard
work, his upward mobility, his fraternal sensibility,[166] and his faith in a natural
partnership between labor and capital. "America is the pre-eminently the land of
great possibilities," he wrote in 1883. "Look around us, no matter what a man
may be, we all stand on the great field of renown, with a free and equal chance to
go to the supreme height of all that can be achieved of earthly grandeur. We all
have a have fair chance and an open field. Long may it so remain."[167]

Yet even before he wrote these words, there were indications the chances were becoming less fair and the field less open—or, to put it in Lincolnian terms, that workers had ever less control over the mode of their work, the manner of their employers, or hope they would receive "a fair day's wages for a fair day's work." As many observers have noted, Lincoln may have had the ironic good fortune of dying in 1865 before the economic system he so passionately embraced, industrial capitalism, began to oppress the people he cherished most. Even before the Civil War, there had been indications this emerging order was perhaps less harmonious than its champions claimed. (We've already seen how proslavery Southerners were among the first to perceive this.) But, in the years after the war, the new plutocratic order became increasingly unmistakable as a few men—John D. Rockefeller in oil, Andrew Carnegie in steel, and James J. Hill and others in railroads, to name three prominent examples—gained control over large segments of entire industries and the people who worked for them.

For much of the 1870s and 1880s, Debs' vision of the Brotherhood of Locomotive Firemen was one of fraternal-minded cooperation, and, in this, he and his colleagues could still view a Rockefeller or a Carnegie in a relatively charitable light, especially because these two in particular went out of their way to be charitable (so long as no one challenged the legitimacy of their sometimes-questionable business practices). Yet even in these years, newer organizations like the National Labor Union (1869), the Knights of Labor (1879), and the American Federation of Labor (1886) adopted an increasingly hardheaded approach that emphasized protecting endangered rights rather than promoting industrial harmony. These groups and others differed in their negotiating strategies and competed with each other, sometimes viciously. But for all their differences, the members of these organizations had largely come to the conclusion that when dealing with increasingly large corporations, contracts were better than handshakes, and collective bargaining was more effective than paternal management. If you couldn't join 'em—and Lincoln notwithstanding, this no longer seemed possible—it was better to beat 'em.

Many workers were convinced the prospect of a strike was the only thing that might prevent capitalists from exercising dictatorial control over their lives. The Panic of 1873, one of the great depressions of American history, led to mass unemployment in a society without insurance, health benefits, or pensions. Wage cuts for those workers who still held jobs pushed even them to the brink of starvation. After a series of relatively local brushfires, the labor landscape erupted in flames in 1877 after wage cuts on the Baltimore and Ohio Railway led to sympathy strikes across the United States. The strike was crushed after President Rutherford B. Hayes sent federal troops to Pittsburgh, where strikers were fighting with local militia. In this, the first major industrial conflict in U.S. history, the federal government had for the first time decisively acted on behalf of management. It would not be the last.

Americans of the nineteenth century were fond of invoking so-called questions: the Woman Question, the Negro Question, and the like to frame important issues of the day. But by the 1880s no question loomed larger in the national imagination than the so-called Labor Question, which, simply put, asked what the proper relationship between capitalist and worker should be. The very variety and intensity of answers, which ranged from Christian charity to a Darwinian struggle of the fittest, is part of what made the issue so momentous and even ominous.

So too were the accents of those answers, many of which came from immigrants, and some of whom had relatively radical ideas. For factory owners, immigrants represented cheap labor (and, in their more worried moments, a political threat). For workers, immigrants were family, friends, and neighbors (who, they sometimes feared, would drive down wages). The tensions surrounding labor, immigrants, and radical politics exploded in Chicago in May 1886, when a bomb at a labor demonstration at Haymarket Square led to the death of a police officer and the wounding of six others. After a travesty of a trial, eight anarchists were convicted of murder. Four were hanged, one committed suicide, and three were pardoned by the governor of Illinois, John Peter Altgeld, himself an immigrant who took a good deal of abuse for the pardons. Long before the terrorist attacks of 2001, Americans were denouncing, and using questionable legal tactics to retaliate against, people with tenuous connections to heinous crimes.[168]

In the years that followed the Haymarket Riot, itself an event whose backdrop was a series of major strikes, the national atmosphere became even more tense. In 1892, federal troops crushed a strike of silver miners in the Coeur d'Alene region of Idaho. Also that year, Andrew Carnegie lowered the wages of the workers at his steel works in Homestead, Pennsylvania by about twenty percent and then left town, leaving his lieutenant Henry Clay Frick to lead an armed band of detectives in battle against workers, who were finally defeated when the governor of Pennsylvania called in the state militia. Meanwhile, a surging Populist movement of farmers was making a visible impact in the nation's statehouses and even in Congress, where their agitation for currency reform—the so-called Money Question—challenged the verities of conservative fiscal management. In the very year the nation celebrated the 400th anniversary of Columbus' voyage to America, many thoughtful Americans believed the nation was on the verge of a major revolution.

And where was Eugene Debs in these years? Gradually—just how gradually is a little hard to gauge—moving to the left. Restless with the political process, he gave up his city clerkship and legislative seat when their terms were up and focused most of his energy on his posts as secretary, treasurer, and editor of the Brotherhood. Like many of his fellow Americans, Debs was troubled by what he saw as the increasingly rapacious American business community, ever more removed from local ties and ever more concerned with shareholders than workers. But his response was somewhat different than many of his peers in the labor movement—and even his own union. In the aftermath of an unsuccessful Brotherhood strike against the Chicago, Burlington, and Quincy railroad in 1888, Debs began working toward a different approach. While organizations such as the American Federation of Labor placed great emphasis on the effectiveness of tightly organized unions centered on skilled workers in particular crafts (like, say, train engineers or metal workers), Debs was inclined to pursue institutions that united workers across craft lines in entire industries—an organization of *all* railroad workers rather than loosely affiliated ones of, say, firemen or engineers, whose cooperation was uncertain at best.

Such an approach was simultaneously more radical and conservative than that of more mainstream movements like the American Federation of Labor. On the one hand, its egalitarianism, a leveling approach toward work reminiscent of European-based movements such as communism, suggested a more thorough critique of industrial capitalism than traditional craft unions. Yet that very egalitarianism also harkened back to a preindustrial past in which a person's identity wasn't primarily defined through work, but rather a shared sense enterprise in an organization and a sense of citizenship in a broader community of *people* as well as workers. Indeed, Debs had a belief, respect, and even affection for the political process that puzzled even many of his allies. Wages were important, he asserted, but American workers were "not to be silenced by any per diem." Their goal should be electing officials "who will see that just laws are rightly administered."[169] Debs believed the power of the voting booth was greater than that of the picket line, a premise that, despite his occasional embrace of the picket line, he would maintain for the rest of his life.

In 1892, with Coeur d'Alene and Homestead dominating the nation's headlines, Debs resigned his position as secretary and treasurer of the Brotherhood of Locomotive Firemen. (Its members refused to allow his resignation as editor of its magazine, a post he held for a few more years.) In June 1893 he helped found the

American Railway Union, of which he was elected president. As he explained to Indiana University economist John Commons, the ARU was modeled on the United States constitution, in which workers in each railroad occupation made up "states" in the union.[170] Organized in a manner similar to that of brewery workers and conductors (who may have provided a model), ARU cut across occupational categories. Members were required to pay a dollar in initiation fees, a dollar annually to the national organization, and whatever local dues were fixed by each lodge. In return they received a weekly paper and magazine, a low-rate insurance plan, and representation to protect and augment wages (all benefits typical of unions at the time).[171] The one significant exclusion was African-Americans (again typical), which Debs opposed. Race was one of many internal divisions that factory owners would be able to exploit in decades to come.

The ARU grew rapidly. Within months, charters had been issued to almost a hundred lodges and a series of important railroads had been organized. The union's victory in reversing a wage cut and injunction against a strike by the Union Pacific railroad in March 1894 was followed a month later by a strike against the Great Northern Railroad, owned by the notoriously tightfisted James J. Hill. The eighteen-day walkout resulted in the ARU winning the overwhelming majority of its demands and the congratulations of Hill himself for its shrewd management of the strike. Debs, delighted at a victory achieved without violence, told a press conference, "I don't thing there will be any more strikes for a long time. I hope not."[172]

And then came Pullman.

◆   ◆   ◆

As I've already suggested, there were a number of answers to the Labor Question from labor's side of the table. There were a number of answers from management's side, too. One involved actually negotiating with workers about pay and conditions—generally a last resort. Another involved confrontation, enlisting allies, like government, when conflict erupted. Still another involved longer-term cooperation within industries, which, like labor unions, were often divided in destructive ways. (John D. Rockefeller, for example, saw his monopolistic practices as a means of imposing stability in a volatile oil industry in ways that benefited everyone.) Some industrial leaders, such as Carnegie, still believed a kind of natural harmony between labor and capital was possible, and his fabled philanthropy, such as the hundreds of libraries he built for communities willing to shoulder the cost of maintaining them, represented what they regarded as their good faith effort to promote that harmony. The Lincolnian dream of effortless cooperation seemed to die hard for Americans of all kinds.[173] Indeed, many Americans today continue to cherish it. But that dream, as Debs himself was learning, could be extraordinarily elusive.

George Pullman had a somewhat different solution to the Labor Question. Pullman, who was born in upstate New York in 1831, moved to Chicago in 1859—a good place at the right time. After working as a contractor on buildings and roads, Pullman became intrigued by the rapidly expanding railroad business, and was particularly engaged by the effort to build railroad cars in which passengers could sleep during long journeys. Through a series of innovations, Pullman's sleeping cars soon set the industry standard in the way Cadillac or Apple would in later generations. "Pullman" became a byword for luxury travel, and truly rich or distinguished VIPs, such as the President of the United States, would have their very own railroad cars. In 1883, Debs boasted to Brotherhood of Locomotive Firemen that Pullman had donated free sleeping cars for its delegates to attend its convention in Denver.[174]

Pullman was involved in a variety of industries and philanthropies, but there was one project in particular that captured his imagination. In 1880, he acquired a large tract of land on the outskirts of Chicago and broke ground in a model town he named after himself.[175] The town of Pullman had many of the things you might expect: a train station, a hotel, and, of course, roads, factories, utilities, houses, apartments, stores, and parks. What made it unusual was that George Pullman owned all of it. Pullman workers would live in Pullman homes (rent and utilities were deducted from their paychecks by Pullman's bank), buy Pullman groceries, borrow books from Pullman's library, and so on. Pullman would also maintain the town's cultural, hygienic, and living standards. Whether or not this was the preferred style of living of its inhabitants, Pullman clearly had some appeal: by 1885, the town census showed almost 1,400 families and over 8,600 residents living under his rule.[176]

Pullman's approach drew extravagant praise from a variety of quarters. Much of the approval focused on the cleanliness and order that were apparent to visitors, but a lot of it went further to celebrate Pullman's resolution of the Labor Question. One writer, for example, called the town "a fresh illustration of the identity of interest which subsists between capital and labor and the mutual advantage which comes from recognizing it." Another argued that Pullman had in effect rebutted the explosive claim of the Haymarket bomber. "No agitator in view of the provision that have been made here for the amelioration of the condition of the laborer—to minister to his comfort and add to his enjoyment, and at the same time furnish the means for his intellectual improvement—can prate about the irrepressible conflict between capital and labor."[177] Attuned to the public relations dimension to his project, Pullman was careful to cultivate informed opinion.

Informed opinion, however, tended not to speak with actual Pullman residents. To be sure, there were those who reported satisfaction. "We have a clean and comfortable house, and plenty of pure air," one resident explained. "My children are healthy, and as far as my wife, she has seemed like a different woman."[178] Turnover in Pullman tended to be high, however; in particular, the fact that residents could not own their own homes discouraged long-term settlement. Economist Richard Ely, who did an intensive piece of investigative journalism on Pullman for *Harper's New Monthly Magazine* published in 1885, had a number of good things to say about the town, but he finally found its impact on residents as dispiriting, describing it as "well-wishing feudalism" that led residents to adopt an attitude of sullen servility. Ely's "unavoidable conclusion" was that "the very idea of Pullman is un-American."[179]

Whatever the merits or flaws of Pullman, its founder could not insulate the town from broader national influences. The most obvious of these was the Panic of 1893, which ushered in hard economic times—among the hardest the nation has ever known. Pullman initially tried to keep his economic operations steady, even taking on some contracts at a loss, but by 1894, the decline in business led him to cut his workers' wages by as much as half, along with widespread layoffs. Significantly, however, Pullman did *not* lower prices for rent, food, water, and home heating. All the town's operations were expected to generate a target six percent annual profit—even the churches Pullman built. (He prided himself on simultaneously providing for the welfare of his residents as well as providing a reliable return to investors.) In December 1893, a short strike by steamfitters and blacksmiths was quashed in days, and all workers who did not return to work were blacklisted. But the rising pressures finally crested the following spring when a committee of railway workers asked to meet with Pullman to discuss labor conditions. Nothing much came of it—except that Pullman broke his promise not to punish anyone on the committee and fired three workers. On May 11, they walked out on the job. And then they turned to the ARU.[180]

Would the ARU support the Pullman workers' strike? Debs hoped not. He had long had reservations about the usefulness of strikes given their costs in money and public opinion, and he wished his new organization would catch its breath in the aftermath of its early victories. But the ARU rank and file, heady with its success against Great Northern less than three weeks earlier, wished to press forward. They voted to join the struggle in June 1894, and Debs, reservations notwithstanding, took charge of the effort. No railway train hauling Pullman cars—which was virtually every train in the United States—would be handled by ARU men.

The early days of the strike were heady ones for the 150,000 members of the union. Rail traffic in the United States virtually ground to a halt, even more decisively than in 1877. An estimated 260,000 sympathizers joined the boycott of Pullman cars, and another half-million may have been idled as a result. A steering committee made of up representatives from local unions coordinated the effort from Chicago with impressive discipline. The nation was stunned.

Pullman may have been down, but he wasn't out. He too had outside resources, notably the General Managers Association, an organization of twenty-six different railroads. Most important, though, was the federal government under President Grover Cleveland (a Democrat Debs had once supported) and his Attorney General of the United States, Richard Olney, a former railroad lawyer. At the request of the General Managers Association, Olney issued an injunction in early July that declared further labor action illegal. (A key justification was the federal government's authority to ensure postal delivery.) Meanwhile, federal troops and state militia were dispatched across the country; the U.S. Army arrived in Chicago on Independence Day. Yet the presence of the army may have intensified rather than stifled disorder. Violence erupted in twenty-six states. Freight cars and train equipment burned in rail yards, as did the goods that could not be brought to market. By July 11, an estimated thirty-four people had died.

Meanwhile, Debs and other ARU leaders were indicted and arrested on two different occasions in mid-July, once for conspiracy to obstruct the mails, and again a week later, for contempt of court for failing to obey the injunction. Refusing bail, he and other strike leaders remained in jail until late July, when they were freed pending a trial. The arrests proved to be a turning point. The strikers' organization began to break down. By mid-August, the Pullman strike was essentially over.[181]

Debs himself also collapsed. The strain of leading the strike led him to go home to Terre Haute and spend two weeks in bed. In November 1894, a judge working without a jury sentenced him to six months in prison for violating the injunction. A second trial for the more serious conspiracy charge was never tried after a juror became ill. (It appeared likely Debs would have been acquitted, particularly after Pullman refused to honor a subpoena to testify, probably to avoid embarrassing revelations.) After failed appeals for his injunction conviction, Debs reported to prison in early 1895.[182]

On the face of it, the Pullman strike was a victory for Pullman and his allies. A rising union had been smashed in a showdown—the ARU would never recover—and state and local governments had demonstrated yet again they would intervene forcefully on the side of management. Yet success seemed hollow to many of the winners. The town of Pullman was now a byword for the most backward kind of feudalism (it would eventually be absorbed into Chicago), and Pullman himself was criticized for his inflexibility even by people whose interests were similar to his. Mark Hanna, the famed Republican political fixer who coached William McKinley to victory over the Populist Democrat William Jennings Bryan in the presidential election of 1896, called Pullman a damn fool for refusing to listen to his workers.[183] Clearly, most corporate leaders felt, there had to be at least the appearance of listening to labor if business as usual was going to be possible.

Meanwhile, many ordinary Americans were beginning to think events like the Pullman strike suggested that something was going to have to limit the arrogance of men like Pullman. Instead of depending on handouts from Carnegies and Rockefellers, maybe their own government—which *the people*, in theory, controlled—could be a better representative of their interests. Even as the Pullman strike was getting underway, a so-called "industrial army" of workers under the direction of Ohio businessman Jacob Coxey marched to the nation's capitol to demand public works projects that would create jobs and build a more civically-minded democratic society. Just as he would do in Pullman, Attorney General Olney dispatched troops to stop the marchers (some of whom rode trains); only about 500 actually made it to Washington, whereupon they were dispersed. Yet "Coxey's Army," as it was known, was a sign of a shifting political wind—and the first of many subsequent Marches on Washington in the next century.[184]

For Debs, the Pullman affair was a watershed event that, literally and figuratively, cleaved his life in half. While its effect was more a matter of confirming trends in his thinking than a sudden shift, the speed and intensity with which the strike was crushed nevertheless had a permanently radicalizing effect on him. "There was delivered, from wholly unexpected quarters, a swift succession of blows that blinded me for an instant and then opened wide my eyes—and in that gleam of every bayonet and the flash of every rife *the class struggle was revealed*," he would later explain in characteristically theatrical language. (One affinity Debs did not have with Lincoln was a gift for hard, lean prose.) "This was my first practical lesson in Socialism, though wholly unaware it was called by that name."[185] During his time in jail, Debs began to read a wide variety of radical literature, and came under the influence of immigrant Socialist Victor Berger.

Shortly after his release from prison, he announced publicly he was now a Socialist, and in 1897 gathered the fragments of the ARU and folded them into a new organization, the Socialist Democratic Party of America (SDP).

Over the course of the next two decades, Debs threw himself headlong into political work, navigating his way through an often-confusing maze of internecine battles between competing socialist factions, unions, and their relations with each other. In 1905, he became a Founding Father of the International Workers of the World, also known as "the Wobblies," perhaps the most militant union this country has ever seen. And after backing William Jennings Bryan in 1896, Debs himself became the Socialist Party candidate in the next four presidential elections. His political clout crested in 1912, when he received almost a million votes in a four-man field that included Woodrow Wilson (who won), Theodore Roosevelt (a renegade Republican running in the "Bull Moose" Party), and the incumbent, Republican William Howard Taft.

This was, however, his high-water mark. Significantly, the three men who ran ahead of Debs in 1912 all called themselves Progressives. Progressivism, yet another product of the ferment of the 1890s, had first taken root at the municipal and state level and became truly national under the leadership of Roosevelt in the first decade of the twentieth century. (Roosevelt ran against Taft, his handpicked successor in 1912, because he decided Taft wasn't Progressive enough.) Defining what Progressivism actually means is something that has bedeviled generations of historians. It nevertheless seems safe to say the movement was more about reform than revolution, more about expertise than equality, and more top-down in its approach than bottom-up. (Populists *dreamed* up ideas like railroad regulation; Progressives *implemented* them.) Progressives agreed with Debs that there was something seriously wrong in American life that needed to be changed. But Debs wanted to go a good deal farther than they did, and suspected that people like Roosevelt, a child of hereditary privilege, were more interested in preserving their own prerogatives and saving capitalists from their own excesses than really understanding, and helping, ordinary working people.

By this point, the forces of change, broadly construed, had become a major force in American life. Though never a principal player, Debs was nevertheless an important and popular one, a reference point even for those who disagreed with him. A man labeled a radical subversive in much of the mass media during the Pullman strike, he was nevertheless greeted in Chicago by one of the most remarkable demonstrations in the history of the city upon his release from prison in 1895.[186] His train tour in 1908 on the "Red Special" attracted sustained national attention, something he would continue to draw for the next decade.

The outbreak of the First World War in 1914, however, proved to be the beginning of the end. The Wilson administration struggled to remain neutral for the first two-and-a-half years of the war, a position that represented the majority view. (Indeed, Wilson was reelected in 1916 on a peace platform in a campaign in which the ailing Debs declined to run.) But a series of foreign and domestic pressures, combined with Germany's calculation that it could afford to alienate the United States by resuming unrestricted submarine warfare and winning the war in one final push, led the United States into the conflict in 1917. "The war to end all wars," Wilson called it, turning the struggle into a Progressive crusade—and showing its least attractive qualities, as his administration's desire for efficient management led it to take a harsh stance on any form of dissent.

Many explanations have been offered to explain the causes of the First World War, among them a belief it represented a rising Germany's bid for global mastery and another that it represented a tragic miscalculation brought about by too many secret treaties. Yet for Debs and millions of people around the world, the war was simply a giant squabble among elite military, corporate, and government leaders in which ordinary people were expected to pay the cost in blood. This position became ever harder to maintain as one nation after another, the United States among them, was sucked into the vortex. Many Socialists around the world eventually supported their native countries.

Debs refused to conform. His experiences, most recently the mass arrests of comrades who tried to express the constitutional right of free expression, steeled his dissent. If, in fact, the United States was ever going to change for the better—if it was ever going to move *forward* by going *back* to the traditions of freedom represented by the Founding Fathers, the abolitionists, and Abraham Lincoln—then he was going to have to speak out. And so it was that, after recovering from another of his occasional bouts of exhaustion, he mounted the platform at Nusimilla Park in Canton.

◆   ◆   ◆

There are all kinds of limitations in the political vision of Eugene Victor Debs. The primary problem was his uncritical embrace of government intervention as a panacea for all social ills. He seemed to think socialism would not only bring capitalists to heel, but would pretty much solve the problem of racism, anchor women comfortably in place, and usher in an order pleasing to both God and man. (One wonders whether such a cheerful vision could survive a single afternoon at in a contemporary Department of Motor Vehicles office.) Even if one assumes such wonderful results would indeed be the result of a socialist revolution, one must nevertheless wonder about his cheerful confidence that for all their hard-knuckle tactics on picket lines, corporate leaders would meekly accept the voice of the people at the ballot box and step aside—as if slick lawyers and lobbyists weren't hard at work even 100 years ago.

Nor was Debs especially incisive about some of the people in the causes he called his own. Many of his contemporaries showed justifiable skepticism about the violent tactics of the Bolsheviks during the Russian Revolution or even those of the Industrial Workers of the World's Bill Haywood. While Debs ultimately publicly repudiated the tactics of both, his uncritical initial embrace of them raises questions about his judgment.

So does his failure to sustain his commitment to many of the organizations he joined or even founded. More comfortable on the edges of institutions than in the middle of them, more interested in speaking than in organizing, he was criticized even by many of his warmest supporters for his failures to weigh in decisively when ideological disputes were at their hottest. For all his communitarian values, Debs was also an instinctive individualist—yet one more way he was a representative American.

Above all, Debs seriously underestimated the nation's ability to reform itself, a phenomenon he might well have had mixed feelings about because reform also foreclosed deeper structural changes. For all their limitations, the Progressives did restrain the worst abuses of capitalism, and when capitalism was on verge of destroying itself in the Great Depression of the 1930s, a new generation of reformers under President Franklin Roosevelt ushered in a half century in which the ordinary workers Debs so cherished enjoyed a generally rising standard of living that made more radical solutions, like those represented by the Russian Revolution, seem irrelevant at best and menacing at worst.

And yet, for all this, Debs remains an important figure for his time—and for ours. While his answers to the Labor Question were deeply flawed, few people framed that question more vividly. And the key to that framing was his deep and abiding love for the nation and its history, a love that suffused his harshest criticism. The speech he gave in Chicago upon his release from jail after the Pullman strike captures that love, and his burning energy to make freedom (something a once and future inmate would savor) a meaningful term in his world:

> Manifestly the spirit of '76 survives. The fires of liberty and noble aspirations are not yet extinguished. I greet you tonight as lovers of liberty and despisers of despotism. I comprehend the significance of this demonstration and appre-

ciate the honor that makes it possible for me to be your guest on such an occasion. The vindication and glorification of the American principles of government, so proclaimed in the Declaration of Independence, is the high purpose of this convocation.

Debs' second prison term left him a good deal less ebullient than his first. A much older man (he was sixty-three years old when he went to jail), the experience was much more physically and psychologically punishing. Yet if he was humbled, his chastening took a form that deepened and textured his commitments, once again leading him to cast his ideological commitments in terms of older rebels (like Jesus) rather than newer ones (like Marx). In his posthumous 1927 book *Walls & Bars*, Debs highlighted his creed: "While there is a lower class I'm in it; While there is a criminal element; I'm of it; While there's a soul in prison I'm not free."[187] A later American patriot—one who would lead a March on Washington considerably more successful than that of Jacob Coxey—would adopt a similar creed. His Dream was a lot like that of Debs. Both men recognized their love of country also had to be grounded in something beyond it.

Despite a good deal of lobbying, Woodrow Wilson resolutely refused to free Debs from jail. "I'll never consent to the pardon of this man," he said at the end of his presidential term in 1921, when Wilson, himself a sick and broken man, was at the nadir of his popularity. "This man was a traitor to his country, and he will never be pardoned during my administration."

His successor, however, felt differently. Most historians agree Warren Harding was one of the most corrupt presidents in American history—and one its most good-natured men. A Republican who generally worked at the behest of archcapitalists, he nevertheless lacked the vindictiveness of Wilson. He arranged for Debs to come to Washington, unaccompanied, for an interview in March 1921. Harding planned to pardon Debs on July 4; when informed this would cause an uproar among the president's supporters, he waited until Christmas. Debs had served about two-and-a-half years (he had also permanently lost his citizenship). Twenty-three hundred inmates gathered at the gates of the prison to cheer him as he left prison in tears. On the way to the train for another meeting with Harding, Debs wrote a note, took the five dollar bill given to every freed prisoner out of his wallet and sent it off to the committee of activists working for the release of Niccola Sacco and Bartolomeo Vanzetti, two Italian immigrants who were tried, convicted, and ultimately executed for murder under highly dubious legal proceedings.[188]

Whatever his personal or political limitations, Eugene Debs knew one thing that remains as relevant as it ever has: The United States is more than a market or a flag. Those who act otherwise are the real radicals, who true patriots are right to resist. We learned that lesson once. Can we learn it again?

6

Mr. Sinatra Gets Rejected

Whatever the term "American Dream" may mean—and it's safe to say it's a far more complicated and ambiguous term than is commonly recognized—it's pretty clear that Frank Sinatra embodied most observers' idea of it. Beginning in relatively modest circumstances, he became one of the richest and most famous people in American history, a celebrity on a scale that has rarely been equaled and perhaps never surpassed.

In his most famous song, a song he once plausibly called "our national anthem," Sinatra insisted he achieved this success "My Way." Yet his way, as even a cursory look at his life suggests, wasn't always very nice, let alone inspiring. Selfish, arrogant, and downright frightening when angry, some saw him as a monster. But whatever you might say about Sinatra, he was deeply human, and as emotionally vulnerable as we all can be, did have his feelings hurt. What he did with those hurt feelings—for worse as well as for better—is worth considering, even for people who were not as gifted as he was. Here is a portrait of a diminutive giant for the cynical beginner.

CHAPTER 6:
MR. SINATRA GETS REJECTED

*in which we see a hurt, angry, and not altogether likable man
master the art of voicing pain*

FRANK SINATRA IS FURIOUS. He's got a sledgehammer in his hands, and he's swinging away, the blows landing on newly hardened concrete. (Do his hands feel the vibration of the handle as the sledgehammer pounds the ground? Does he notice his valet, George Jacobs, witnessing his rage? If so, he probably doesn't care.) Sinatra is destroying the heliport he's just had built on the grounds of his house in Palm Springs.[189]

It was supposed to be Jack's house—or, at any rate, the house Jack lived in when he left the White House for the West Coast. Three years before, when he was running for president, he had visited, and Sinatra had installed a plaque on the door of the guest room: "John Fitzgerald Kennedy Slept Here."[190] In the months that followed, Sinatra had been one of Kennedy's most visible and effective supporters. Using his extensive contacts in entertainment, he had organized Kennedy's spectacular inaugural gala, and had served as Jacqueline Kennedy's escort at the event. Perhaps more importantly, he had served as a conduit for JFK's mistresses, notably Judith Campbell [later Exner], whom Kennedy shared with Sam Giancana, the notorious organized crime chieftain.[191]

Now, in the winter of 1962, Kennedy is well into the first of what he hopes will be a two-term presidency. Sinatra, for his part, expects their friendship to continue. To that end—but without any formal request that he do so—he's made extensive renovations in his home: separate cottages for the president and the Secret Service; a dining room for about forty guests; twenty-five extra phone lines; enough cable to support teletype services; a switchboard to handle the incoming communications traffic; and a heliport to serve air traffic. He's even installed a flagpole like the one in Hyannisport so that he can fly the presidential flag when Kennedy arrives for a weekend visit in March and a vacation in June.

But Kennedy never does. He defers to his brother Robert, who insists he cannot go. The reason, in a word, is Giancana. In late February 1962, Attorney General Kennedy receives information from FBI Director J. Edgar Hoover showing Judith Campbell has not only been calling the White House, but also Giancana and fellow mobster Johnny Roselli. (In Hoover's mode of operations, this intelligence is as likely to be a covert threat—I've got dirt on you people—as it is a matter of passing data up the chain of command.) No one at the Justice Department yet knows for sure that Sinatra is the connecting link between Giancana, Campbell and JFK, but a series of bureau reports document personal calls by Giancana, the focus of a major investigation of organized crime, to Sinatra's unlisted phone number. These reports also claim that Giancana has been a frequent guest at Sinatra's house in Palm Springs. This in itself is a reason that Robert Kennedy says JFK can't go there: The president cannot politically afford to be entertained by a man who also hosts gangsters.[192] His brother reluctantly agrees. The presidential party will instead stay with (Republican) Bing Crosby, who also has a house in Palm Springs. Security considerations are the official reason given for changing the previously announced plan to stay with Sinatra.

The president delegates his brother-in-law, Peter Lawford, a member of the so-called Rat Pack (Sinatra had changed its name to the "Jack Pack" during the 1960 campaign) to give Sinatra the news. One result of the conversation is that Sinatra wields a sledgehammer. Another is that he shoots the messenger: Lawford is literally written out of two movies in which he is to appear, and Sinatra refuses to speak to him ever again. Twenty years later, upon learning that Lawford and his wife were in the audience for a show at the Sands Hotel, Sinatra delegates two security guards to remove him from the premises. "Mr. Sinatra refuses to perform until you're gone," he is told.[193]

Sinatra's response to JFK is milder, though still cool. Upon his arrival in California at the end of March, Kennedy asks Lawford how Sinatra has taken the news. "Not very well," Lawford replies. "I'll make it up to him," Kennedy responds. He calls Sinatra and invites him to Crosby's for lunch. Sinatra declines. Too busy, he explains. He's on his way to Los Angeles to visit some friends (one of whom, Marilyn Monroe, will soon be an intimate of the Kennedy brothers).

The bloom is off the rose. In May, Sinatra sends the president a birthday gift, which Kennedy acknowledges in a thank-you note. In August, Sinatra telegraphs his readiness to send a print of *The Manchurian Candidate* if desired. But Kennedy keeps his distance. Sinatra does not attend his funeral. He does call the White House to offer his condolences. (The call is taken by Lawford's wife, Patricia, who is also JFK's sister).[194] But for all intents and purposes, Sinatra's stay in Camelot is over by the spring of 1962. In 1968, he supports Hubert Humphrey, not Robert Kennedy, for the presidency.

"The thing was this: Frank was hurt," Sammy Davis Jr. told Sinatra biographer Randy Taraborelli decades later. "He thought it was chickenshit, the whole goddamn thing. And for the president to stay at Bing's, well, that looked to Frank like a slap in the face. A Republican! In other words, it looked to Frank like Kennedy was saying 'I'd rather stay *anywhere* than with you.' I think Frank felt like the whole thing was designed to humiliate him, and you know what, pal? I fucking agree. I do. The way Frank helped the Kennedys, man, that whole thing they did was *cold.*"[195]

Other perhaps more neutral observers were less outraged by what happened. "Why the fuck would the president stay with Sinatra?" Giancana said at the time. "He ain't crazy."[196] One might argue that, appearances notwithstanding, simple loyalty might have led the Kennedy people to stand by those who helped them get where they were. But as Giancana, a man whose work behind the scenes in Chicago allegedly secured JFK's razor-thin electoral margin could testify, this wasn't the Kennedy style. The real problem, one can easily infer him arguing, was that Sinatra had trouble accepting his dispensability.

Which leads to what I regard as an interesting question: How did Frank Sinatra come to see himself as a man entitled to consort with Kennedys and Kings (from Martin Luther King to the royal family of Monaco)?[197] Twenty years before, he was "a little guy from Hoboken" thrilled to shake President Roosevelt's hand. Clearly, he had come a long way since then. Unlike FDR, JFK was a contemporary of Sinatra's, and, while Sinatra clearly admired Kennedy, their relationship was at least initially reciprocal—and Sinatra may have even had more to offer the then-senator than vice versa. But the issue goes deeper than personal contacts or generational protocols; it has more to do with Sinatra's apparent belief he could pretty much go, do, and act as he pleased with anyone he wanted to. By the early 1960s, this assumption—undoubtedly rooted in actual experience—was so strong that learning otherwise, even from the President of the United States, was infuriating.

But when did this assumption actually take root? When he began singing at the Rustic Cabin, a small New Jersey nightclub, in the 1930s? When the girls began screaming at the Paramount in the 1940s? When his comeback was secure in the 1950s? No doubt all of these turning points contributed toward shaping his outlook. But I suspect the series of thoughts and experiences that led him to wield a sledgehammer that March day originated in a relatively unprepossessing house in Hoboken. The real groundbreaking took place there.

◆   ◆   ◆

"He didn't dream. He said, 'I'm gonna do it. I'm gonna get across this river. I'm gonna go there [New York City] and make a name for myself.'"

—Tina Sinatra on her father's youth in Hoboken[198]

"As I left the theater, with the shriek of young lungs still ringing in my ears, I was bothered by a strange discovery—that you could become a public idol simply by looking young, sad, and undernourished, then by skimming off a certain amount of your misery and pouring it into a microphone."

—journalist Jack Long after a Sinatra performance, 1943[199]

It may be a perverse tribute to the elasticity of the American Dream that by the early twentieth century, Martin Sinatra would adopt an Irish name—O'Brien—as a means of upward mobility. Of course, he probably didn't think about his situation exactly this way. For the young Sicilian immigrant, it was probably more a matter of common sense: There was no way an aspiring boxer was ever going to get into a gym, never mind a ring, with a name like Sinatra. Perhaps he was aware there was a time when people with names like "Kennedy" had been viewed with the same degree of disdain and dismay that the Italians like him were. Perhaps he could anticipate a time when there would be those (Puerto Ricans? Koreans?) who would take their place at the bottom of the pecking order along with a fixed underclass of Negroes. But he probably didn't spend a lot of time thinking about it.

Not much came of Marty O'Brien's boxing career. Still, the O'Brien name continued to have its uses, particularly when wielded by his bride, the Genoan-born Natalie "Dolly" Garavante, who apparently did most of the family's thinking. It was she who, as a major backstage player for the Democratic party in Hoboken, orchestrated Marty's appointment as a city fireman. It was she who, after borrowing money from her mother, opened a saloon she named "Marty O'Brien's" (this during Prohibition). And it was she who, when her only child was born in December 1915, made sure he had an Irish godfather, Frank Garrick, to someday get him a job for *The Jersey Observer*. Garrick got him hired to bundle papers, but when young Francis was fired for posing as a sportswriter, Dolly never forgave Garrick for failing to get the paper to take him back.

You get the idea: Francis owes a lot of what he became to Dolly. Part of this is sheer economic privilege. Later in life Sinatra would emphasize the gritty urban milieu of his youth, but without underestimating the insularity and widespread poverty that surrounded him, it must nevertheless be said he lived a life of relative affluence. In 1932, with the Depression at its height, the Sinatra family moved into a four-story $13,400 house (a price tag of affluent Westchester County proportions). Young Frank, an only child, had so many pairs of pants that he had the nickname of "Slacksey O'Brien." But the advantages in life that Dolly gave Frankie were more than just material; they had more to do with a sense of confidence that would lead a high school dropout to believe he could pass himself off as a sportswriter, and to later make both his high school and journalistic "experiences" fixtures of his official publicity biography. Here, truly, was a child with great expectations.

Still, an ambitious mother will only get any child so far, particularly a child who, much to that mother's dismay, was indifferent about education and lacked an obvious channel for yearnings that remained inchoate well into his adolescence. Anyone reading a Sinatra biography looking for a childhood incident that would foreshadow his future will be largely disappointed; while there are scattered references to him singing to friends or at family gatherings, there's little here to distinguish such an activity from a passion for baseball or a knack for drawing. Most accounts of his youth emphasize Dolly's and Martin's skepticism about their son's growing interest in a singing career (they hoped he would attend nearby Stevens Institute and become an engineer). Though Dolly eventually bought him a sound system and a car to allow him to pursue his avocation, one suspects this had less to do with her belief that he could become a singing star—who, after all, could really make a living doing that?—than it did her long-standing strategy of making sure her son had enough money in his pocket to treat, and thus make, plenty of friends.

The epiphany, virtually everyone agrees, took place in the spring of 1935 when the nineteen-year-old Sinatra took his girlfriend, Nancy Barbato, to see Bing Crosby, the premier popular singer of his day. Crosby's appeal had less to do with the pure beauty of his voice than his ability to exploit the cultural possibilities of new technology, specifically that of the microphone. By singing in a smooth, subtly modulated voice, a style that came to be known as "crooning," Crosby distinguished himself from more powerful vocalists such as Al Jolson and Sophie Tucker, who attained their preeminence as "belters" who could project their voices to the far corners of a room. Moreover, Crosby's image matched his singing style—that of an elegantly dressed, pipe-smoking man of leisure. Ironically, the effect of Crosby's understated image on young Frank Sinatra was electrifying. "When I saw that guy on stage," he reputedly told Nancy, "something happened to me. It was like I was really up there, not Crosby. I've got to be that singer." As the magazine writer who related this anecdote related, "Probably a thousand other youngsters who heard Crosby that night painted the same mental picture—themselves in the spotlight, thrilling millions. But Sinatra was the one out of a thousand with the courage to chase the rainbow."[200]

Courage, certainly: There's a lot to be said about that. But it's also worth considering the particular rainbow Sinatra was chasing. It had its own arc, and one can confidently say that, if he had be been born in a different place or time it would have been situated—and chased—differently. As his chroniclers tirelessly assert, Frank Sinatra was very much a man of his time.

What time was that? My answer, despite the fact that he is dead and buried, is now.

Why is Sinatra *now*? When did *now* begin? And why hasn't *now* ended? To put it simply, I believe the basic texture of modern American life emerged during Sinatra's youth, that he embodied it with unusual clarity, and that its contours, despite its myriad variations, remain largely in place. Far more than extraordinary events of his childhood (like the stock market crash) or the leading figures of his era (like the so-called Lost Generation), there's something accessibly familiar about the rhythms of everyday life in the years following the First World War, a time known by those who lived it as "The New Era."

That familiarity is almost palpable, for example, in this description of a day in the life of the fictional John Smith, "a typical citizen of this restless republic," written by an ad agency copywriter in 1928, when Sinatra was twelve years old:

> Yanked out of bed by an alarm clock, John speeds through his shave, bolts down his breakfast in eight minutes, and scurries for a train or the street car. On the way to work his roving eye scans, one after another, the sport page, the comic strips, several columns of political hokum, and the delectable details of the latest moonshine murder.
>
> From eight to twelve, humped over a desk in a skyscraper, he wrestles with his job to the accompaniment of thumping typewriters, jingling telephones, and all the incessant tattoo of twentieth century commerce. One hour off for a quick lunch, a couple of cigarettes, and a glamorous glance at the cuties mincing down the boulevard. Jangling drudgery again from one until five. Then out on the surging streets once more.

Clash, clatter, rattle and roar! Honk! Honk! Honk! Every crossing jammed with traffic! Pavements fairly humming with jostling crowds! A tingling sense of adventure and romance in the very air! Speed-desire-excitement—the illusion of freedom at the end of the day! The flashing lights of early evening—Clara Bow in Hearts Aflame! Wuxtry! Wuxtry!—Bootlegger Kills Flapper Sweetheart! Clickety-click, clickety-click—John Smith homeward-bound, clinging to a strap and swiftly skimming through the last edition.[201]

The point of this little tableau was to illustrate the fast pace of life in The New Era. What may first strike a reader now, however, is how quaint it all seems: the virtual bragging about technology that's now commonplace, if not obsolete (alarm clocks, skyscrapers, typewriters); the dated slang and references ("hokum," "wuxtry," movie star Clara Bow); behavior that was once racy but is now regarded as distasteful, if not unacceptable (cigarette smoking, alcohol consumption, leering at women). Moreover, this sketch wasn't as fully representative as it was clearly meant to be; a "typical citizen," if there is any such person, did not necessarily live in a city, ride a subway, work in a skyscraper, or even have a lunch hour. Ironically, perhaps, what it most accurately depicts is the provincialism inherent in this writer's assumption that he can render a "typical" American experience.

Such limits notwithstanding, there nevertheless does seem to be much in this description that not only rings true of what many observers at the time and since have observed of the twenties, but also in the way John Smith's life resembles that of, say, his great-granddaughter Juanita Smith. The essential shape of the day shows striking similarity to ones experienced today: a morning routine followed by a rush-hour commute to work, with a subsequent workday punctuated by daily rituals that culminate in a trip home and "an illusion of freedom." One can grasp the fundamental continuity of John and Juanita's time by imagining alternatives on either side of the temporal divide: These are not people who begin their day by milking cows or drawing water from a well. Nor do they put food on the table by telecommuting from computer terminals in their homes or attached to their clothing.

Perhaps more importantly, John and Juanita's lives are also paralleled in the extraordinary range of the mass media in suffusing their days. Driving home from work, Juanita may be less likely to get her news from a newspaper than by listening to the radio, a medium that came into its own in the twenties, but the content of what she absorbs, right down to the sensational murder trials and entertainment news, is much the same in its intense, but fleeting, interest. Even the evocative phrase "jangling drudgery" continues to describe the combination of hectic activity and numbing repetition that characterizes the workaday lives of most Americans.

Changes in family life were also important. While women gained the right to vote in 1920, it was the developments that occurred in the domestic sphere—smaller families, more sexual freedom, and the replacement of servants by laborsaving devices like vacuum cleaners and washing machines—that were more obviously transformative. While it's possible to overstate the impact of the changes (not all young women were gin-swilling flappers; laborsaving devices were accompanied by rising housekeeping standards),[202] one nevertheless senses the *issues* of the time gave rise to assumptions and language that have been with us ever since. In *Only Yesterday*, his history of the 1920s published in 1931, journalist Frederick Lewis Allen noted "married women who were encumbered with children and could not seek jobs consoled themselves with the thought that home-making and child-rearing were really 'professions' after all."[203] One does not have to strain very hard to find an identical sentiment expressed today or to find women, like Dolly Sinatra, who left much of their child care in the hands of others while they made their way in a so-called man's world.

If women were increasingly going into the outside world, that outside world was also increasingly coming into the home. The first commercial radio station, for example, was established in 1920; by 1922 there were 508, and by the end of the decade Americans were spending $850 million a year on radio equipment.[204] What's significant here isn't the technology itself (radio broadcasting, like other technological innovations such as automobiles, were developed well before the 1920s), but rather the way these once cutting-edge inventions had become a part of everyday life on a mass scale.

What's also significant is the *way* this technology became part of everyday life: through fully mature mass-market industrial capitalism. Chain retailing, buying on credit, and, especially, the rise of pervasive national advertising came into their own in the 1920s. Nothing better illustrates the impact of this new consumer culture than the development of radio, a crucial medium in the rise of Sinatra's idol, Bing Crosby. Originally developed for its shipping and naval uses for wireless communication between two points, the industry evolved toward broadcasting in 1920 when a Westinghouse engineer in Pittsburgh played records (yet another industry that boomed in the twenties) for the enjoyment of those with receivers. The nascent broadcast industry was a patchwork quilt of stations and programming run by churches, unions, and other institutions at the start of the decade. But the use of national networks created for private profit, as well as the use of advertising to pay for programming, not only quickly became the dominant way of structuring the industry and its programs (for example, the soap opera, an entertainment genre that got its name from its sponsor), but also laid down the political, organizational, and financial tracks that would be followed by television (in its infancy in the 1920s) and even the Internet.

These social, economic, and technological developments also had a decisive impact on American values. Until around the time Sinatra was born, the United States was predominately a culture of *production*. Its social values (for example, the Puritan work ethic), material conditions (an abundance of raw materials), and economic realities (such as relatively high labor costs, which fostered technological innovation as well as the immigration of intellectual capital from abroad) helped create a society in which making things was paramount. Starting in the 1920s, the first decade in which more Americans lived in cities than in rural areas, the United States became a culture of *consumption*: As many government and business leaders recognized, the future success of capitalism depended on nation's ability to absorb incredible productive capacity via buying, spending, using up. Indeed, it was precisely the difficulty in absorbing this capacity that was widely blamed for the advent of the Great Depression.

This new culture of consumption had important psychological ramifications that reached deep into the roots of mass consciousness. In the words of cultural historian Warren Susman, a society that once placed emphasis on "character" now prized "personality." "Character" has a moral connotation; it suggests the essential nature of an individual in a way that transcends surface appearances. But "personality" suggests the allure of precisely such surface appearances, whether via the acquisition of cosmetics or a newly styled automobile. (Alfred Sloan's General Motors Corporation was finally able to beat Henry Ford at his assembly-line game by subtly changing his models every year.)

Here again, the example of Crosby is instructive. While he no doubt had to work hard to establish himself, a large part of Crosby's appeal was that he made it all seem so easy. He was one of the first modern celebrities—a man famous in large measure for being famous, and one whose fame allowed him to cross into media like film and television with what seemed like effortless ease, even though his primary claim to fame was music. As a young man, Sinatra smoked a pipe and wore a hat in conscious emulation of his hero. (Upon finding a picture of Crosby in his room, an exasperated Dolly threw a shoe at her son and called him a bum.) What he wanted, very clearly, was to become a show business personality just like Crosby.

Significantly, however, there is one thing Sinatra pointedly did *not* copy from Crosby—his style of singing. "I was a big fan of Bing's," he later told his daughter. "But I never wanted to sing like him, because every kid on the block was boo-boo-booing like Crosby. I wanted to be a different kind of singer. And my voice was higher anyhow and I said, That's not for me."[205] To that end, Sinatra cultivated a more expressive approach. It was comparatively mild to what came later in his career, but it was distinctive enough to win him attention, and, eventually, accolades.

Of all the mysteries in Frank Sinatra's career, few are more perplexing than the nature of his talent. To put it simply: how was it that a man who could not read music should be celebrated as an unparalleled interpreter of popular song? How did someone with virtually no formal training come to be seen as a musician's musician, winning the admiration of unquestioned geniuses like Duke Ellington and Miles Davis? Actually, in the context of American popular music, these seeming anomalies are less contradictory than they might appear. Musical ability is often as much about instinct as it is about training, and it's likely that much of Sinatra's originality came precisely from the absence of formal models to follow. Moreover, much of what made him unique had less to do with music than drama, specifically his much-celebrated ability to convey emotion and conviction. In other words, Sinatra was a great actor with music long before he became an occasionally convincing actor with a script.

And yet for that very reason it's almost possible to believe he wasn't really an artist but rather a celebrity pretending to be one. After all, anyone can be a singer, and the difference between one who sings well and one who does not very often has nothing to do with hard work or personal character but rather a roll of the genetic dice. The many musicals in which young Sinatra appeared, often as an ordinary loser who would periodically break into song, could almost reinforce this belief there wasn't anything to it. It's almost as if his presence there is random, and that you too could be in that spotlight, thrilling millions. There's nothing to it.

In fact, of course, Sinatra worked extremely hard. Indeed, even if you factor out the elements in his personality that effectively disqualified him from the mellow, Bing Crosby school of effortless poise—his almost compulsive work ethic, that temper—Sinatra's cool public image could never wholly disguise his energy, even his edge. As William Herndon said of his law partner Abraham Lincoln, his ambition was a little engine that knew no rest.

That ambition emerged from the mists of his childhood shortly after the Crosby concert in 1935 when Sinatra made his first serious effort to break into show business by trying out for the *Major Bowes and his Original Amateur Hour*, a nationally broadcast radio show. ("Round and round she goes," went Bowes' signature saying, referring to the wheel of fortune, "and where she stops nobody knows.") It isn't clear whether it was Bowes' inspiration or Dolly's machinations that led him to join another auditioning group, The Three Flashes, which was rechristened The Hoboken Four. The group took first place on the September 8 show, and was invited to tour with a series of other acts in Bowes's national company. Sinatra stayed on until the bullying of other group members led him to quit at the end of the year.

Marty Sinatra was disappointed in his nineteen-year-old son. Here was one more failed attempt to make something of himself. But for Frank the Hoboken Four had never been much more than a necessary detour on the road to becoming a solo act. As usual, Dolly supported him. "The two of you're driving me nuts," she said of the fighting between father and son. "Frankie wants to sing, Marty. Jesus Christ, let him sing, will ya?" Once more, it appears that mother knew best.[206]

The next stage in Sinatra's career began in 1937 when a song promoter named Hank Sanicola became his unofficial manager and got him a job waiting tables and singing with the house band at the Rustic Cabin, a club in Englewood, New Jersey, right on the shore of the Hudson River. But even Dolly was dubious about this idea. "His salary was only fifteen dollars a week, and I used to give him practically twice that so he could pick up the tabs of his friends when they dropped in," she said. "When he got a five dollar raise, I told him 'This isn't getting me anywhere. It would be cheaper to keep you at home.' 'Mama,' he said, it's going to roll in someday. I'm going to be big time.' He always believed that."[207]

While the Rustic Cabin was hardly a major musical showcase, it offered a number of crucial advantages to Sinatra. One was its strategic location near the George Washington Bridge, which provided him easy access to the most important New York City venues, where he could see and learn what was going on. The other was that the Rustic Cabin had a direct radio wire to radio station WNEW in Manhattan, where the house band could be heard on weekly Saturday Dance Parade broadcasts. This, in turn, brought important bandleaders like Jimmy Dorsey to the Rustic Cabin, who then saw Sinatra for themselves.

Not that these people always liked what they saw or heard. "He was such a nuisance, hogging the mike all the time and singing every chorus when he was only supposed to do an occasional vocal," a musician who worked with him later told Kitty Kelly. "Finally we started taking the microphone away from him. We ridiculed him because he just wasn't that good." Sinatra, however, kept at it, picking up a vocal coach and rejecting any criticism. "When we'd tell him how bad he was, he'd get furious and start cursing and swearing at us. 'Son of a bitch,' he'd yell. 'You bastards wait. One of these days you're going to pay to hear me sing. You just wait.'"208

Sinatra's first important true believer was Harry James, a trumpeter who had left Benny Goodman's band to start his own. He was looking for a singer, a role that, in those days, was secondary to featured players like bandleaders themselves, and thought Sinatra sounded promising. Sinatra signed on and began touring with James in June 1939. But the band struggled to make ends meet. When, six months later, the much more prestigious Tommy Dorsey sought Sinatra's services with a long-term contract, James let him go with a handshake. Dorsey himself would not be quite so accommodating.

Sinatra remained with Dorsey for the next two years. In that time, his status rose steadily from a visible member of Dorsey's ensemble to a featured vocalist. He appeared in a number of films with the band and was named outstanding male vocalist by the bellwether *Billboard* and *Downbeat* magazines, and became a fixture on the pop scene with records like "I'll Never Smile Again" and "I'll Be Seeing You."

In 1942, Sinatra, now twenty-seven, began making his first solo recordings. This was the direction he wished to go—a path blazed by Crosby—but it was by no means clear that anyone, never mind Sinatra himself, could make the transition from a band vocalist to a pop singer. Moreover, Dorsey wasn't particularly interested in making it easy for Sinatra to leave. He ultimately agreed to do so, but not before claiming a third of his gross earnings for the next ten years. (Protracted negotiations the following year between Dorsey, Sinatra's agent, and his new record company, Columbia, untangled him from such onerous terms.)

He had momentum now. Most of it came from adolescent girls, or "bobbysoxers," as they were called for their distinctive apparel, whose growing adulation of the singer was described as "Sinatrauma" and "Sinatramania" in a mass media voracious for stories to cover. The climax occurred on in his first solo appearance on December 30, 1942, when he appeared as an "extra added attraction" to Benny Goodman's Band at New York's Paramount Theater. "Who the hell is Frank Sinatra?" Goodman asked upon learning of the addition to the program, which featured the Bing Crosby movie *Star-Spangled Rhythm*. Goodman soon found out. The screaming, applauding, and urine-stained seats made clear that Frank Sinatra, wearing his signature bow tie, had arrived. In fact, the girls refused to leave when the show was over, preventing the next scheduled performance from getting underway. ("Whatever he stirred beneath our barely budding breasts, it wasn't motherly," one bobby-soxer later reminisced.)209 Theater man-

agement resorted to showing the dullest films they could find in the hope of getting the audience to leave.

With an army of managers, publicists, and promoters, Sinatra pushed on,
expanding his dominions. A series of nightclub appearances at New York's
Riobamba Club and the Waldorf-Astoria in 1943 established his appeal with
older, more serious audiences. His appointment as a host of the weekly radio
show *Your Hit Parade* made him a household word across the country. Signed to
Metro-Goldwyn-Mayer, the most prestigious of the movie studios, he prepared
for his first major musical, *Anchors Aweigh*, by learning how to dance under the
tutelage of Gene Kelly.

But his core constituency remained the bobby-soxers. On Columbus Day of
1944, tens of thousands of them rioted at the Paramount, where Sinatra returned
for a series of performances, and where the refusal of those with seats to vacate
them led to the arrival of the police. By now, all the adulation generated by "The
Voice," as he was known, had become familiar, alternately amusing and irritating
to those who constantly heard about it. Others, however, were perplexed, even
troubled. In a piece for *The New Republic* shortly after the Columbus Day riot,
writer Bruce Bliven groped to understand what all the fuss was about:

> My strongest impression wasn't that Frankie means so much to the bobby-
> socksers, as that everything else means so little. Our civilization no doubt
> seems wonderful to the children of half-starved, dictator-ridden Europe; our
> multiplicity of gadgets is the envy of the world. And yet, if I read the bobby-
> socksers aright, we have left them with a hunger still unfulfilled: a hunger for
> heroes, for ideal things that don't appear, or at least not in sufficient quanti-
> ties, in a civilization that's so busy making things and selling things as ours.
> Whatever else you may say of the adoration of The Voice, it is a strictly non-
> commercial enterprise, a selfless idolatry which pays its 75 cents at the box
> office and asks in return only the privilege of being allowed to ruin its vocal
> chords. Perhaps Frankie is more important a symbol than most of us are
> aware.[210]

In retrospect, of course, most of us *are* aware that Frankie was an important
symbol, but we're no more able to fix exactly what he was a symbol *of* than Bliven
was. As he suggests, it has something to do with the longing engendered by the
very promise of American life, the incalculable price dreams exact by the mere
fact of their (often ill-formed) existence. "It was the war years, and there was a
great loneliness," Sinatra has said in explanation of his own appeal." But, while
that sounds poetic and true in as far as it goes, it's too clichéd and incomplete to
really be a satisfying answer. Yes, as Sinatra explained, he surely was "the boy in

every corner drugstore, the boy who'd gone off to war."[211] But even so, why did that loneliness persist for so many even after the boys had come home? (Hadn't it long preceded their departure?) And even if that loneliness had come and gone, why was *Sinatra* the voice of it?

My own guess is that Sinatra had an unusually clear understanding of this loneliness, which has something to do with the sense of isolation that results when you have high hopes in a land where you're is told anything is possible, and where, no matter what you do, the perception of plenty always seems most vividly in view somewhere *else*. Sinatra was literally the voice of these hopes, and had inhabited them with an intensity that few of us have the stomach for. Because let's face it: Dreams wear you down. Even if you have confidence, talent, opportunity, energy, courage, and luck (things I've spent the last few pages tracing), there's no guarantee you'll get what you want, or you'll be satisfied once you do.

Indeed, even after achieving more fame, wealth, and admiration than any sane person could ever hope to achieve, Sinatra—like many before and after him—seemed to regard mere success as somehow unworthy of serious consideration. "Happy? I don't know," Sinatra once responded to a query about the early days. "I wasn't *un*happy, let's put it that way. I never had it so good. Sometimes I wonder whether anybody had it like I had it, before or since. It's was the damnedest thing, wasn't it? But I was too busy ever to know whether I was happy or even to ask myself."[212]

More than anything else, it was Sinatra's busy-ness—his legendary work ethic that cut through the culture of personality in which he came of age—that was cornerstone of his success. And that busy-ness, in turn, rested on an assumption that his (often remarkably focused) actions would make a difference as to the outcome of his life. The American Dream has been many different things to many different people in the last four centuries, but its inexhaustible ends have tended to obscure its indispensable means: a sense of agency. Not everyone can become a star, but those who do usually believe that will is the engine of success. "Luck is fine, and you have to have luck to get the opportunity," Sinatra once told columnist Earl Wilson. "But after that, you've got to have talent and know how to use it."[213] There's little doubt where the emphasis is here. But as Sinatra would learn, luck and opportunity (not to mention to actions of others) will continue to haunt even those most intent on banishing them from the dominions of fortune.

It had now been a decade since Sinatra went to that Crosby concert. Reading about it in the space of a few minutes can obscure that it really was a fairly long time, and there must have been long moments, especially in those early years, when it would have been hard even for Sinatra himself to believe he was going to get to that place he had never been but knew he wanted to go. At some point he must have sensed he had caught a wave, one that would carry him from a sea of pure potential straight to the shore of recognized achievement (and once there, he would just keep going). And while he might not be happy, but he could at least ride out his personal demons. One thing was certain: There was no going back.

◆   ◆   ◆

"He kept saying, 'My career is over. I'm fucking washed up, and now I have to go out and face these people—the same goddamn people who aren't buying my records, who aren't seeing my movies.'"

—Sinatra bodyguard Jimmy Silvani,
quoting Sinatra backstage at the Copacabana, 1950[214]

He couldn't sing. Frank Sinatra was onstage for his third show of the evening at the Copacabana in New York City on April 26, 1950 when he lost the power to do what he did best. "No words would come out—absolutely nothing—just dust," he later told his daughter. "I was never so panic-stricken in my whole life. I remember looking at the audience, there was a blizzard outside, about seventy people in the place—and they knew something serious had happened. There was absolute silence—stunning, absolute silence." Sinatra looked at pianist Skitch Henderson, whose face was white with fear. "Finally I turned to the audience and whispered into the microphone 'Good night,' and walked off the floor."[215] The problem was attributed to bleeding in Sinatra's vocal chords. He canceled the rest of the engagement to regain his voice, and did. But there was a serious question about how much that mattered. For in the eyes of many observers, and even Sinatra himself, his career was finished.

The stages of Sinatra's fall from commercial grace seem to have occurred as imperceptibly as his meteoric rise. To all outward appearances, he was still at his peak in 1945 when he was the lead (with higher billing than Gene Kelly) in *Anchors Aweigh*. He won an Academy Award for his 1945 short film promoting wartime tolerance, *The House I Live In*, the following year. (It remained a staple of high school assemblies for decades.) He also enjoyed a string of top ten hits and was named "America's Favorite Male Singer" in *Downbeat* magazine in 1946.

Still, there were signs of slippage. In 1945 Sinatra was dropped from *Your Hit Parade*. Although he had come to hate the drudgery of hosting the radio program, he found it doubly irritating to be replaced by opera star Lawrence Tribbett.[216] He returned to the show in 1947, but by that point his output of hit singles had noticeably declined to one that year ("Mam'selle") and none in 1948. Meanwhile, a new group of singers like Frankie Laine and Johnny Ray were attracting attention that had generally been Sinatra's five years before. And while some of his movies, notably *Take Me Out to the Ball Game* (1949), another musical with Kelly, continued to perform well at the box office, most of his films in the second half of the decade were regarded as middling at best by critics and moviegoers. By the time of his Copacabana engagement in 1950, there was an established public perception that Sinatra wasn't quite the celebrity he had been during the war. Indeed, Sinatra took the gig in part because he needed the money, and the mental and physical stresses of multiple shows a night over a period of weeks was no doubt a major factor in the vocal health of a not-quite young thirty-four-year-old who simply lacked the effortless ability he exuded a decade earlier.

Sinatra's fall from grace can plausibly be attributed to shifts in public taste and a real decline in the quality of his singing (though the latter, as I plan to make clear later, is a partial explanation at best). Strictly speaking, these were both matters beyond his control. But the most important cause of his fall may well have been his own personal conduct. In part, this was a matter of comeuppance by those who had been neglected and during his rise, and who were now only too happy to see him fall. "It was pathetic," a Columbia Records engineer said of Sinatra's recording sessions at mid-century. "Sinatra would open his mouth and nothing would come out but a croak. Usually, when a singer is in bad shape, we can help him by extending his notes with an echo chamber. But Sinatra was one of the meanest men we ever worked for, so we engineers and musicians just sat on our hands and let him go down."[217]

However widespread or fair such comments may have been, they were essentially a private matter concerning Sinatra's workaday world. Far more problematic was public behavior that could be witnessed—and reported. Rumors over Sinatra's involvement in organized crime can be dated to 1947, when he visited the notorious gangster Lucky Luciano in Havana. Long fascinated by gangsters, Sinatra ate, gambled, and even posed for pictures with Luciano and fellow crime chieftains Carlo Gambino, Vito Genovese, Joe Bonanno, and others. "The curious desire to cavort among the scum is possibly permissible among citizens who are not peddling sermons to the nation's youth and may even be allowed to a mealy-mouthed celebrity if he is smart enough to confine his social tolerance to a hotel room," columnist Robert Ruark of the Scripps-Howard chain wrote after seeing Sinatra in Havana. "But Mr. Sinatra, the self-confessed savior of the country's small fry, by virtue of his lectures on clean living and love-thy-neighbor, his movie shorts on tolerance, and his frequent dabblings into the do-good department of politics, seem to be setting a most peculiar example."[218]

As the tone of such comments suggests, Sinatra wasn't especially popular in some quarters of the media, particularly by conservative writers and publishers under the control of the powerful Hearst syndicate. Few were more powerful—and more contemptuous of Sinatra—than Lee Mortimer, who taunted him mercilessly. (In fact, Sinatra had only taken the stage that painful night at the Copa in April 1950 after five previous cancellations because Mortimer had bet club owner Jack Entratter $500 he wouldn't show again.) Mortimer, who described Sinatra's fans as "imbecilic, moronic, screaming-meemie autograph kids," was also the primary source of unconfirmed reports in the dossier the FBI compiled on him. Sinatra, aware of this, threatened Mortimer with violence, and considered planting stories that he was gay. (Mortimer's FBI contact, Clyde Tolson, was rumored to be the lover of FBI Chief J. Edgar Hoover.) On April 8, 1947, Sinatra saw Mortimer at Ciro's, an exclusive Hollywood nightclub, and accosted him as he left. Calling Mortimer "a fucking homosexual," he punched him, and continued to slug away as two of Sinatra's bodyguards held the writer down. "Next time I see you, I'll kill you, you degenerate!" he allegedly said. Mortimer had Sinatra arrested, and sued him for $25,000. Sinatra claimed Mortimer had called him a "dago," but under pressure from MGM studio chief Louis B. Mayer, he retracted that allegation and settled out of court. Though he would later atone for the act by paying a visit to William Randolph Hearst himself, Sinatra would be viewed for the rest of his life as a man prone to resort to violence when he felt he was crossed, a perception that would only be augmented in barely concealed incidents that would continue to surface in the media for decades to come.[219]

But Sinatra's biggest offense against a public he had so assiduously cultivated was probably his now-legendary love affair with Ava Gardner. Sinatra had married Nancy Barbato in 1939, and she had borne him a daughter the following year, facts which figured prominently in shaping his public image as a husband and father. In truth, of course, Sinatra had never been a traditional family man, not only because a mid-century celebrity lifestyle largely foreclosed that possibility, but also because it was a more-or-less open secret that Sinatra was a notorious womanizer. (In the memorable words of Dean Martin, "When Sinatra dies, they're giving his zipper to the Smithsonian.")[220] For the most part, however, Sinatra kept his sexual activity from the prying eyes of gossip columnists.

Ava Gardner, however, was different. By most accounts, she was truly the love of his life. Moreover, the thrice-married Gardner was something of a larger-than-life figure herself who wasn't always inclined to discretion even when Sinatra was. (There's a salty edge to her 1992 autobiography that distinguishes it from the typical Hollywood memoir).[221] This isn't the place for a detailed examination of their romance, not only because its highlights—which include abortions, possible suicide attempts, gunplay, and highly public temper tantrums—have been covered in detail elsewhere, but also because there are parts of it that can never (and probably *should* never) be known to anyone but the now-dead principals. Sinatra's relationship with Gardner matters here, however, to the degree it affected the course of his career. In terms of his commercial power, that impact was largely negative. His long and highly publicized struggle to obtain a divorce from Nancy in the late 1940s, his short and stormy marriage to Gardner from 1951 to 1953, and his protracted (and also highly public) separation and divorce from Gardner from 1953 to 1955 all considerably damaged Sinatra's public image, and consolidated a view of him as a mercurial and irresponsible celebrity who simply rode roughshod over social rules most Americans felt compelled to honor. Perhaps only Ingrid Berman, whose relationship with film director Roberto Rossellini scandalized the nation at around the same time, attracted more censure than Sinatra and Gardner did.

Ironically, however, Gardner may well have been the pivotal figure in rescuing Sinatra from a future of disdainful oblivion. By the time of their marriage she had far more cultural caché than he did, thanks to her work in films like *The Snows of Kilimanjaro*, *Mogambo*, and *The Barefoot Contessa*. A celebrated beauty in a Hollywood culture that took good looks for granted, she used that power to make studio executives want to keep her happy. When Sinatra learned a movie was going to be made from James Jones's 1951 novel *From Here to Eternity*, he began lobbying hard for the part of the defiant, but doomed, Angelo Maggio. Harry Cohn, head of Columbia Studios, which was making the movie, was initially unmoved by the prospect. But Gardner played a role in bringing him around. "You know who's right for that part of Maggio, don't you?" she told Cohn after finagling a dinner invitation with him. "That son-of-a-bitch husband of mine, that's who. If you don't give him this role, he'll kill himself." Cohn reluctantly agreed to a screen test, and asked Sinatra to "call off the dogs, and Ava too."[222]

He got the part in *From Here to Eternity*, which was released with great fanfare generally (and for Sinatra specifically) in late 1953. It proved to be a turning point, not only in Hollywood (where he won an Academy Award for Best Supporting Actor in 1954), but also in the music industry, where he had been wholly absent from the charts since 1951. From the mid-1950s on, Sinatra became a man "who took up permanent residence in his success," in the evocative words of John Lahr.[223] Occasionally, one could get glimpses of the ravaged figure Sinatra had been at his nadir in films like *Young At Heart* (1954) in which he played a songwriter down on his luck, or in *The Man with the Golden Arm* (1955), in which he played a heroin addict with harrowing credibility. But for the most part, even that door would shut by the end of the 1950s, as his film work became ever more complacent, and his far more interesting music took on a more aggressively masculine edge. "When he was down and out, he was so sweet," Gardner said toward the end of their relationship. "But when he got back on top again, it was hell. Now that he's successful again, he's become his old arrogant self. We were happier when he was on the skids."[224]

Henceforth, Sinatra would play a Man in Control so effectively that it often seemed even he himself was convinced of his omnipotence. So it must have been all the more shocking when his friend Jack "Chicky Boy" Kennedy would teach him otherwise in that breezy way Sinatra himself, despite decades of trying, could never quite master.

◆   ◆   ◆

"I think he solved it—whatever he was going through—
by keeping it inside of him and filing it, putting it aside to use later
in his art."

—Sammy Davis Jr. on Sinatra's fall and later comeback[225]

The most dramatic point in the history of an American Dream isn't its moment of conception. Nor is it the moment of realization, or (as some might suppose) that moment just before it is realized. Rather, it is that essential moment of adversity when the attainability—or, perhaps even worse, the legitimacy—of the Dream is called into serious question. It's at moments like these that the true costs of dreaming begin to come into focus: of energy not allocated to other purposes, of potential disappointment that has accumulated in direct proportion to hope. It's also the same time when crucial questions—like the difference between growing up and giving up, between being persistent and merely being pathetic—become honestly confusing. You begin to find out (without really intending to ask, and without really wanting to find out) who you really are: a person of real, but limited, talent; a self-deceived poseur; someone of accomplishment whose achievements, as it turns out, are not as important as they seemed; or perhaps one happy with—and maybe even humbled by—success.

Confronted with such possibilities or realities, some will strike the tent of aspiration, wisely redirecting their energies toward the obviously attainable. Others will hold out at least a while longer, insecure with the new knowledge that stakes are now higher than ever. Some will learn from their experiences, and others will descend into mindless self-destruction (like wielding a sledgehammer against concrete). The really amazing thing, though, is the way any person seems to remain capable of both in lives that, to invoke Sinatra's contemporary Yogi Berra, are never quite over until they're over.

When Sinatra entered Columbia Recording Studios on March 27, 1951, his career had just about bottomed out. The label hadn't dropped him yet, but the writing was on the wall. This was the period in his life when he was producing his most embarrassing work—a time when, in collaboration with Columbia executive Mitch Miller, he recorded novelty songs like "The Huckle Buck" and "Mamma Will Bark" that generated ridicule perhaps most vociferously from Sinatra himself.

And yet, as those who have examined Sinatra's work closely have long noted, mid-century was also a major artistic turning point in his career. In 1951, for example, Sinatra recorded "The Birth of the Blues," a remarkable musical snapshot that captured the fluidity of his youthful voice as well as the more assertive style that would characterize his later work with Capitol and Reprise Records and more than compensate for any loss of vocal purity in the next decade. Confident yet melancholy, clearly patterned on the blues and yet bearing the stamp of his own inimitable style, "The Birth of the Blues" almost single-handedly illustrates the difference between Sinatra's commercial decline and artistic decline. Here, quite simply, is a hitless pop singer near the height of his powers.

In my mind, however, the actual summit was reached on this March night. Sinatra was reputedly miserable. His wife Nancy was refusing to give him a divorce, and a notably unsympathetic Gardner, who had a weakness for Spanish bullfighters, was making it clear to Sinatra she would not wait indefinitely to get married. Interestingly, the song scheduled for the evening's session was one—the only one, in fact—for which Sinatra claimed a songwriting credit. It was called "I'm a Fool to Want You."[226]

To borrow a term of psychoanalysts, the tone of "I'm a Fool to Want You" was "overdetermined" before he ever sang a note. Arranger Alex Stordahl opened the song with dark, almost weeping strings, a mood augmented by haunting backup vocals. When Sinatra himself enters, the emotion escalates even as the arrangement recedes; the intensity he brings to the words takes the feeling beyond heartsickness into bona fide grief. The death in question isn't that of a relationship, but rather the self-respect of a man who hates himself for what he has become. Mere words can't express this loathing: You have to hear it to believe it. Although a composer and lyricist also worked on the song (and probably were the primary writers), it seems unusually apropos for Sinatra to receive songwriting credit for "Fool." His contribution to it is utterly unmistakable.

One of the more remarkable aspects of "Fool" is that it does not simply capture a powerful inner experience. It also charts a trajectory of emotion from resistance to capitulation. At first, the singer acknowledges that indulging longing is counterproductive. But by the bridge of the song, there's a slippage between past and present, and it becomes increasingly clear its lovelorn protagonist has not gotten over the relationship. In the end, he lapses into a capitulation made all the more awful by the self-knowledge that accompanies it: "Pity me: I need you." Never before and never again would Sinatra sing with the tremulous intensity that he sings these words—especially "need"—and the song ends with an assertion that his man simply can't carry on without his lost love.

"Frank was worked up," Ben Barton, the head of his music company, later said. "So worked up he couldn't do more than one take. But that take was so tremendous it didn't need more than one."[227] Indeed, an emotionally overwrought Sinatra reputedly fled the studio that night.

It has been customary in (mostly brief) discussions of "I'm a Fool to Want You" to emphasize the obvious autobiographical dimensions of the song, as indeed I've done here. But such an approach, however valid and useful, also has the effect of obscuring the nature of Sinatra's achievement. The really striking thing about "Fool" isn't that Sinatra was able to spontaneously express his pain in song. (This underestimates the decades of applied passion and discipline that Sinatra brought to the studio that night.) Nor is it that "Fool" is an especially intelligent or insightful piece of music. (Considered solely on the basis of lyrics or music in isolation, it would undoubtedly seem both melodramatic and trite.)

Here's what's really great about the song—and, by extension, much of Sinatra's best music: a kind of emotional honesty that closes a gap between people. The protagonist of "Fool" has no lesson or advice to offer; indeed, the unresolved ending is part of what makes it so harrowing. And yet for reasons that aren't entirely clear, a powerfully rendered rendition of an inner life, even an anguished one, can bring comfort to those with whom it is shared: You are not alone. You are not alone in your feeling of deprivation, and perhaps more importantly, you are not alone in feeling foolish for wanting things you had no real right to expect, but could not help but want anyway. The best popular music makes the world a bigger place, not simply by validating common feelings (though that inevitably is what attracts most listeners), but also by illuminating an unseen community and tapping the wellsprings of empathy.

In short, Sinatra's performance in "I'm a Fool to Want You" is a profoundly creative act, one that falls more into the realm of character than personality. He took the pain of an unrealized longing and shaped it not only into an experience that could be shared, but one whose beauty transcends the pain that inheres in it. Maybe it isn't surprising that, as Sinatra grew older, he seemed to become increasingly less interested in performing such productive work. Destroying things is sometimes an easier way to deal with frustration than making things.

So we probably shouldn't blame him for wielding that sledgehammer. It's enough that some of the time, anyway, he gave us a love that's there for others too.

7

Lieutenant McCain Says No

As he has often said, John McCain has not led a perfect life. And although he survived a wartime experience that many of us would consider heroic, McCain has pointed out there have been many people who have been more heroic than he. And yet it seems fitting to make subject of the final chapter of this book a man who, perhaps more than any other living American, has embodied not only courage, but a defiance of cynicism that sustains the belief that yes, really, we can do better.

CHAPTER 7:
LIEUTENANT MCCAIN SAYS NO

*in which we see a human hero
define the meaning of courage in our time*

JOHN McCAIN THINKS American intervention in the Vietnam War was honorable, and the war should have been fought more aggressively than it was.[228]

I don't.

John McCain believes the policies of former President Ronald Reagan, the defining political figure of recent United States history, add up to a decisive change in the right direction for the country in the 1980s and beyond.[229]

I don't.

John McCain agrees with President George W. Bush that the invasion of Iraq in 2003 was justified, and continues to believe it is justified despite often-fierce resistance by some Iraqis and the evidence of false and misleading facts used to promote that invasion.[230]

I don't.

Of course, what I think isn't terribly consequential. John McCain is an important U.S. Senator, and I'm merely a high school teacher. He certainly doesn't need my approval. Nor, of course, do you.

Perhaps more interesting are some of the things John McCain has said and done that *he* disagrees with, things that he and I (and probably you) agree show, shall we say, questionable judgment:

- John McCain committed serial adultery against his wife of more than a decade, a wife who waited for him for over five years (more on this shortly) and who through great dint of effort, recovered from a crippling car accident while he was away.[231]

- John McCain accepted large sums of money from, and attended private meetings with regulators arranged to get assistance for, a corrupt business executive whose reckless behavior cost the American government $2.6 billion and helped bring about the much larger Savings and Loan scandal of the late 1980s and early 1990s, a scandal that you'll be paying for with payroll deductions from *your* wages for decades to come.[232]

- John McCain once joked that Chelsea Clinton, daughter of the president and a future colleague in the Senate, was ugly because Attorney General Janet Reno was really her father.[233]

Oh, by the way: There is no person in American politics today that I admire more than John McCain. As a liberal Democrat from New York, I'm very sorry to say I never got the chance to vote for this conservative Republican from Arizona when he ran for president in 2000. I regard this victory in the New Hampshire primary that year to be the most exciting event in my generally bland political life, a shining moment of possibility I'll always cherish. I'm reasonably confident there are many Americans of all political stripes who feel the same way.

How can that be?

The answer to this question usually begins with a prisoner of war camp in Hanoi, North Vietnam, where McCain was incarcerated between 1968 and 1973. This is indeed an important event in making him who he is today, and I mean to tell you about it. But I want to emphasize this prison ordeal *begins* to answer the question. I also want to emphasize this is a story that, as of this writing, lacks an ending, because—unlike George Washington, Ida Wells, Eugene Debs, or the other people you can read about in this book—the defiance of cynicism embodied here is ongoing.

◆   ◆   ◆

When we think of the word "elite" in American life today, it's usually imagined in terms of money: People at the top of the social order are rich, whether that money is "old" (typically generated as interest on long-term investments) or "new" (the product of entrepreneurial pluck—or good connections). Yet money has never been the sole measure of status in American life, and among the different elites in our history have been those of arts and letters, the clergy, and the military. Over time, many of these people acquired a substantial measure of comfort, but that has been a by-product of successfully pursuing vocations with long-term, generational passion.

John McCain comes from a family with a burnished military pedigree. He traces his ancestors on both parental lines back to the Scottish Presbyterian Clansmen who were persecuted by Queen Elizabeth I of England after she murdered her cousin Mary (Queen of Scots). In the following century, one branch of his family fought for Oliver Cromwell in the English Civil War; another sided with King Charles I. The latter migrated to Virginia in the aftermath of their defeat. One of his American relatives fought on the staff of General George Washington. His McCain forebears settled on a plantation in Mississippi and were slaveholders before the Civil War. They fought for the Confederacy.[234]

McCain's more immediate roots are in the U.S. Navy. His grandfather, John Sidney "Slew" McCain, was an admiral in World War II who became a naval aviator late in life and commanded ships against the Japanese from Guadalcanal to Tokyo Bay. He was on hand to witness their surrender aboard the USS *Missouri* in 1945. Slew's son, John Sidney McCain, Jr., was a submarine commander during the war who briefly reunited with his father a few hours after the surrender; the old man dropped dead of a heart attack at a welcome home party in California four days later. McCain Jr. went on to become an admiral himself and attained command of the entire Pacific fleet during the Vietnam War—the first four-star father-son succession in U.S. naval history.

So when John Sidney McCain III was born in the Panama Canal Zone in 1936, it was clear he had a legacy to live up to. And he did—the hell-raising part of it, anyway. Like his father and grandfather, McCain was a mediocre student with a chip on his soldier—his friends in high school called him "McNasty" and "a tough, mean little fucker."[235] Like both, he attended the U.S. Naval Academy in Annapolis, and like both, he continued the family's undistinguished academic tradition, graduating near the bottom of his class. The problem wasn't really his intellect exactly (McCain usually enjoyed his English and history classes in particular), but his refusal to tow the often-brutal line of hazing and hierarchy at the academy, a culture purposely designed to break the will of headstrong boys who resist becoming military men. McCain had many friends, and was notable for the degree to which he stood up to people who demanded he perform petty, demeaning tasks. But his refusal to conform to academy rules (for example, he was a legendary slob) meant he racked up demerits to a point where he came dangerously close to flunking out (the ultimate fate of his brother).

Upon graduation in 1958, McCain set his sights on becoming a naval aviator, and attained the necessary training to pilot his own plane. He quickly acquired a reputation as a daredevil, flying so low during one run over Spain that he knocked down power lines. He was forced to eject from an aircraft near Norfolk when its engine died, and survived a crash in Corpus Christi, Texas. (He was out carousing again that night.) McCain also attained notoriety as a ladies' man, dating a well-known Brazilian model; bringing an exotic dancer, the so-called "Flame of Florida" to a staid affair for married officers; and serving as the so-called "vice-commodore" of the Kay Fess Yacht Club, a kind of ongoing frat party at a Mississippi naval air base.[236]

Yet there were also some signs of seriousness as well. McCain showed increasing interest in attaining a position of command, as well as settling down, marrying a Philadelphia model named Carol Shepp and starting a family. McCain also survived at least one close call that could not be attributed to machismo. While preparing for a routine flight on the U.S. naval carrier *Forrestal* in July 1967, a missile from a nearby plane accidentally ignited, smashed into his aircraft, and sparked a gigantic fireball that left 134 men dead or missing. McCain escaped with shrapnel in his legs and chest, but he was deeply shaken by the experience, which was taped by video cameras. (The footage evokes a terrible sense of awe.)[237] McCain accepted reassignment to another carrier, yet was concerned about his future. "I may have to get out of the Navy," he told a friend at the time. He was dismayed by his reputation for recklessness—apparent, for example, when he gave his name to the majordomo of a Hawaiian resort and people in the room suddenly lifted their eyes and locked them on this well-known high roller. "If I can't get people to take me seriously," he said, "maybe I'll have to try something else."[238]

By this point the Vietnam War was at its height. American involvement could be traced back to secret advisers and technical training the United States had offered South Vietnam in its civil war with the North in the late 1950s and early 1960s. But the U.S. role had exploded into all-out war in 1964 when President Lyndon Johnson claimed American naval vessels had been fired upon in the offshore Gulf of Tonkin. Though the circumstances were murky, Johnson used the incident to justify a massive intervention in the conflict. About 500,000 American troops would ultimately serve there.

Among other things, members of the military regard war as an opporutunity, a chance to show what they can do, to make a difference, and to achieve goals (and receive promotions) that can be attained no other way. Certainly McCain saw Vietnam in this light, volunteering for bombing raids that were quick but very dangerous.[239] On October 26, 1967 he was on one such raid when his luck finally gave out. On a flight to bomb a Hanoi power plant, he bobbed and weaved to avoid Soviet-made surface-to-air (SAM) missiles when one hit his right wing and sent his plane into a death spiral at 550 miles per hour.[240]

Realizing the plane was going down, McCain pulled the ejector handle. Upon doing so, his body smashed against the plane, breaking his left arm, his right arm (in three places), and his right knee. Knocked unconscious, witnesses later said his parachute had barely opened when he landed in a lake saddled with fifty pounds of equipment. This woke him up, and he pushed against the floor of the lake to reach the surface, dazed and unclear why he couldn't move his arms to activate his life vest and thus sinking down again. He managed to open the vest with his teeth and resurfaced.

Yet drowning may have seemed more attractive to what happened next. A crowd of angry Vietnamese yelling, "Get him! Get him right away!" hauled McCain ashore using bamboo handles and began beating the American pilot who minutes before had been bombing them. A rifle butt smashed his shoulder. A bayonet entered his ankle. Another one entered his groin. Stripped naked, he was lying on the ground when a woman, possibly a nurse, fought her way to the front of the melee and applied splints to his damaged limbs. As a truck came to take McCain away, she held a cup of tea to his lips. These were the last kind gestures he would know for some time to come. The scene of his capture, recorded by photographers, would make front-page news back in the United States.

McCain was taken to the notorious prison nicknamed "the Hanoi Hilton." There he was interrogated by his captors but refused to provide any information. He begged them to take him to a hospital, but was told, "It's too late." Believing death was approaching, he drifted into an unconsciousness that he later said "blessedly relieved me of the dread I was feeling."

He was awakened by the bustle in his cell. The North Vietnamese realized their prisoner was the son of an important U.S. admiral and, as such, had propaganda value. He was hospitalized and received minimal care. The government made an English-language radio broadcast denouncing him, and a French journalist was permitted to visit McCain and videotape him, though he rejected his captors' demands he say how badly he wanted to go home.

The images from this footage, later broadcast on American television, show a gaunt, hollow shadow of a man on a hospital bed.[241] Because of dysentery, McCain often weighed less than a hundred pounds. He spent months in a dirty body cast. An operation performed on his leg a few weeks later was botched, and he lost most of the mobility in his knee. His arms were useless appendages, except to the North Vietnamese, who tied them with ropes as part of a torture technique they used from time to time. (To this day, he cannot raise them above shoulders.) He was, and in many ways would remain, a physical wreck.

The ensuing months were a blur of pain and isolation punctuated by spells of relief in which he had the company of other prisoners, who raised McCain's spirits and, in some cases, nursed his wounds. One prisoner named Norris Overly took particularly good care of McCain, who he credits with saving his life. In early 1968, Overly was released and went home.

McCain was sorry to see Overly go, but not simply because he missed his company. According to the Code of Conduct for American Fighting Men developed by the military after the Korean War, American prisoners of war were not supposed to accept release before any longer-held prisoners (by this point, there were about 300) were let go. While he felt lifelong gratitude to Overly, who left out of turn, McCain said at the time that he "wouldn't even consider any kind of release. They'll have to drag me out of here." [242]

As it turned out, McCain was wrong: He *did* consider release. By the summer of 1968, he realized his captors, believing him to be a chit they could cash in, were holding back in their cruelty toward the man they mockingly called "the Crown Prince." They were careful, for instance, when beating him to not exacerbate his old injuries. As a result, McCain was all the more fierce, cursing them every chance he got and refusing to give them any kind of satisfaction, never mind information. [243] One day that June, he was summoned for a series of meetings in which an offer of freedom was dangled before him. He said he would think about it. McCain then talked with a close friend he admired who asked him what he should do. The friend pointed out the Code of Conduct did not apply to seriously wounded men. "I don't know if you can survive this," he told McCain. "The seriously wounded can go home." McCain believed he would survive.

His friend then asked what the North Vietnamese wanted in return for his release. McCain said he didn't know—nothing had been discussed. The two agreed they sometimes demanded a statement of some kind, and neither of them wanted to McCain to gain his release at the cost of saying something dishonorable. His friend suggested, however, that he should continue conversations to see just what the North Vietnamese wanted.

Yet in discussing the matter with his friend, McCain realized such discussion could prove to be a slippery slope. Nothing might be demanded, but through a series of incremental steps he might find himself somewhere he didn't want to be. "No matter what I agree to, it won't look right," he concluded. Moreover, although he didn't know exactly what was prompting this sudden development, he suspected something fishy about it. (In fact, McCain's father had just been named commander-in-chief of the Pacific Fleet, and the North Vietnamese were looking to embarrass him by promoting an image of special treatment.) Finally, McCain felt some loyalty to his fellow prisoners, and a desire to see himself, and be seen by others, particularly his father, as honorable.

And so, in a second meeting in June 1968, McCain said no. His captors told him that President Johnson himself had ordered him home. It was a lie that McCain didn't believe. They gave him letters from his wife that had been previously withheld, letters in which she pined for his return. Still, he maintained his resolve.

A week later—July 4, 1968, the day his father's assumed command in the Pacific—McCain was again brought in to them for a third interview, and was asked one more time if he would like to be released. "My final answer is no," he said. The pen his interrogator was holding snapped, spilling ink on the *International Herald-Tribune.* "They taught you too well, Mac Kane," McCain remembers being told. "They taught you too well!" he shouted as he left the room.[244] (It sounds like a bad James Bond movie.)

There was quiet in the days following this refusal, but McCain feared there would be retribution. He was right. In August 1968, he began the darkest hour of his captivity, marked by beatings over a period of four days that were so severe that his resolve finally broke. On the third day, he tried unsuccessfully to commit suicide by hanging himself by using his shirt as a rope that he threaded through a window. Physically and emotionally shattered, he was ordered to copy the hand-written confession that was written for him. Yet, even then, he argued over the assertion he was to admit bombing a school and purposely added stilted phrases so that it would be clear his confession of being a "black criminal" and "air pirate" was forced. After he finally capitulated, he was thrown into a solitary cell for two weeks. This was the price he paid for choosing to remain a prisoner of war.[245]

McCain would remain a prisoner for another four-and-a-half years. While he and his fellow inmates would endure indescribable physical and emotional pain, the overall trend was better. His memoir from this phase of his captivity sometimes sounds like an episode of the 1960s sitcom *Hogan's Heroes*, as prisoners enacted scenes from movies, gave lectures, and made each other crude gifts. While there was surely little that was actually amusing in his life in these years, he nevertheless drew solace from his strength and particularly that of those around him. More than ever, McCain was inclined to value solidarity more than the solitude, recognizing, for the first time in his life, the limited strength of the individual.[246]

Though it was cause for much chagrin back home, McCain reacted with glee to the Nixon administration's carpet bombings of North Vietnam during peace negotiations in late 1972. While they endangered his life, McCain believed they would hasten the end of the war. He may well have been right. In any case, he gained his release on his terms, in the order in which he was captured, in March 1973. The Vietnam War—John McCain's war—was over.

New fights beckoned.

◆   ◆   ◆

John McCain returned from Vietnam determined to get his life back, and went about it in a way that reflected his fierce intensity before his capture and the forged discipline he acquired because of it. With the help of a talented physical therapist, he regained much of the mobility in his damaged knee, and much of his strength generally—so much so that was able to able to meet the stressful physical challenges of flying an airplane again. He returned to his wife, who had kept their family together in his absence, even amid a devastating automobile accident, and bought a beachfront house. Carol McCain said at the time she thought "we would live happily ever after."[247]

Not quite. In some ways, it would be more surprising if McCain simply did resume his former life after the kind of ordeal he had survived. Many people had considerably more difficulty amid even less adversity. There were two evident signs that things had changed. The first was the collapse of his marriage, which ended in divorce in 1980. (He has since remarried and had more children). The second was his departure from the Navy. Notwithstanding his comeback as a naval aviator—he was promoted to captain—McCain quickly concluded he wasn't really fit for the service anymore, and unlikely to attain anywhere near the level of his forebears. He wore his uniform for the final time at his father's funeral in 1981. Now it was time for a new career: politics.

In some ways, this was a logical evolution. McCain's father had been a naval liaison to Congress, a job that had traditionally been ceremonial. Much of it involved arranging travel and serving as an escort for traveling legislators, but McCain II had turned into a post of considerable influence. McCain III would resume that tradition by making his final tour of duty as the Navy's emissary to the Senate. In this capacity, he befriended a number of senators, notably John Tower, Gary Hart, and Bill Cohen—a conservative Republican, a liberal Democrat, and a Republican who eventually served as Secretary of Defense in the Clinton administration. McCain also felt a considerable affinity with conservative Democrat Henry "Scoop" Jackson.[248] Such ties suggest McCain's broad popularity. He was a much a much sought-after traveling companion, attractive not only because of his heroic stature, but also his sense of humor. (He once joked after attending a Chinese opera that it was "the most fun I've had since my last interrogation.")[249] When he remarried in 1980, Cohen was his best man, and Hart was an usher. Even in an age when collegiality across the aisle was more common than it became later, McCain—befriended by California governor Ronald Reagan, whom he considered his political mentor as early as 1973—was notable for his ability to make and keep friends.

McCain decided to take the electoral plunge himself in 1982. His wife Cindy's family was from Arizona, and he settled there. His father-in-law, a wealthy beer distributor, gave him a high-profile public relations job that allowed him to circulate around the state. When census redistricting created a new seat in the House of Representatives, McCain worked aggressively to secure the Republican nomination—perhaps a bit *too* aggressively. When one of his competitors called his ex-wife seeking dirt on him (she refused to play along), McCain approached him and told him, "Politics aside, you ever do anything like that again against a person in my family, and I'll beat the shit out of you." McCain was similarly frank about those critics who claimed he was a carpetbagger simply using Arizona as a perch from which to fly into Congress. Irritated by such a charge during a debate during the campaign, he replied, "I wish I could have had the luxury, like you, of growing up and living and spending my life in a nice place like the first district of Arizona, but I was doing other things. As I matter of fact, when I think about it now, the place I lived longest in my life was Hanoi."[250]

McCain won that race handily. And four years later, upon the retirement of one of the Senate's old lions, Barry Goldwater, he made the leap from the House to the Senate. Yet McCain encountered considerable turbulence shortly after taking office in a scandal that he called "the absolute worst thing that ever happened to me"[251]—no small statement coming from a man of his experiences.

It all began with a social relationship with a man named Charles Keating. McCain's capacity for making friends did not always include close scrutiny of their character. One of his early pals in Arizona, for example, was a newspaper publisher who fabricated a war background that McCain never questioned.[252] Keating, one of the largest homebuilders in Arizona, appealed to McCain because of his fun-loving generosity, which extended to vacations in the Bahamas and well over $100,000 in campaign contributions to his House and Senate races. Keating's company, American Continental Corporation, acquired a small financial institution, Lincoln Savings and Loan of Irvine, California, in 1984. Such savings and loan companies were known as "thrifts," functioning as small banks that made loans to individuals with relatively modest returns. (Jimmy Stewart's character ran one in the classic 1946 movie *It's a Wonderful Life*, enabling people like Italian immigrants to buy their first homes.) A series of rule changes in the 1980s simultaneously allowed such thrifts to make riskier investments while simultaneously providing government backing of depositors' money. People like

Keating exploited this situation, behaving recklessly because they knew the government would cover their losses. And those losses proved colossal.

Senator John McCain felt loyalty to Keating, but he wasn't willing to help him simply fleece the government. Indeed, McCain made a reputation for himself as a prominent critic of wasteful spending. But because Keating's business interests employed a lot of people in Arizona, he attended two private meetings with federal bank regulators along with four other senators—the so-called Keating Five—a decision that at least created the appearance of impropriety. An intensive investigation followed, and McCain was cleared of any crime other than poor judgment. "I still wince thinking about it," McCain later wrote. "I had lost something very important, something that was sacrificed in the pursuit of gratifying ambitions, my own and others', that I might never again possess again as assuredly as I had once had."[253]

To at least some degree, that fear proved exaggerated. McCain was reelected to that seat in 1992, and again in 1998, and yet again in 2004. In the process, he became something of an old lion himself.

A question arises, however: How much does this matter? John McCain is neither the first nor the last war hero to ride his exploits into politics—nor the first or last elected official to survive a political scandal. We can respect such people, whether or not we agree with their views. But has John McCain really made a difference? Has he been truly admirable? My answer is yes.

I'll try to give you three specific reasons why. The first is that McCain has time and again demonstrated he is a man of conviction, someone who says—and acts—on what he professes, even when it means displeasing his friends. One good example of this was his stance toward the Reagan administration's use of Marines in Lebanon, with a largely American fleet offshore, in 1982. Divided by factions and caught between Syria and Israel, Lebanon was essentially a failed state, and the American military was serving as a buffer between warring parties. But when the Reagan administration sought a war powers measure that would allow the president to keep troops there for another eighteen months, McCain balked. He felt the nation had failed to clarify the basis of its presence there, and that American troops were sitting ducks. The freshman congressman (and former military man) thus rejected the wishes of his powerful patron and voted against his commander-in-chief. Less than a month later a powerful bomb exploded near Marine barracks in Beirut, killing 241 Americans and forty-one French soldiers. Soon thereafter, Congress cut off money for the deployment and the administration brought the troops home. McCain's stance had been prescient.[254]

As McCain himself noted, he didn't pay much of a personal or political cost for this vote. But time and again he has bucked powerful interests—and powerful allies—in causes that ranged from holding tobacco companies accountable for promoting deadly behavior to (unsuccessfully) proposing the abolition of special parking privileges for U.S. Senators at Reagan National Airport.[255] The former pilot argued strenuously against a sweetheart deal for the aviation industry. This user of firearms has spoken out passionately against the excesses of the gun lobby. McCain has also been a vocal opponent of the concentration of corporate power in the media. Unlike Republicans who talk about the importance of limited government but then embrace a range of pork barrel handouts for their states and their friends, McCain embraces the entrepreneurial capitalism of Abraham Lincoln and Theodore Roosevelt rather than the crony capitalism of Ronald Reagan and the Bush family.

Yet for all his iconoclasm, McCain is also distinctive in another way that has already been noted and worth saying more about: the expansiveness of his relationships. Liberal Democrats and conservative Republicans alike find him to be honorable as well as likable. This fusion of the personal and political has won him many friends, people who reached out to him and people who, in turn, to whom he expressed his gratitude. One of the most striking examples of this was McCain's relationship with the powerful House member Morris Udall, a former NBA basketball player and giant in Arizona politics when McCain was elected to the House in 1982. Udall, a classic liberal and unsuccessful presidential candidate, took McCain under his wing in the early 1980s, and influenced his thinking about environmentalism and government policy toward Native Americans. Udall was later stricken with Parkinson's disease, and lived out his final days, largely alone, in a hospital room before his death in 1998. One of his few regular visitors was John McCain, who would bring along newspaper clippings about local politics and other subjects and read them to the mute figure in bed with his eyes closed.[256]

McCain's sense of camaraderie isn't limited to his peers. As the veteran *New Yorker* reporter Elizabeth Drew has noted, most senators situate themselves hierarchically in their offices. McCain runs a notably egalitarian ship. His staff refers to him as "John," and his office sits in the middle of the action rather as part of an inner sanctum. Perhaps most importantly of all, there is little staff turnover in jobs notorious for burnout.[257] One of his aides, Mark Salter, has been with him since 1989 and served as his cowriter on each of his three books.

It's one thing to be a principled man. It's another to be a nice one (though McCain reputedly has a temper). But perhaps the most important question from a political standpoint is: Can you get something done? In McCain's case, it's a little too early to say. What is clear is that he has one other quality worth noting here—persistence—that has allowed him to accomplish things that some have said could not be done.

Exhibit A in this regard is campaign finance reform. In the aftermath of Richard Nixon's resignation from the presidency in the Watergate scandal in 1974, Congress passed a series of laws designed to limit the role of money in politics. Yet as is so often the case, the cure lawmakers imposed created its own problems. (This is one reason why Conservatives are skeptical of government power in the first place.) After large direct contributions to candidates became illegal, politicians began to cultivate relationships with political action committees (PACs) that bundled and funneled cash to candidates. The former process was known as hard money; the latter was called soft money. Soft money, it was believed, was less corrupt.[258]

For a time, perhaps, it was. But by the 1990s both political parties were engorged with soft money, and incumbents in particular used it to stay in power. At the same time, however, those very incumbents had to spend more and more of their time doing fund-raising instead of governing, and even some of them felt the process had become oppressive. More importantly, special interest groups were commanding more and more of candidates' attention—it's an open secret of politics that no one gives money to politicians without wanting something in return. In the mid-1990s, President Bill Clinton reigned without peer in generating cash—with the possible exception of the money machine engineered by House Speaker Newt Gingrich.

John McCain wanted to change all that. Shortly after the congressional elections of 1994, he reached out to someone who felt similarly, freshman Senator Russell Feingold of Wisconsin. (McCain has said he has tried to mentor Feingold the way Udall mentored him.)[259] The two drafted a bill, known as McCain-Feingold, to limit the power of soft money in politics. Year after year, McCain-Feingold was debated and voted on in the Senate. And, year after year it was shot down. Yeah, it's a nice idea, they were told, but it would never work: We need to catch up to the other side. Or: The other side wouldn't respect it. Or: There's nothing wrong with the system—we need *more* money in politics. (This was the position of McCain-Feingold's principal antagonist, Republican Senator Mitch McConnell of Kentucky.)

But McCain wouldn't let the subject drop. And Feingold went a step further, running for reelection in 1998 without accepting soft money advertising—and barely surviving the contest. (He did so more easily in 2004.)[260] Through a concerted strategy of wheedling, buttonholing, shame and praise, McCain finally got their bill through the Senate in 2002. A similar bill was passed by the House and a compromise measure was reached, reluctantly signed by President George W. Bush, who like many politicians, supported it out of fear of looking bad in the eyes of voters for rejecting such an obviously appealing reform. Though hard money limits are now higher, soft money is more tightly regulated, and candidates are required to give their explicit approval for any ads that run on their behalf, among other provisions. There are doubts these campaign finance reforms will ever work; the 527 committees (named after a provision in the tax code) that formed in response may let even more money in through a different door. But McCain himself always viewed the law as a beginning—one that would work a whole lot better if the corrupt Federal Elections Commission actually did its job. He continues to work on this issue.

As a politician, however, McCain's truly shining hour came in 1999–2000 when he made the decision to run for the Republican presidential nomination. He dubbed his candidacy the "Straight Talk Express," and toured the country in a bus, talking endlessly with reporters and citizens who were used to highly screened, prepackaged candidates who stringently limited contact with the outside world. Voters of all political persuasions were excited, even moved, by this singularly authentic man whose love of country—and love of the political process itself—was so emphatically evident. The McCain tide crested in New Hampshire in February 2000, when he won a surprise victory over George W. Bush, the well-financed favorite of party regulars and son of a former president. For a moment, it looked like McCain was going to liberate the nation from venality and cynicism. I remember jumping up and down in my living room, watching a smiling McCain before a podium and thanking his supporters. It seemed like there was an opening here of the kind Abraham Lincoln or (McCain's hero) Theodore Roosevelt[261] squeaked through when they became president despite entrenched opposition.

The gates slammed shut later that month in South Carolina. The Bush forces rallied and poured immense sums of money into the state, using it, among other ways, for a sustained campaign of telephone innuendo. Calls to voters raised questions, for instance, about the Asian child McCain had adopted. Was she parented out of wedlock by McCain and a prostitute? (The answer is no. His wife had brought the orphan back from a humanitarian trip abroad and made her their own.) Such strategies proved regrettably effective, and McCain's dream died in the heart of the old Confederacy. By his own admission, McCain made a misstep himself on the stump in South Carolina, fudging his own opposition to the state's use of the Confederate flag out of a desire not to lose votes.[262] Though he managed a win in blue-collar Michigan, he was out of the race by early March.

Nowadays, McCain seems to be all over cable television, sought for his views on any matter of subjects. He was repeatedly offered, and rejected, the vice-presidential slot on Democrat John Kerry's ticket for the presidency in 2004. (Many wish he would embrace one important aspect of Theodore Roosevelt's legacy—his decision to leave the Republican Party in 1912 and strike out on his own.) Alas, John McCain doesn't always do what we want him to. He supported President Bush for reelection in 2004, but he resumed his criticism of the administration's environmental and war policies immediately after the election. Yet such surprising stances sometimes seem like a kind of integrity. In a country where even beginners are justifiably cynical, he seems both deeply human and deeply admirable at the same time. This former prisoner of war seems to understand the meaning of freedom, which appears to involve an independent mind that chooses to commit, rather than a conformist mind that seeks to avoid commitment. His bravery enlarges the world of possibility, and makes us want—even as we fear—comparable challenges.

These are some of the reasons why he's a hero of mine.

Who's one of yours?

Conclusion:
Feeling Better

In the introductory essay of this book, I asserted the point of studying history is to find sources of hope. But, you may plausibly ask, hope for what? That we will see world peace in our time? That the United States will close the gap between its often-soaring ideals and its often-tawdry realities? That you'll vanquish the anxieties that gnaw away at you each day, anxieties that are all the worse because you know they're often really silly, even unworthy of you? (And that there are some that aren't silly at all?)

I know you're going to be absolutely crushed when I tell you the answer is no. But I'm also going to tell you that history can really help you feel better.

What, you may wonder, do I mean by "feel better?" Am I saying that history has therapeutic value, that you can study it for some of the same reasons people eat chocolate or read romance novels or get psychotherapy? Yeah, to at least some degree, I'm. Like many things, history is a taste you can acquire to fill time, keep demons at bay, or build social bridges. Like many things too, you can do it at a pretty basic functional level—most people don't need to be experts about real estate, fashion, or baseball to engage with them pleasurably and profitably—or you can savor the experience of developing a more refined palate. We all know people that get excited by wines or stock car racing or cinematography in ways we find utterly mysterious.

But without insisting it's true for everyone all the time, I'd like to suggest a passion for history may well pay more satisfying psychic dividends than any of these alternatives. I believe the lessons you can learn from history have broad applications that can enrich your understanding of everyday life. They can help you understand the people around you ("What I have to remember about Grandpa is that he was born during the Great Depression"); give you an escape from the people around you ("There was a time not long ago when even the people of this town thought differently about this situation"); and help you conceptualize your life in compelling ways ("Maybe I should take a page from Grandpa's book, save some money, and get the hell out of this town").

Principally, I think that what history can do is enlarge your world. By that I mean it can broaden your notion of what is "realistic," your sense of the humanly possible. I myself have a hard time believing I can overestimate the evil that's humanly possible, but I think I may sometimes underestimate the good that people can do. One of the reasons why I wanted to tell you about the people featured at this book is that the process of learning about them has led me see them as fallible, even frail people—and that their very fallibility makes their unmistakable accomplishments all the more impressive. And all the more real. I'm not sure I could stop a conspiracy, endure a prisoner of war camp, or even convert my private anguish into public art. But maybe I can do good things too—not great or grand things, necessarily, but worthwhile ones. God help me: I'd like to think this little volume might qualify.

Which brings us to another meaning of "feel better," that is, to be better at feeling, to develop a sympathetic imagination. Reading about admirable figures will probably not, in itself, make you a better person. But it may engender habits of thought that nurture a desire to do good things. Back in the 1990s, the sportswear company Nike promoted its products using NBA star Michael Jordan as its pitchman. "Be Like Mike," was the company's slogan. I've got nothing against Michael Jordan—he's always struck me as a sane, generally reputable citizen—but I've never felt much desire to be like him. But I think there's something to an admonition to "Be Like Harriet" or "Be Like Ida." In some sense, that's really what the various chapters of this book have been all about.

Look, I'm not going to tell you that you need to go forth and love history. Love doesn't work like that: You can't command people to be passionate. Nor am I going to tell you that many of the things you can get from history are unique to history. Literature, for example, can enlarge your world as surely as history can (so might hip-hop or ice-skating—my vision here is ecumenical, not sectarian.) In the end, I can only offer you my own testimony, which takes the form of a book I felt compelled to write for really no other reason that an innate desire to do so. You'll do with my example what you wish. *My* wish is that you'll indeed *do* something with it, if in no other way than to *make* sense of it in your own way.

Thanks for the privilege of your attention.

J.C.

Endnotes

1. Robert Middlekauff, *The Glorious Cause: The American Revolution, 1763-1789* (New York: Oxford University Press, 1982), 510; Richard H. Kohn, "The Inside History of the Newburgh Conspiracy: America and the Coup d'Etat," *William and Mary Quarterly* 27:2 (April 1970): 189 (henceforth Kohn). Kohn also discusses the Newburgh Conspiracy in Eagle and Sword: The *Beginnings of the American Military Establishment* (1975; New York: Free Press, 1985).

2. Kohn, 197.

3. Kohn, 203.

4. Kohn, 205–207; James Thomas Flexner, *George Washington in the Revolution, 1775-1783* (Boston: Little, Brown, 1968) 503–504. This is the second in a four-volume biography Flexner published between 1965 and 1972. A one-volume condensed edition, *The Indispensable Man*, was published in 1974.

5. For more on this point, see Bernard Bailyn's chapter on this subject in *To Begin the World Anew: The Genius and Ambiguities of the American Founders* (New York: Knopf, 2003), 3-36.

6. Flexner, *The Indispensable Man*, 54.

7. One important exception was the Quakers. But their relatively brash political approach to abolition, combined with their pacifism during the Revolution, made them an unattractive model for Washington.

8. Flexner, *The Indispensable Man*, 386; GW to Brian Fairfax, 158.

9. Richard Brookhiser, *Founding Father: Rediscovering George Washington* (New York: The Free Press, 1996), 182; Washington to Tobias Lear, in *George Washington: Writings*, ed. John Rhodehamel (New York: Library of America, 1997), 868. The tensions within Washington's family over his opposition to slavery is discussed at length in Henry Wiencek's well-researched and elegantly written study, *An Imperfect God: George Washing-*

ton, His Slaves and the Creation of America (New York: Farrar, Straus, and Giroux, 2003).

10. Flexner, *Indispensable Man*, 390; Brookhiser, 183. The will provided for the slaves to remain in bondage until his wife's death, but Martha Washington freed them a year after her husband's death. Washington also provided pensions for his slaves; the last payment was made in 1833. Not surprisingly, some of Washington's slaves regarded freedom as more attractive than even the mildest form of slavery, and he, like other slave owners, faced the problem of runaways. Yet the only effort he ever made to recover one involved a girl whose flight hurt his wife's feelings—a naïve perspective on the part of the Washingtons, though not exactly a crassly materialistic or especially vindictive one. See Flexner, 390–394.

11. For a detailed account of the Conway Cabal, see Flexner, *GW in the Revolution*, 241–280.

12. John C. Miller, *Alexander Hamilton: Portrait in Paradox* (New York: Harper & Brothers, 1959), 71–75. For Hamilton's version, see his letters to his father-in-law, Philip Schuyler, and James McHenry, in *Hamilton: Writings*, ed. Joanne B. Freeman (New York: Library of America, 2001) 93–97.

13. Flexner, *GW in the Revolution*, 491–492; Nicola to GW, in *GW Writings*, 1106; GW to Nicola, in *GW Writings*, 468–469.

14. GW to Benjamin Lincoln, in *GW Writings*, 472.

15. GW to James McHenry, in *GW Writings*, 476.

16. GW to Joseph Jones, in *GW Writings*, 479.

17. Flexner, *GW in the Revolution*, 501.

18. AH to GW, in *Hamilton: Writings*, 121–122.

19. GW to AH, in *GW Writings*, 489.

20. Washington, "General Orders" (March 11, 1783), in *GW Writings*, 490.

21. GW to Boudinot, 495–496; GW to Jones, 493–95.

22. Hamilton replied almost immediately upon receipt of the letter in a postscript updating him on the situation in Congress. "Your Excellency mentions that it has been surmised the plan of agitation was formed in Philadelphia," he notes, admitting he was among those pressing hard for

action. But, he asserted, "I have expressed the same sentiments out of doors" (*Writings*, 125). The concept of "plausible deniability," coined in the 1980s amid some nefarious military activity by the Reagan presidency, was clearly in practice 200 years earlier.

23. GW to AH, in *GW Writings*, 491–492.

24. Kohn believes Gates was deeply involved in the Newburgh Conspiracy, though this has been contested. For one such view, See Paul David Nelson, "Horatio Gates at Newburgh: A Misunderstood Role," *William and Mary Quarterly* 29:1 (January 1972), 143–158.

25. Kohn, 208–209.

26. Widely reputed to be Gates's aide, John Armstrong, Jr.

27. GW, "Speech to the Officers of the Army," in *GW Writings*, 496–499.

28. Kohn, 210; Flexner, *GW in the Revolution*, 507.

29. Kohn, 210–211.

30. See, for example, John Ferling's treatment in *The First of Men: A Life of George Washington* (Knoxville: University of Tennessee Press, 1988), 309–312. With a bit more emphasis, a puckish Joseph Ellis calls the Newburgh Conspiracy, "the last temptation of Washington" in *His Excellency: George Washington* (New York: Knopf, 2004), 141. Richard Brookhiser gives the affair all of a paragraph in his *Alexander Hamilton, American* (New York: The Free Press, 1999), perhaps because it puts this man he regards as a hero in a good deal less than a heroic light. Ron Chernow also tends to downplay any questions of treachery in his magisterial biography *Alexander Hamilton* (New York: The Penguin Press, 2004), 183–186. As far as I could tell, the subject was entirely avoided in the ambitious Hamilton exhibition that ran at the New York Historical Society in 2004–05, perhaps because Brookhiser was one of the exhibition's advisers.

31. Middlekauff, 582.

32. Kohn, 217–219.

33. Paul Nagel, *John Quincy Adams: A Public Life, a Private Life* (1997; Cambridge: Harvard University Press, 1999), 13.

34. *The Diary of John Quincy Adams, 1795-1845*, ed. Allan Nevins (New York: Longmans, Greens & Co, 1929), 157 (Feb. 7, 1815), 133 (Sept. 8, 1814); Robert Remini, *John Quincy Adams* (New York: Times Books,

2002), 45. The Nevins' edition is a one-volume abridgment of the twelve-volume set, itself abridged, edited by JQA's son, Charles Francis Adams (himself a distinguished diplomat and U.S. ambassador to England during the Civil War). The Remini book is part of a fine series of short biographies on the presidents edited by Arthur Schlesinger, Jr.

35. In those days, senators were chosen by state legislators, not voters, a procedure that wasn't changed until the Seventeenth Amendment to the Constitution in 1913.

36. John F. Kennedy, *Profiles in Courage* (1955; New York: Harper & Row, 1964), 27–54. Although I, like many observers then and since, regard the embargo as a stupid move on the part of the Jefferson administration, I don't doubt his or JQA's integrity in supporting it. Yet, in writing this book, the embargo issue does not speak to me with the same urgency as it apparently did to John F. Kennedy. The episode I'm choosing to focus on, by contrast, involves race relations. This was a topic Kennedy did his best to avoid for as long as possible while senator and president (for some very understandable political, if not necessarily moral, reasons). Among other things, our respective choices reveal something of the way generational politics shape what we find interesting and important.

37. *Diary of JQA* (May 8, 1824), 322–323.

38. The Democrats were the party of smaller government until the 1930s when the administration of Franklin Delano Roosevelt assertively used the federal government to fight the Great Depression. Ever since, the Democrats have been the party of a strong central authority and Republicans the champions of local control (except in matters of national security, which increasingly seems to justify a federal presence in just about everything except welfare programs).

39. Remini has a nice, short gloss on the tariff in John Quincy Adams, 109–116. Oddly, Nagel doesn't even mention this standard episode his otherwise graceful and deeply researched biography of JQA.

40. Adams was one of the principal figures, amid much congressional opposition, who steered the $500,000 bequest of James Smithson into the founding of a national museum: The Smithsonian Institution.

41. *Diary of JQA* (June 18, 1833), 439.

42. The Bank was re-created in modified form as the Federal Reserve in 1913.

43. Joseph Ellis, *Founding Brothers: The Revolutionary Generation* (New York: Vintage, 2000), 81–119.

44. Hammond quoted in William Lee Miller, *Arguing About Slavery: John Quincy Adams and the Great Battle in the United States Congress* (1995; New York: Vintage, 1998), 39. This magisterial work by a magisterial historian (actually, he was trained as an ethicist) is a crucial source in the discussion that follows. For more on Hammond's role as a proslavery theorist, see Drew Gilpin Faust, *A Sacred Circle: The Dilemma of the Intellectual in the Old South* (1977; Philadelphia: University of Pennsylvania Press, 1986).

45. Hammond quoted in Miller, 134.

46. More militant Southerners, such as Senator Calhoun, a major influence on Hammond, wanted the resolution to assert that it would be *unconstitutional* to end slavery in the District. See Miller, 144.

47. Miller, 144–49; Miller, 515.

48. For a brief overview of JQA's attitudes toward slavery, see George Lipsky's chapter on the subject in *John Quincy Adams: His Theory and Ideas* (New York: Thomas Y. Crowell Company, 1950), 120–127.

49. Robert Remini, for example, describes JQA as having "shown little concern about slavery during his early career, and although he had no love of the institution, he in no way condemned it" (137). Yet, as William Lee Miller has observed of his presidency, "the latent issue of slavery ran silently—usually silently—underneath everything about it." Miller notes that JQA's advocacy of a strong national government "would have enlarged federal powers in a way that might one day threaten slavery" and that his policy toward Indians "implied a dangerous touch of humanity that might apply to blacks as well" (175). The argument here, as you can probably tell, hews closer to that of Miller, though these views don't necessarily contradict each other.

50. *The Book of Abigail and John: Selected Letters of the Adams Family, 1762-1784*, ed. L.H. Butterfield (Cambridge: Harvard University Press, 1975), 120.

51. Samuel Flagg Bemis, *John Quincy Adams and the Foundations of American Foreign Policy* (New York: Knopf, 1949), 122–123; Worthington

Chauncy Ford, "John Quincy Adams," *Dictionary of American Biography* (1928; Macmillan Reference Library CD-ROM).

52. *Diary of JQA* (Feb. 24, 1820), 228–229.

53. Adams quoted in Miller, 198, 203.

54. Miller, 206–209.

55. Miller, 142–149.

56. Miller, 225–230.

57. Miller, 230–236.

58. Miller, 349, 364–365.

59. Miller, 318–320, 268, 420. The subsequent account draws heavily, though not exclusively, from Miller, 429–444.

60. Miller, 444–446.

61. *Diary of JQA* (March 29, 1841), 519.

62. The circumstances surrounding the start of the Mexican War, like those of this (related) story, are quite complex. Suffice it to say, the President of the United States (our friend James K. Polk) made a dubious claim that American forces were attacked in a border dispute and used it as a justification for war. By a large majority, most of Congress went along with him.

63. *Diary of JQA* (Feb. 11, 1820), 226.

64. Andrea A. Lunsford and John J. Ruszkiewicz, *Everything's an Argument* (Boston: Bedford/St. Martin's, 1999).

65. Harriet Beecher Stowe, *Uncle Tom's Cabin, or Life Among the Lowly* (1852; New York: Bantam Books, 1981), xviii. (Henceforth *UTC.*)

66. Thomas Gossett, *Uncle Tom's Cabin and American Culture* (Dallas: Southern Methodist University Press, 1985), 4.

67. Joan D. Hedrick, *Harriet Beecher Stowe: A Life* (New York: Oxford University Press, 1994), 25–27; Forrest Wilson, *Crusader in Crinoline: The Life of Harriet Beecher Stowe* (Philadelphia: J. B. Lippincott & Co., 1941), 61.

68. Hedrick, 32–40. Hedrick's biography, a superb piece of scholarship, is notably good on the culture of girls' education in the early nineteenth century.

69. Hedrick, viii.

70. A long excerpt of Stowe's piece is included in Wilson, 184–185.

71. Hedrick discusses the story on pp. 171–172.

72. Wilson, 193–194.

73. *The Life of Harriet Beecher Stowe, Compiled from Her Letters and Journals, by Her Son, Charles Edward Stowe* (Boston: Houghton Mifflin, 1896), 144; Lyde Cullen Sizer, *The Political Work of Northern Women Writers and the Civil War, 1850-1872* (Chapel Hill: University of North Carolina Press, 2000), 20.

74. Stowe quoted in Hedrick, 193.

75. One such story became the basis of Nobel-prize winning laureate Toni Morrison's 1987 novel, *Beloved.*

76. For more on the story as an antecedent for *Uncle Tom's Cabin,* see Gossett, 88–89.

77. *The Life of Harriet Beecher Stowe,* 144; Gossett, 91.

78. For one such version of many, all based on C.E. Stowe's *Life of Harriet Beecher Stowe,* see Sizer, 55.

79. Hedrick records an incident in which Stowe and the husband of a friend had an extended argument in which Stowe repeatedly asked the man, who was mildly antislavery, what he would do if a fugitive slave showed up at his door. He prevaricated. The very next day, this happened, and the man gave the slave money, his wife gave him provisions, and the two sent him on the way to Canada—a felony under U.S. law. As Stowe later wrote to her sister, such stories show that for many Northerners, "Their hearts are better on this point than their heads." (205–206). She includes a similar line of reasoning in her novel when Senator John Bird's wife replies to his own prevarications by saying, "O, nonsense, John! You can talk all night, but you wouldn't do it. I put it do you, John,—would *you* now turn away a poor hungry creature because he was a runaway? *Would* you, now?" (He will not.)

80. Jefferson Davis, excerpt from message to the Confederate Congress (April 29, 1861), in *The Causes of the Civil War*, 3rd revised edition ed. Kenneth Stampp (1959; New York: Touchstone, 1991), 154.

81. In her next novel, *Dred* (1856), Stowe would push the envelope still further in her title character, a Southern nightmare—the bloodthirsty slave.

82. *UTC*, 15. While writing the book, Stowe wrote Douglass for information about life on a plantation (see Hedrick, 218) and consulted burgeoning literature of slave narratives that began appearing in large numbers in the 1840s and 1850s.

83. *UTC*, 48.

84. *UTC*, 127.

85. Flannery O'Connor, author's note to the second edition of *Wise Blood* (1952; New York: The Noonday Press, 1962), n.p.

86. *UTC*, 181.

87. *UTC*, 312.

88. Charleston customs collector quoted in James McPherson, *Battle Cry of Freedom: The Civil War Era* (New York: Oxford University Press, 1988), 99; Muscogee, *Georgia Herald* excerpt in Stampp, 210.

89. *UTC*, 92–93; *UTC*, 304–305.

90. *UTC*, 33.

91. *UTC*, 338.

92. *UTC*, 64.

93. Gossett, 146; *Mary Chesnut's Civil War*, ed. C. Vann Woodward (New Haven: Yale University Press, 1981), 168.

94. *UTC*, 338–339.

95. *UTC*, 30.

96. *UTC*, 77, 13.

97. *UTC*, 181, 313.

98. *UTC*, 230–231, 267.

99. *UTC*, 440.

100. *UTC*, xvii.

101. Gossett, 365.

102. David Reynolds makes this point by contrasting Stowe with more psychologically complex writers such as Herman Melville or Nathaniel Hawthorne in *Beneath the American Renaissance: The Subversive Imagination in the Age of Emerson and Melville* (Cambridge: Harvard University Press, 1988), 77. The fact that neither Hawthorne nor Melville—nor, for that matter, Thoreau of Whitman—ever mentioned the *Uncle Tom's Cabin* (see Gossett, 166) strikes me as a failure of imagination on *their* own part, however. How could these writers have nothing to say about what was arguably the most important book of their time?

103. Ibid.

104. Much of the letter is reproduced in Wilson, 259–260.

105. Gossett, 164–165, 239; *Edmund Wilson, Patriotic Gore: Studies in the Literature of the American Civil War* (1962; London: The Hogarth Press, 1987), 3.

106. Gossett, 190. For a collection of some of the most important reviews of the novel at the time of its publication as well as some influential subsequent reappraisals, see Elizabeth Ammons, *Critical Esssays on Harriet Beecher Stowe* (Boston: G.K. Hall, 1980).

107. For a survey, see Gossett's chapter on Anti-Tom literature in *Uncle Tom's Cabin and American Culture*. He includes a bibliography of such novels on p. 430.

108. Baldwin's essay is included in Ammons, 92–97; the quote appears on p. 94. The piece was originally published in *Partisan Review* in June 1949. In *Uncle Tom's Cabin and American Culture*, Gossett argues that Baldwin is too severe with Stowe on this and other points. "How many characters of any race in nineteenth-century American literature are adequately portrayed in terms of their sexual nature?" he asks.

109. Wilson, *Patriotic Gore*, 3, 6, 35.

110. Gerald Early, "*The Color Purple* as Everybody's Protest Art," in *Tuxedo Junction: Essays on American Culture* (New York: Ecco Press, 1989), 44. Hughes's more appreciative remarks, originally published as an introduction to a 1952 edition of the novel, can be found in Ammons (102, 104).

111. For more on *Gone with the Wind* as a refutation of *Uncle Tom's Cabin*, see Leslie Fiedler, *What Was Literature? Class Culture and Mass Society* (New York: Touchstone, 1984); see also the chapter *GWTW* in Jim Cullen, *The Civil War in Popular Culture: A Reusable Past* (Washington DC: Smithsonian Institution Press, 1995), 65–107.

112. The facts surrounding this event have been widely discussed in the literature surrounding the life and work of Ida B. Wells-Barnett. The principal primary account relied upon in the discussion that follows is *Crusade for Justice: The Autobiography of Ida B. Wells*, ed. Alfreda Dunster (Chicago: University of Chicago Press, 1970), 47–59. Among other sources, I have also drawn on Linda O. McMurry, *To Keep the Waters Troubled: The Life of Ida B. Wells* (New York: Oxford University Press, 1998), 130–137 ff, which draws on contemporary newspaper accounts of the incident.

113. This quotation, which may well be the most incendiary piece of journalism published in the second-half of the nineteenth century, is widely cited in all literature about Wells. It is most easily accessed and contextualized in her pamphlet *Southern Horrors: Lynch Law in All Its Phases*, included in *Southern Horrors and Other Writings: The Anti-Lynching Campaign of Ida B. Wells, 1892-1900*, ed. Jacqueline Jones Royster (Boston: Bedford Books, 1996), 52. This book, part of the Bedford Series in History and Culture, is the best single-volume introduction to Wells' work.

114. *Commercial* editorial quoted in McMurry, 147. Wells herself quotes the *Evening Scimitar* and the destruction of the *Free Speech* in *Southern Horrors*, 52.

115. Wells' autobiography presents her departure as unrelated to the editorial, as she was engaged to attend an African Methodist Episcopal conference in Philadelphia (Dunster, 58–61). But, as Patricia Schechter points out, her actions mirror those of newspaperman Jesse Chisholm Duke, who wrote a similar editorial about "white Juliets" and "colored Romeos" for a Montgomery paper before fleeing to Memphis, and that Wells notes his case in *Southern Horrors*. Wells herself acknowledges at one point that someone with her views might have to "hop, skip, and jump." See Schechter, *Ida B. Wells and American Reform, 1880-1930* (Chapel Hill: University of North Carolina Press, 2001), 78.

116. This biographical account relies on a number of sources, principal among them Dunster and the first chapter of McMurry.

117. In a diary entry from 1886, Wells lamented "my tempestuous, rebellious, hard headed wilfulness (sic)" and noted she had no hard feelings about the president who expelled her. See *The Memphis Diary of Ida B. Wells: An Intimate Portrait of the Activist as a Young Woman*, ed. Miriam DeCosta-Willis (Boston: Beacon Press, 1995), 78.

118. This distillation of the incident relies on Dunster, 18–20; McMurray, 25–31; and Schechter, 43–44, 51, 71–72.

119. *Memphis Diary of Ida B. Wells*, 141.

120. McMurry, 118–119; Dunster, 35–40.

121. Dunster, 42–44. Schechter places particular emphasis on the gender politics that shaped, and constrained, the life of Wells. See in particular 15–18.

122. *The Memphis Diary of Ida B. Wells*, 102.

123. Wells cites statistics on this point from the *Chicago Tribune* in her 1900 pamphlet, *Mob Rule in New Orleans*, included in Royster, 206.

124. See Jacqueline Jones Royster's Introduction to *Southern Horrors and Other Writings*, 8.

125. See Ida B. Wells' chapter on Lynch Law in the multiauthored pamphlet *The Reason Why the Colored American Isn't in the World's Columbian Exposition* (1893, included in *Selected Works of Ida B. Wells-Barnett*, compiled with an introduction by Trudier Harris [New York: Oxford University Press, 1991]), 75.

126. For more on this point, see Chapter 3, "Mrs. Stowe Writes Wrongs."

127. This 1893 account is cited in Joel Williamson, *A Rage for Order: Black-White Relations in the South Since Emancipation* (New York: Oxford University Press, 1984), 123–124. Wells also wrote about the Smith case in her 1895 pamphlet, *A Red Record* (in Royster, 91–93). She emphasized the father's ill-tempered reputation (he was a police officer), the lack of evidence against Smith, and the likelihood he was an "imbecile" unlikely to be capable of committing murder against a child. Of course, even if one assumes Smith was guilty of murder, a lynching—as a public spectacle, no less—defies any tenet of a democratic legal system of the kind Americans like to profess. Calling attention to such gaps between principle and reality was the cornerstone of Wells' work.

128. See table in Wells, *Mob Rule in New Orleans* in Royster, 206. Royster attributes the 3,318 figure to NAACP statistics. See her "Wells Chronology" on p. 212.

129. Dunster, 62.

130. Gail Bederman cites this *Times* piece in her insightful chapter on Wells in *Manhood and Civilization: A Cultural History of Gender and Race in the United States, 1880–1917* (Chicago: University of Chicago Press, 1995), 45.

131. Wells, *A Red Record*, 90.

132. Dunster, 62; Schechter, 84.

133. *Southern Horrors*, 52; *A Red Record*, 91.

134. *A Red Record*, 112; Bederman, 63.

135. *Southern Horrors*, 54–59; *A Red Record*, 80–81. Emphasis added. For more on the gendered strategies of Wells' writing, see Bederman's chapter in *Manliness and Civilization*, Schechter's chapter on "The Body in Question" in *Ida B. Wells-Barnett and American Reform* and Hazel Carby, *Reconstructing Womanhood: The Emergence of the Afro-American Woman Novelist* (New York: Oxford University Press, 1987), 107–120.

136. Wells, *Mob Rule in New Orleans*, 206; Schechter, 127.

137. Bederman, 69.

138. Dunster, 414.

139. Thomas C. Holt, "The Lonely Warrior: Ida B. Wells-Barnett and the Struggle for Black Leadership," in *Black Leaders of the Twentieth Century*, ed. John Hope Franklin and August Meier (Urbana: University of Illinois Press, 1978), 44; McMurry, 263, 256.

140. Patricia Schechter is particularly good in articulating the way the Progressive vision of race differed, and finally displaced, that of Wells. See, in particular, her chapter "Progress Against Itself" in *Ida B. Wells and American Reform*.

141. McMurry, 210–212; Schechter, 110–111.

142. Dunster, 255.

143. Dunster, 221–223.

144. Schecter, 22.

145. McMurry, 336–338.

146. Schechter, 124.

147. Schecter reconstructs the publishing history of the book in a detailed footnote on p. 257.

148. Hazel Carby's *Reconstructing Womanhood*, which deals with Wells' career in part of one chapter, was published in 1987. This influential study was nevertheless the leading edge in a new wave of publications that surged in the decade-and-a-half that followed.

149. Quoted in McMurry, 180–181.

150. Martin Luther King, Jr. used very similar language toward the end of his famous "I Have A Dream" speech at the Lincoln Memorial on August 28, 1963: "With this faith we will be able to transform the jangling discourse of our nation into a beautiful symphony of brotherhood…This will be the day when all of God's children will be able to sing with new meaning—'my country 'tis of thee; sweet land of liberty; of thee I sing; land where my fathers died, land of the pilgrim's pride; fro every mountain side, let freedom ring." See "I Have a Dream," in *A Testament of Hope: The Essential Writings and Speeches of Martin Luther, King, Jr.* (New York: HarperSanFrancisco, 1996), 219–220.

151. Ray Ginger, *The Bending Cross: A Biography of Eugene Victor Debs* (New Brunswick, NJ: Rutgers University Press, 1949), 353–355; Nick Salvatore, *Eugene V. Debs: Citizen and Socialist* (Urbana: University of Illinois Press, 1982), 291; *Eugene V. Debs: Spokesman for Labor and Socialism* (Chicago: Charles H. Kerr Publishing Co., 1978), 151 (this book was published for the Eugene V. Debs Foundation). Provisions of the Espionage and Sedition Acts came from Donald B. Cole, ed., *Handbook of American History* (New York: Harcourt, Brace & World, 1968), 200.

152. Ginger, 355–357; Eugene V. Debs, "The Canton, Ohio Speech," in *Writings and Speeches of Eugene V. Debs* (New York: Hermitage Press, 1948), 417–418. Crowd reactions are indicated in brackets.

153. Salvatore, 294; Debs, "Address to the Jury," in *Writings and Speeches*, 435.

154. "Address to the Jury," 436.

155. Debs, "Statement to the Court," in *Writings and Speeches*, 439.

156. Debs got more votes (919,000 to 900,000), but a smaller percentage of the vote (6% to 3%) than when he ran against Roosevelt, Wilson, and William Howard Taft in 1912. See Salvatore, 264, 325. Data also drawn from the "Facts in Summary" electoral tables included in *The American Heritage Book of the Presidents and Famous Americans*, vol. 9 (New York: Dell, 1967), 764, 787. The larger point here, in any event, is that while Debs never captured more than a decided minority of voters, he nevertheless had a relatively large and durable following, one whose size and influence was probably not measured in votes in any case.

157. *The American Heritage Dictionary of the English Language*, 4th ed. (Boston: Houghton Milfflin, 2000), 1649.

158. Salvatore, 223.

159. W.J. Ghent, "Eugene Debs," in *The Dictionary of American Biography* (1928; American Council of Learned Societies/Charles Scribner's Sons, 1998) CD-ROM; Salvatore, 225; Harold Currie, *Eugene V. Debs* (Boston: Twayne, 1976), 51.

160. "John Higham, 82, Historian of Nation's Role as Melting Pot," *New York Times*, August 18, 2003, B9.

161. Salvatore uses the term "deferential democracy" on p. 10. The first chapter of his biography evocatively sketches the world of mid-nineteenth century Terre Haute (as does Ginger's *The Bending Cross*). McKeen and Hulman serve as touchstones in Salvatore's biography, as does Terre Haute itself, to which Salvatore returns at the start of every section.

162. This affinity between Debs and Lincoln is one Debs himself often cited in his speeches and in some of his letters, and comparisons between the two were made by a number of observers. After Debs gave a speech at New York's Cooper Union in 1894, thirty-four years after Lincoln had done so, journalist John Swinton (1829–1901) wrote, "Debs in Cooper Union reminded me of Lincoln there. As Lincoln, of Illinois, became and efficient agent of freedom, so, perchance might Debs, of Indiana, become in the impending conflict for the liberation of labor." (Swinton quoted in Ginger, 183). Such comparisons were particularly common after Debs' imprisonment in 1919. "You're honored and will never be forgotten and your Worthy Name will go down in history the same as Abraham Lincoln, as a true lover for Freedom and Principal [sic]," a "Brother Socialist" wrote him in February 1921. Eight months later, a Minnesota woman

wrote Debs to tell him "you're the greatest man since Lincoln." No less an authority than Carl Sandburg, author of a multivolume Pulitzer Prize-winning biography of Lincoln and a friend of Debs, wrote him shortly before his death to say, "I hope to do an extended sketch of you that will have some of the breath and feel of the Lincoln [bio]." See *Letters of Eugene Debs*, vol. 3, ed. J. Robert Constantine (Urbana: University of Illinois Press, 1990), 184–185, 256, 573 for these and other examples. Deb's reply, "[That] is most generous in you and flattering to me," can be found in Penelope Niven, *Carl Sandburg: A Biography* (New York: Scribner, 1991), 436.

163. Abraham Lincoln, "Fragments on the Tariff," in *Lincoln: Speeches and Writings, 1832-1858* (New York: Library of America, 1989), 153.

164. Lincoln, "Speech at Cincinnati, Ohio," in *Lincoln: Speeches and Writings 1859-1865* (New York: Library of America, 1989), 84. For more on this passage and its larger significance in Lincoln's vision, see Jim Cullen, *The American Dream: A Short History of an Idea that Shaped a Nation* (New York: Oxford University Press, 2003), Chapter 3 (esp. 84–85).

165. While most biographers emphasize the degree to which Debs was a dedicated family man, Salvatore describes the couple as unhappily married and Debs as having a long extramarital affair with Mabel Dunlap Curry, the wife of a Terre Haute English professor. The affair wasn't made public, and Debs never divorced, but his wife at least suspected his infidelity. See 277–280 ff.

166. It has often been noted that Abraham Lincoln was, in many ways, a man's man who enjoyed the comradeship of a largely male world of work. For an excellent evocation of this world, see Robert Wiebe, "Lincoln's Fraternal Democracy," in *Abraham Lincoln and the American Political Tradition*, ed. John L. Thomas (Amherst: University of Massachusetts Press, 1986) 11–30.

167. Debs quoted in Salvatore, xv.

168. The fullest account of the riot is Paul Avrich, *The Haymarket Tragedy* (Princeton: Princeton University Press, 1984).

169. Debs quoted in Salvatore, 103.

170. Ginger, 92.

171. See editor J. Robert Constantine's "biographical sketch" in the first volume of *Letters of Eugene V. Debs*, vol. I, lxii.

172. Ginger, 100–106.

173. This point is a major theme of Carl Smith, *Urban Disorder and the Shape of Belief: The Great Chicago Fire, The Haymarket Bomb, and the Model Town of Pullman* (Chicago: University of Chicago Press, 1995).

174. Salvatore, 50.

175. On the origins, design, and outcome of Pullman is Stanley Buder, *Pullman: An Experiment in Industrial Order and Community Planning* (New York: Oxford University Press, 1967). Though dated, it is still widely cited as an authoritative source.

176. Buderman, 89.

177. Smith, 187.

178. Buder, 95.

179. Ely quoted in Buder, 103.

180. Salvatore, 127; Buder, 67, 159–160, 152; Smith, 235.

181. Statistics on the strike taken from the American Social History Project, *Who Built America? Working People and the Nation's Economy, Politics, Culture, and Society*, 2nd ed., vol. II (1992; New York: Worth, 2000), 127–128. This classic text is a treasure trove on many of the incidents discussed in this chapter.

182. Salvatore, 137–138.

183. Buder, 199–200.

184. *Who Built America?* 124. For more on Coxey's political heirs, see Lucy Barber, *Marching on Washington: The Forging of an American Tradition* (Berkeley: University of California Press, 2004).

185. Eugene Debs, "How I Became a Socialist" (1902), in *Writings and Speeches*, 43.

186. Ghent, "Debs," in *DAB*.

187. Eugene V. Debs, *Walls & Bars: Prisons and Prison Life in the "Land of the Free"* (1927; Chicago: Charles H. Kerr Publishing Company, 2000), xxi.

188. Ginger, 404–414; Salvatore, 328.

189. Kitty Kelly, *My Way: The Unauthorized Biography of Frank Sinatra* (1986; New York: Bantam, 1987), 329. The planning and subsequent cancellation of President Kennedy's visit to Frank Sinatra's house in Palm Springs is described in all major Sinatra biographies. The specific details vary, though all—with one exception—agree the result was "a big Sinatra tantrum," in the words of a "longtime associate" quoted by J. Randy Taraborelli, *Sinatra: Behind the Legend* (New York: Birch Lane Press, 1997), 267. The exception is Nancy Sinatra, who, as usual, offers a less dramatic account in *Frank Sinatra: My Father* (1985; New York: Pocket Books, 1986). Yet even she acknowledges the event was "a disappointment in Dad's life" (157). The sledgehammer incident is attributed to Jacobs, who personally witnessed it and later described it to Peter Lawford, the bearer of the bad news and the focus of Sinatra's rage in the aftermath of the affair. Lawford, in turn, was interviewed by Kelly in 1984. Regardless of which of these accounts are most credible, I believe all support the basic point I'm trying to make here: By 1962, Frank Sinatra believed himself to be a man with virtually unlimited access to privilege in American life, and he was deeply hurt when it became apparent this wasn't the case. I use the sledgehammer to make this point because it seems so, well, poetically vivid.

190. Nancy Sinatra, *Frank Sinatra: My Father*, 155.

191. Though shrouded in controversy and misinformation—Judith Campbell Exner herself disavowed her 1977 memoir *My Story*, claiming fear of retribution—a basic Giancana-Campbell-Sinatra-Kennedy connection has now been largely accepted by those who have studied both Sinatra and Kennedy extensively. For a good brief overview of the matter, see Taraborelli, pp. 221–223.

192. For versions of this story from the Kennedys' perspective, see Peter Collier and David Horowitz, *The Kennedys: An American Drama* (New York: Summit Books, 1984), 294–295 and Richard Reeves, *President Kennedy: Profile of Power* (New York: Simon & Schuster, 1993), 292–293.

193. Taraborelli, 267–268. "I tried several times to apologize for whatever it was that I had done to Frank, but he has not spoken to me for over twenty years," Peter Lawford told Kitty Kelly in 1983. "He wouldn't take my phone calls and wouldn't answer my letters. Wherever I saw him at a party or in a restaurant, he just cut me dead. Looked right though me with those cold blue eyes like I didn't exist." Lawford talked about the

problem with Sinatra's daughter Tina, who encouraged him to keep try-ing, but to no avail (592).

194. Earl Wilson, *Sinatra: An Unauthorized Biography* (New York: Macmillan, 1976) 171–172; Taraborelli, 268.

195. Taraborelli, 268.

196. Taraborelli, 267.

197. Sinatra held a fund-raiser for Martin Luther King Jr. in the early 1960s; his ties to Monaco stem from his friendship with (future princess) Grace Kelly, which took root during their work together in the 1956 film *High Society.*

198. John Lahr, *Sinatra: The Artist and the Man* (New York: Random House, 1997), 4.

199. Jack Long, "Sweet Dreams and Dynamite," *The American*, September 1943 (included in *Legend: Frank Sinatra and the American Dream*, ed. Ethlie Ann Vare (New York: Boulevard Books, 1995), 9.

200. Long, "Sweet Dreams and Dynamite," 13.

201. Roland Marchand, *Advertising the American Dream: Making Way for Modernity, 1920-1940* (Berkeley: University of California Press, 1985), 3.

202. For more on the role of technology in housekeeping standards, see Susan Strasser, *Never Done: A History of American Housework* (New York: Pantheon, 1982).

203. Frederick Allen, *Only Yesterday: An Informal History of the 1920s* (1931; New York: Harper & Row, 1981), 81.

204. Mary Beth Norton, et. al., *A People and a Nation* (Boston: Houghton Mifflin, 1998), 703–704.

205. Nancy Sinatra, *My Father*, 13.

206. Dolly Sinatra quoted in Taraborelli, 23.

207. Dolly Sinatra quoted in Kelly, 45.

208. Quoted in Kelly, 45–46.

209. Martha Weinman Lear, "The Bobby Sox Have Wilted, but the Memory Remains Fresh," *New York Times*, October 13, 1974, sec. 2, p. 12.

210. Bruce Bliven, "The Voice and the Kids," *The New Republic*, 6 November 1944, 593.

211. Quoted in Taraborelli, 55.

212. Quoted in Taraborell, 56.

213. Quoted in Wilson, 117.

214. Taraborelli, 115.

215. Nancy Sinatra, *My Father*, 73. "I thought for a fleeting moment that the unexpected pantomime was a joke," Henderson is quoted by Kitty Kelly as saying without attributing a source. "But then he caught my eye. I guess the color drained out of my face when I saw the panic in his." (*His Way*, 165–166).

216. Wilson, 77.

217. Quoted in Kelly, 168.

218. Kelly, 134.

219. Sinatra's assault on Mortimer has been widely recounted; I have relied principally on Wilson, 69–76 and Taraborelli, 92–95. Kitty Kelly based her knowledge of a Sinatra-Hearst meeting on an interview with Hearst's grandson, John Hearst. See *My Way*, 139–140, 575. Years later, a drunken Sinatra found Mortimer's grave and urinated on it. See Lahr, 43.

220. Martin quoted in Wilson, 140.

221. Ava Gardner, *Ava: My Story* (New York: Bantam, 1992).

222. Nancy Sinatra, *My Father*, 94–96; Taraborelli, 147

223. Lahr, 52.

224. Gardner quoted in Kelly, 225.

225. Davis quoted in Nancy Sinatra, *My Father*, 91.

226. For factual background on "I'm a Fool to Want You," see Ed O'Brien with Robert Wilson, *Sinatra 101: The 101 Best Recordings and the Stories Behind Them* (New York: Boulevard Books, 1996), 33

227. Arnold Shaw, *Sinatra: Twentieth Century Romantic* (New York: Holt, Rinehart & Winston, 1968), 145.

228. "There is much to regret about America's failure in Vietnam," McCain wrote at the end of his 1999 book, *Faith of My Fathers: A Family Memoir*, written, like all three of his books, with his legislative aide Mark Salter (New York: Random House, 1999). "The reasons are etched in black marble in the Washington Mall [McCain is referring to the Vietnam memorial, which contains the names of the 52,000 Americans who died in the war]. But we believed the cause that America served was a worthy one, and millions who defended it had done so honorably (348). As journalist Robert Timberg notes, "McCain never turned against the war, or apologized for his role in it." See *John McCain: An American Odyssey* (New York: Touchstone, 1999), 59, 117. This book is an excerpted from, and expands upon, Timberg's widely hailed book *The Nightingale's Song* (New York: Simon & Schuster, 1999), which traces the careers of McCain and four other graduates of the U.S. Naval Academy and the influence of the Vietnam War on them.

229. See, for one example among many, McCain's discussion of Reagan in *Worth the Fighting For: A Memoir* (New York: Random House, 2002), 85. Timberg also discusses McCain's admiration for Reagan in An *American Odyessey*, 119–122.

230. I base this assertion of seeing McCain making statements to this effect many times on television. But one can also see various speeches on his website to this effect: http://mccain.senate.gov/ (accessed June 27, 2004).

231. See Timberg, 123–125. McCain elliptically, but unmistakably, attributes his divorce from Carol McCain in 1980 to "my own selfishness and immaturity."

232. For McCain's version of this widely reported story, see *Worth the Fighting For*, 59–61, and his chapter on the Keating Five scandal, 159–206. Timberg cites the $2.6 billion figure on p. 174.

233. See Timberg, 193. The joke is quoted on a web site, "John McCain's Skeleton Closet" at http://www.realchange.org/mccain.html (accessed June 27, 2004).

234. McCain, *Faith of My Fathers*, 18–21. McCain did not discover his Mississippi relatives were slaveholders—which should not have been surprising, as plantations in the South were not typically supported without slave labor—until much later. *See Worth the Fighting For*, 385.

235. Timberg, 24–25.

236. See McCain, *Faith of My Fathers*, Chapter 13, and Timberg, 68–70.

237. The footage can be seen in the episode on McCain in the MSNBC series *Headliners & Legends* periodically broadcast on cable television.

238. Timberg, 75–76.

239. McCain describes himself as "eager to build my reputation as a combat pilot, and I looked for any opportunity to hurry the day I would deploy to Vietnam." See *Faith of My Fathers*, 168.

240. Much of the following account of McCain's crash and capture comes from Chapter 16 of *Faith of My Fathers*. See also R.W. Apple Jr., "Adm. McCain's Son, Forrestal Survivor, Is Missing in Raid," *New York Times*, October 28, 1967, http://www.Proquest.umi.com (accessed June 29, 2004).

241. See the *Headliners & Legends* episode on McCain.

242. Timberg, 85–87.

243. McCain, *Faith of My Fathers*, 225.

244. McCain's account of his offer of release can be found in Chapter 19 of *Faith of My Fathers*, 232–238.

245. McCain, *Faith of My Fathers*, 241–244; Timberg, 94–95.

246. This is a theme that threads much of McCain's writing. See, in particular, *Why Courage Matters: The Way to a Braver Life* (New York: Random House, 2004), 106–109.

247. McCain, *Faith of My Fathers*, 302. Timberg, 112–116.

248. McCain writes at some length about his admiration of Jackson in *Worth the Fighting For*, 14–28.

249. Timberg, 129.

250. McCain, *Worth the Fighting For*, 63.

251. Timberg, 179.

252. See Timberg, 157–159.

253. McCain, *Worth the Fighting For*, 204.

254. McCain discusses his role in Lebanon policy in Chapter 5 of *Worth the Fighting For*. See also Timberg, 147–149.

255. For examples of this and other iconoclastic stances he has taken, see McCain, *Worth the Fighting For*, 327–365. McCain also refused to avail himself of a perk for most Senators—a chauffeur. See Elizabeth Drew, *Citizen McCain* (New York: Simon & Schuster, 2002), 131.

256. McCain, perhaps characteristically, has little to say about these visits in the chapter he devotes to Udall in *Worth the Fighting For*. I first learned about them in Michael Lewis, "The Subversive," *New York Times Magazine*, May 25, 1997, 62. It was from this piece, which also discusses McCain's leading role in campaign finance reform, that I first realized that McCain was no ordinary politician.

257. Drew, *Citizen McCain*, 21–22.

258. For a good history outlining the reforms of the 1970s and how they failed, see Elizabeth Drew, *The Corruption of American Politics: What Went Wrong and Why* (Woodstock, NY: Overlook Press, 1999). *Citizen McCain* is in effect a sequel to *The Corruption*, as it traces—using Drew's usual approach of narrating the twisting legislative pathways of a bill's fate—the trajectory of campaign finance reform.

259. Lewis, 62.

260. Feingold was the beneficiary of advertising of outside groups that ran ads without his consent, however. See Drew, *Citizen McCain*, 11.

261. McCain tirelessly invokes TR as his political inspiration when he appears on television. For a prose tribute, see *Worth the Fighting For*, 305–326.

262. McCain discusses this and other aspects of his presidential campaign in the final chapter of *Worth the Fighting For*.

For ancillary materials related to this book—illustrations, timelines, discussion questions, and the like—see the American History for Cynical Beginners *Web site at* www.ecfs.org/projects/jcullen.

0-595-34342-2

Printed in the United States
27225LVS00003B/247-285

9 780595 343423